The White House Is Compromised

"Lost Memorandum"

Prologue

Unfortunately William Wright's last briefing two weeks ago was tainted by instructions for the ace spy to welcome a team of cleaners, along with a liaison officer, appointed by the White House Communications Director. Clairvoyant feelings causing consternation from that briefing, with a number of eavesdroppers about to infiltrate the ASA(Army Security Agency) headquarters in Frankfurt along with the substation in Bad Aibling, also in West Germany. A fire destroying all the files on William Wright was fortuitous while suspicious at the time.

No one knew for sure, Will's intentions of overtaking the running of the American Government through the Capitol, if we had a President who was proven to be easily corruptible, and a threat to the U. S. security. Wright's next promotion was in the incubator waiting to hatch into the job of CIA Director, Washington D.C., with the present Chief, General Thibodeau having life ending health problems.

Twelve agents placed nn an American Army Base and overseas were being groomed and shaped into a stealthy force of super spies. The group being paid from an offshore account, would make sure they will not be discovered while waiting to become fully operational at the right time.

Five of these agents were being trained on a base inside a North Carolina jump school. Their next posting is 37 weeks in Kentucky, training with a Ranger Team. Another 5 agents attending an American University in Amman, Jordan, becoming acclimated to Middle Eastern Culture, and having a goal of speaking the language as proficient as a local city dweller or tribesman. All ten prospective agents were recruited because they were far above the rest, physically and mentally adept in a CIA class several months ago, along with obtaining high marks in psychological exercises, while at Langley.

The Ranger trainees are to be a five man kill team, stationed close to the Sinai Desert, where they have to be within two hours of the cities where we will have agents gathering vital intelligence on terriorist.

Major General William Wright's success rate of one hundred percent on numerous covert assignments into the Soviet Union, as well as the Orient, South America and the Middle East. In endless briefings, his opinion was the Middle East will be America's largest threat, from Armenia, to Egypt, and all of the Arabian Peninsula.

The final two operatives are Pierre Farouk, a French Algerian Jew, who looks the part, fitting into many Islamic neighborhoods. Paul Combs, a retired Green Beret Colonel, a 5 tour veteran of Vietnam, having served each tour advising the montagnards, making him a person who seems to have the ability to adapt to most situations.

Wright's spies and informants

	Agent	Attributes	Nationality	Job
1	Jeff	CIA Trained	USA	White House,staff
2	Combs	Green Beret	USA	Contractor
3	Lt. Donnie	PHD	USA	ASA Control
4	Isaac	Multilingual	USA	Kibbutz Res.
5	Seekman	Weapons spec.	USA	Kill Team c/o
6	Hank	Bi-Linguist	USA	Tehran F/officer
7	Darlene	= = BA	USA	Amman F/o
8	Antonin	Multi- = PHD	Czech	Luxor F/o
9	Monika	= =	=	Answam F/o
10	Pierre	=	French/ Algerian	Contractor
11	Loupe	=	Ex-Sandinista-	Tehran, Univ. F/o
12	Aposlolic	CIA Trained	Ukraine-	Double agent/KGB
13	Rover	MI6 Double Agent		ASA MI-5 Mole
14	Josie	BEA Stewardess	Brit-	Courier
15	The Hills- Phil, Alison-British ex CID- Recruited by MI5			

Number 12 Petro Aposlolic is KGB Director/ Wife ex- CIA

General Wright;s Aliases

General Gennady Vagon- Doctored Resume/Field Command
Colonel- Yuri Azarov- = - /KGB
KGB Agent- Gora Demyan- Hard man/assassin
Ludwig Von Wilhem- German National- ASA alias
Malcolm McLeod- Scottish National-alias

Chapter 1

Recollection

I know there will be repercussions from the destroyed files when the cleaning crew start to investigate it's cause along with interviewing underlings. A coming legal battle will definitely stall my agenda, hopefully I will be able to stop or divert this inquiry quickly.

Contemplating the gathering storm on my arrival in Frankfurt, from a hasty arranged briefing in DC, flying overnight from Dulles, I went to the house to rest and think about how to handle the new White House team coming in next week, if the crew found about the dozen secret agents. Evasion plans will be sorted out and started before they visited Frankfurt's ASA Headquarters.

That next morning walking through a cold crisp fall parking lot at 0500, opened my senses and giving me a spark to deal with this looming storm.

Up on the first floor, an idea from last night's planning session was initiated by getting busy in setting up a faux office along with starting hand written replacement dossiers, since the original files were destroyed in a fire.

A large room above the main ASA office used for storage was transformed into where conversations were monitored. Listening device's and miniature camera's were placed into a box. This equipment had to be undetectable by the naked eye or electronic sweeper if a diversion was to succeed.

One may think paranoia was perhaps driving this need to catch out a group of D.C. spies. What could be useful for my agency, is to engage the D.C. team into constructive conversation while studying their body language and what they had to say. How many people were being sent? A mystery at the time, thinking a half dozen was the number. One or two being so entrenched in the Washington fabric could cause an obstacle. It may be necessary to cull the unwilling, from the willing. The last team sent to clean the offices was a party of five that may still be the scenario.

Thinking, Buck would have had to be called to filter all briefing files, especially the ones concerning Israel, contacts throughout Europe and the Middle East. The segregated files had to be taken to the C.O.'s residence in Bad Aibling Village, and hidden in the master bedroom closet, since all of the data was in my head. Destroying files of high ranking Russian aliases used for covert reasons was very important.

Third on the agenda is to plant innocuous transcripts, hoping to frustrate the snooping DC Spies enough for them to move towards other interest.

The files before 1966 survived the fire and those before I was on the scene were also moved to a safe location. After that particular year, my involvement had to be lost in the fire.

The day was spent reading and redacting files upstairs. Replacing meaningless data into new manila folders, and replacing them down in the ASA document room.

Next on the agenda was to set up an activity for a bored crew of Washington insurgents to get involved in. It would have to be an enjoyable exercise that hopefully would entice the participants back again and again, like the ski slopes of Garmisch, with lovely snow bunnies from Frankfurt for company.

Early the next morning my vintage Karmann Ghia was delivered to the front of ASA HQ to use in getting to Bavaria, specifically for traveling to our substation in Bad Aibling. It seems like the three hour trip is a little more enjoyable and quick especially in a sports car, instead of taking a canvas top Jeep. On the way my thoughts were on what the main cleaning crew were going to look like and could they be baited.

Arriving at the Bavarian office, Buck was woken up as he slept with his head in his hands on top of the desk. He was startled to see me so soon after arriving in West Germany.

He snapped to attention and uttered, “Sir, General Thibodeau called to find out where you were, he wants a conference call with you, General Simpson and a Mrs Schultz.”

“Who is Schultz? oh yes, her.”

Buck interrupted, asking, “Sir please let me finish before you start on your reasons for being here. Three other people called in, Fran, Lenka, and Elke called several weeks back. They were told you were on an assignment.”

“Thank you. Mrs. Schultz is our thorn, and the Vice Presidents closest adviser. When is this call going to take place?”

“General as soon as I call him to say you are in this office.”

“Good. I am not here.”

“Please sir, don't do this to me. When Washington calls this morning, they can tell when I am lying. You know sir I will not lie to a General.”

“Take the phone off the hook. I have at least two hours of work for you to do, without interruptions.”

“Sir, The CIA will have an operator cut into the phone anyway,what do I say when they ask if the phone was off left off the hook on purpose?”

“I will take care of it if they get through. Now get me all files from 1966 to the present. Lay them on the conference table in chronological order. Make sure the copier has plenty of ink and paper. When I place papers on the opposite side of the table, you copy, staple them, and file them, understand?”

“Are you okay, sir? Those were taken to Frankfurt and destroyed in the fire.”

“Get me every file that was left, even the amended ones.”

Buck is a piece of work. I can’t lie to a General, what a weenie. They are supposed to be lied to, a way dousing flames and expectations. With the door closed I got two hours of sleep while files were put in the conference room.

Almost two hours later, Buck was heard replacing the phone on its hook, coming into my office and saying, while my eyes were still closed, “Sir, may I take a few hours off, I do not want to hear you explain why your first Sergeant didn't call Washington, as soon as you arrived in this office. My pension will be gone if General Thibodeau finds out I ignored a direct order.”

“Good idea. Do not come back until you see the outside light on. On the way, take all my weapons, have them cleaned, oil and resupplied with ammunition. Then take all of the uniforms to the dry cleaners. Have new Russian documents forged in the name of General Yasif Buran. Take the files I obtained from Washington out of their folders and to my residence, hide them in my bedroom closet.”

“Yes sir, will do, thank you sir.”

I followed Buck out the door, making him look around, salute and shaking his head as he loaded up the jeep, with my gear. Within twenty minutes the phone rang. It was Washington, causing me to hang up and go to the conference room where I could rest my feet on the table when they called again.

The conference room was easier to work in since my desk was full of papers, and its phone had a better speaker system.

Within seconds the call came in with General Thibodeau shouting out, “How long have you been there?”

“Just walked in sir.”

“I want to speak to your first sergeant.”

“Sorry sir, he should be here soon. It's not like him to walk out as I arrived.”

"Did he say I needed you to call me?"

"He said something like that while walking out the door. I'lltell him you called sir."

"Wright don't you hang up on me again, I'll have your stars ripped off your shoulders and replace them with private stripes, do you understand me, soldier?"

"Sorry sir, I did not know it was me you wanted to speak to. You did ask for Buck, sir.

"Don't you parse words with me General Wright you know very well, it is you this phone call was for. Why did you hang up on my secretary?"

"Somehow we were disconnected, sorry sir I did try to answer it quickly."

He was heard muttering to his secretary, "That is the most incorrigible soldier I've had the misfortune to have met. Have him stay on the line, I need a drink."

When Thibodeau was out of the room, she whispered, "General Wright, the director has had it with you and your shenanigans."

What was she trying to say, this was uncalled for or was she acting on someone's behalf. Have to file that conversation into my mind.

Thibodeau was back saying, "Now where were we?"

"Sir, you didn't get a scotch and soda, did you? We shouldn't talk shop while drinking alcohol."

“I swear, one of these days you are going to step to far over the line, you no good SOB. I'll have you frog marched down Pennsylvania Avenue, all the way to the White House gates, you hear me General.”

With him starting to cough and sputter, I answered, “Yes sir, what was it you wanted to ask me.”

“Wait a minute while I catch my breath. You do know the Vice President is sending another team over in two days, don't you interfere with their work. Wright, you listen good. Those people are hand picked to help you in transforming your agency.”

“You mean they are not really cleaners, sir?”

“Did Mrs Schultz say that?”

“That was the way she put it, sir. Who is in charge of her team?”

“Her, P.A., it seems she wants to add that to her resume. Her name escapes me for the time being.”

“It's not that Linda Latta, is it? You know she is still a little green on CIA protocol?”

“Miss Latta yes, do not play games with those people, especially the lady in charge. She is engaged to the assistant ways and means chairman, I warn you Wright, you mess this up your ass is in trouble. Our full funding could be jeopardized if they think you are an obstacle in getting their job done in a timely manner.”

Before Thibodeau could say anything else, I made a crackling noise against the receiver, hearing him say, “No more fires you” -I hung up without hearing anything else about another fire..

Alright, two days to get back to Frankfurt to await the Washington insurgents (W.I.) arrival in three days after flying overnight. How to set up a possible scenario where the WI may want to escape a boring old baby sitting job. Got it, as soon as Buck gets back, I am off to Garmisch, to see if there is enough snow for a skiing holiday.

In the mean time Fran, Alke and Lenka were called to tell them I just got back in Germany, and to set up when we could get together.

Lenka should be the first called to set up a time. No I will surprise her and hope there is room at the Inn. No one was home at Fran's a message was left, saying I hope to be in Florida within two months. Alke was next asking her to book me into the Passau Inn next weekend.

When Buck arrived back, he said, “Sir, your weapons and uniforms should be ready tomorrow morning. Did the General ask how long you have been on the base? Is that why you followed me outside, so you could tell him you just walked in, sir?”

Ignoring his question, I said. “In a week or so, a group of people will be arriving to go over our missing files.”

“Sir, the files are not missing, they were destroyed.”

“That's it Sergeant, you are going on leave with your family for two weeks, have a good Thanksgiving, all expenses paid.”

“Thank you sir. Am I reading you correctly, you want me out of the way.”

“Go pack sergeant.”

After Buck left, I vacated Bad Aibling arriving in Garmisch two hours later. Lenka hurried out of the hotel to greet me with a hug and kisses.

Asking her, “Your Austrian skier is no longer a boy friend.”

“Silly, he is still my favorite, with you Billy a close second.”

“Thanks.”

She giggled while taking me by the hand, leading the way into the lounge area. Her mom and dad were equally pleased to see me, and couldn't wait to say how well the hotel had done in the last ten skiing seasons, and summers as well, with hikers and ramblers using the hotel as a base.

Our dinner took two hours to finish with news about the hotel, the local people, and of course their interest in what was happening in their country of Czechoslovakia.

Lenka didn't act like she had a man friend, wanting to sit so close to me, one would think she wanted to restart our relationship again.

After a night cap at the bar Lenka's father said, "William, you should see the bank manager tomorrow morning, he has good news for you, no more talk now, until the morning. Good night it has been a long day."

Thankfully Lenka went to bed first.

The next morning Mr. Dagmar and I were at the bank when they opened up. We were both given a printout of deposits for the time I was away. With interest and profits from the hotel, I had over 700,000 Duestch Marks in my account, roughly $250,000.

That was a shock. What would Nicola have thought, to know the hotel had done so well.

The bank manager wanted to know if I would be willing to purchase another Guest Haus that he and Herr Dagmar discussed a few weeks ago. I agreed, and with that, my account was now down to 100,000 DM. Oh well easy come, easy go. There is a chance the profit may double.

While in the managers office when we were alone, I said, “There are maybe six American Associates coming to Germany for six months. I would like to have them take a break on odd weekends and see Garmisch through a German's prospective.”

Mr. Dagmar replied, “We are fully booked for the season, saying that the other hotel we are purchasing has plenty of rooms available.”

“Okay, that's fine. Are there any events planned for late November or early December, they could go to? Say maybe parties or celebrations.”

“On weekends there are sleigh rides to the border with Austria, with celebrations on the Zugspitz slopes.”

After rethinking the billeting, I did not want the group to stay at our hotel, for fear of knowing about my business interest. The American enlisted man's hotel in the center of town would be a better place to stay. It was soon set up, rooms were booked in the other hotel as a back up, Garmisch would be a quiet diversion. Now to get back to Bad Aibling to see if my weapons and uniforms were available.

Pulling into the parking lot at the ASA Building, Buck was out to greet me, with a concerned look on his face. What was going on, the man should be in America.

He was beside himself, saying, “General Thibodeau called me at home, just before we were to leave for the States. The General asked me a strange question, he wanted a word with me or my sergeant. Wait a minute, his call had to do something with the Washington Group, didn't it sir?”

“Alright Buck tell me what was behind the General's phone call.”

“He sent two MP”s and a MP Officer to seize all the files in this building, and ones in the I. G. Farben Building. They do not know you beat them to those files, long ago”

“Get Thibodeau on the line, then leave.”

After the phone call was made he left just as Thibodeau's secretary started to speak, saying, “Here he is sir and the General saying, “Is this is General Wright?”

“Yes sir. What is the meaning of wanting my files taken away? I do not need this interruption I have an agency to run, General Thibodeau.”

“They are not your property, end of question. Another item do not interfere this time.”

“Their first and last attempt to frame this agency went awry before their dastardly fraud played out. Had to be a huge embarrassment for the Veep's people.”

“Please, do not act like you are unaware what has caused this intrusion, it isn't the ASA they want, it's your head on a platter, and you know why. While we are at it Wright, you are going to take orders and say yes sir or mam and keep going, do you understand this?”

“Yes sir, one last question, why do this in a backhanded way General. Who is behind this theft?”

“It isn't theft, do you not understand, those files belong to the U. S. Government. As far as where those orders were generated, it is a need to know situation, and you do not need to know.”

“Sir, did the orders generate from the White House? I am leaving soon for Frankfurt to stop those documents being taken.”

Thibodeau with an annoying laugh, replied, “Too late, they are in a secure area, away from your office and the ASA Headquarters hee hee hee. Wright you just don't get it do you? As a department head you have many more superiors now, more than when you were a spy, scampering through hedgerows and over fences. Need to know, Wright, you are out of the loop.”

After hanging up the phone, I was satisfied he took the bait. Those files will have to be taken to a place where six insurgents have the room to spread them out in secret.

Now think, where in Frankfurt could a team of Americans operate without causing a little curiosity by civilian onlookers. Since ASA files are in a secure area, cuts down on available buildings.

Still cannot get over that they may all fell into the trap of taking files. Have to take advantage, go on the offensive with a backup plan, one that has to be initiated by following the team when they arrive at the airport tomorrow morning. Taking off to Frankfurt for a three hour drive, will afford me the time to figure this out, before arriving at the Farben complex."

Pulling into the Frankfurt ASA Headquarters, none the wiser where the Americans are staying for sure. Outside of an airport hotel who would have the facilities to stage a place to have a conference.

My secretary was asked to call all large hotels to see if a Miss. Latta had reservations. While this was going on I went to change clothes at my residence, to make sure personal files were not taken.

Everything looked good, allowing time to call my parents to see how everyone was doing.

Back in the office an hour later, just before the workers left, I was told, there were no hotels holding a reservation for a Miss. Latta, in fact no American groups had bookings this week.

It then dawned on me, Rhein Main Air Force Base, the only possibility. Maybe better to make a call in private, this way the staff could answer no to questions if they were asked about interfering in an official inquiry.

The Base Commander's Adjutant gave out the best news I've had during this upheaval, by saying, "General, your group are taking a MATS plane from Andrews."

That figures, since there are available rooms in the guest barracks, next to the officers mess, where I have stayed many times, it does make sense. Once inside the base, they will have to stay put, unless the base commander issues them a pass to get back in.

A thought came to me, maybe the Base Commander from whom I worked with when Frank's plane went down, could be helpful.

The Commander's office was called, with his secretary informing me she was getting ready to leave.

She said, "Yes General, you just stopped me from walking out the door. How can I help you?"

Being a strident German civilian, and very officious, it was necessary to use a little psychology, to make her think she could not help me.

I asked, " Frau, put me in contact with someone

who knows when the Latta team are arriving."

"I know every zing, no need to go furzer. Zey are landing 2100 hours, in swie hours, vooms vill be ready in the Officers guest barracks. You can see I know every zing."

"Dunka. You are going to be my eyes and ears from now on, is that goot, Fraulein."

"Ya mien General, vie not, call me anytime."

It was now necessary to see where the new battle ground is going to take place. There is time to go get some materials needed for a little eavesdropping. A war room was going to be infested with a few electronic bugs, hoping the playing field will be leveled or maybe tilted in my favor.

Knowing the fix would be discussed if they do not find any dirt it would be easier to stop the fraud now. I had to extract what they had in mind to present to a court martial if it gets that far.

Another uniform with a pair of Captains bars will be needed to access the base, instead of going in as a General where attention needed to be averted, especially if a few junior officers show up hoping to gain favors with a General.

Back again in a familiar area of the guest officers barracks, remembering the past and having to deal with being challenged by security was annoying.

Two hours later, the barracks porter bought my reason for being there, as an Army Officer checking in for a few nights waiting for a hop to Mac Dill in a few days.

Writing down my name, he confirmed the team would be arriving this evening, asking if I needed to be on the same floor.

Taking a chance I said "Yes, the room next to Mr. Latta if it is possible to have connecting doors."

"Sorry sir, no rooms have access to another room. I thought she was female."

"No, Lin Latta, short for Lincoln."

"Thank you sir that could have been embarrassing for the evening shift sergeant. May I ask, who are they?"

"Washington big wigs. They are not to be approached. Instructions are to be left on Latta's desk on how to get to the mess hall and the room for meetings, nothing else."

"Captain, do you also need instructions?"

With a little laugh, I said, "No Sergeant, this place has been like a second home for me over two decades."

"Captain, the conference room is set up as to their instructions. Would you like to approve the set up?"

"Yes, lead the way please."

Security seemed lax, until I noticed two AP's (Air Force Police) standing at parade rest outside the door.

One AP asked to see my ID while the other one unlocked the solid metal door.

When the porter led the way inside, he pointed to a long table with my boxes of files on top, no wonder this room was guarded. A projector was ready, along with a pull down screen, at the front of the room.

Left alone to inspect the layout, the projector was tested. turning it on and placing a miniature listening device inside a speaker, piercing a small hole, by inserting the tip of a ink pen though the paper covering.

If for any reason an electronic sweeper was used, the technician would assume it was the crystals in the machine. Too risky putting a bug anywhere else. Wait a minute the steel door should also cover a bug on the top and back edge.

Thirty minutes later it was time to return to the barracks, where the sergeant asked if there was anything he could do. As soon as he was back down stairs Latta's unlocked room was entered with the door quietly shut,allowing me to survey the area.

A tiny bug was quickly placed in her telephone receiver, with another one into the back of a radio alarm clock.

Within minutes of getting back to my assigned room, the porter started knocking on the door, with me saying, “What is it Sergeant?”

“Your group's flight was directed to Gander for the night.”

That definitely was good news. When they eventually arrive, waiting for a plane to be fixed would exacerbate lingering jet lag. I have heard of flights redirected to a Newfoundland Airport had taken a week sometimes to be repaired, especially if an engine was the problem, having to wait for parts.

After checking out the next day, the porter was told to leave my room as it is. I would be back tomorrow around midnight.

On the fourth day of inquiring about Latta's flight, Rhein Main Operations finally got word another C-130 was leaving Hawaii to pick up the Washington six. They would be arriving within two days. Let’s see, they would have used up almost a week, another two weeks to recover, that is if they didn't catch a chill waiting in a base surrounded by tundra and ice.

Two days later, I was alerted the team was one hour from touchdown. My driver was instructed to drive me out in the Jeep, after placing two stars on the front plate for getting through the front gates.

We were waved though the main gate and asked to wait two minutes for an escort vehicle by one of the AP's. We were eventually led out to the tarmac where the plane was set to park up.

We were allowed to park fifty yards short of the pad where monitoring the group when they deplane out the back ramp. We may have to move where the plane isn't blocking the view. It is essential for me to gauge how they handled themselves while walking and carrying luggage to their bus.

With binoculars the C-130 was seen approaching while flying over the autobahn with its landing gears seeming to barely clear the Base's fence. Five minutes later, watching two of the team sauntering down the long ramp, they looked really in rough condition, enough so, two ambulances arrived with four medical staff. Two of the group were stretchered out, with another two being helped down the ramp. Four down, two too tired to care what happens next. The other two walked ever so slowly towards their bus, waiting for larger cases to be loaded into the bus.

My driver was instructed to drive back to ASA headquarters and have the vehicle gased. There was more work to do than dealing with these silly DC pest right now.

Chapter 2

Washington Spies

Amman was called to get an update on the agents in the university there. No phone log was kept for this call because of the people about to go through this office.

From my office the next morning at ten, the porter in Rhein Main was called for an update.

The porter informed me, the group was not stirring however, a doctor was called to look at them last night, something about some of them infected with the Hong Kong flu. He also said they were now officially quarantined, meals having to be brought in.

More information was needed than what some porter heard second or third hand. My secretary was instructed to find the examining physician to see what the prognosis was.

An hour later a call was put through to my desk from the doctor who inspected the Washington spies.

"General Wright this is Major Zipser, you needed to speak to me?"

"Did you examine the six civilians from

Washington?"

"I did sir. Their diagnoses are in my report."

"Two questions Major, when will your report be sent over to my office and how did they get sick?"

"Sir, I was instructed to send the report to a Mrs. Schultz, however I can tell you that their problems were caused by being exposed to frigid temperatures."

"Major, as you well know, riding in a transport freighter is not what sick people should have to go through."

"Yes General, I know very well what you mean. I made myself a promise to never catch a hop again, after spending most of my leave trying to get to South Florida to see my family one Christmas, and coming down with a horrendous cold. Oh yes, I see what you are driving at. Whoever made the decision to send the six people on to Frankfurt must have been mad. They should have been sent to a hospital right away. This will be in my report."

"Thank you Major."

Three days later, two of the group was taken back to Washington D. C. in another C-130, that had to be equipped with two hospital beds. The rest of the team was still restricted to barracks, causing me to call Buck in the States, and have him come back ASAP so I could fly to London for a meeting with General Simpson and Thibodeau in two days at an Air Base in the UK.

Not worried about this group for now, I decided to go to London and get prepared for another interruption in my schedule. Spending tonight at the Hyde Park flat would be a bonus and Kenny meeting me at Heathrow will be reminiscent to the early days of the cold war.

Kenny met the flight as scheduled and was told to be back at the flat in a couple of days and not tell anyone about me being here, because of the need to go to Harrow and see Nicola's parents tomorrow.

Two days later I was picked up and delivered to the American Embassy for a one pm briefing. It was a relief to have this set up in London instead of Mildenhall RAF Station.

While waiting for our meeting, Simpson's secretary and I were telling stories from the past which annoyed the CIA Director, who was trying to talk with Simpson, who must have overheard us from closed doors in Simpson's office. Over the intercom I was told to go to the conference room, and for the secretary to stay put.

General Thibodeau started with, "Mrs Schultz is livid at her team problems from being exposed to arctic weather, as if a catastrophic fire destroying evidence wasn't enough. Wright, the White House aid is adamant on having you investigated for possible sedition."

"Sir, I take it se is calling the shots and the Vice President, being an ex CIA Chief is kept out of the loop on my inquisition."

"Now see here Wright, you mind your P's and Q's. Remember this is all down to you and your suspicious agenda."

That was such an inane statement, it is what a parent may say to a teenager, when nothing else comes to mind when trying to tell the child why he was in trouble.

By him not responding to the Veep question spoke volumes. Maybe not, it was his way of moving away from the question on the Vice President.

Having to let Thibodeau side tract me, I added another angle, with, "Sir, I must quietly protest Mrs. Schultz considering me a traitor she is the one who has an agenda."

"Look, Wright, It'll blow over, give it a year you will see."

That wasn't like him, to let a slanderous accusation go unanswered, especially towards a Washington insider.

"Alright sir, however, I would like to know, who or

where she came to think I was engaged in nefarious activities."

"Aright, you impertinent ass, you have ruffled more than a few feathers, especially our friendly British Intelligence Community. You did not hear that from me, are we clear on that?"

"As a bell sir?"

So that's the reason for this upheaval. MI5 orMI6 must have noticed my team in Amman, couldn't be anything else. It is starting to come together, Lord Chesterfield was told months ago about an idea of creating a secret unit to watch Middle East hotbeds.

An uneasy feeling is giving me goose bumps on something more sinister is in the air. A cover up on how my personal information was passed on to the Russians back when I was supposed to be living in anonymity with Nicola.

"Stop your dab-burn Clairvoyant thinking. We are getting back to our task at hand. Now tell me, have you compromised the files Schultz's team wants to peruse? Have you ever heard of a Captain Smudgeholder? It seems he inspected the areas where the forensic teams are living and working, must be an Ivy League pansy, with a name like that."

"Sir, only a magician could be in two places at the

same time. When you called me, files were taken away within hours. Did you just say forensic?"

"Did I? That's it Wright I have far better things to do, than wasting time with some amateur magician or wannabe Benedict Arnold. If you are asked about this meeting,just say you were scolded and told to quit whatever you are doing. Is that clear?"

"Yes sir."

Something wasn't adding up, one thing, General Simpson didn't say a word. It was almost like we were being listened to, by outside interested parties.

Humm, I wonder. Another verbal faux pas worth mentioning, so this was now considered a forensic investigation. Maybe Dannie Els could put some light on this situation since this was her major in university.

Back in my flat a couple hours later, Lieutenant Els was phoned in Amman, Jordan.

When she finally got to a phone in her halls of residence, the Jordanian operator was heard saying, "Sorry, he did not give his name."

Before she had a chance to speak, I said, "This is Wright."

The receiver went quiet, thought I'd lost transmission before she could answer.

Taking a chance I quickly said, "I need to ask you

something."

"Who is this please?"

"It's Will, I need to ask you something."

"Go ahead, you're coming in clear now sir."

"Els, can a clerical trail be forensically investigated and is it possible to trace its origin?"

"Yes and no. We studied such things, where an IRS investigation may find files have been tampered with or altered. Without original transcripts, it is difficult to prove intent or compromised by say an adversary."

"Intent cannot be determined unless a psychiatric exam is ordered for a targeted individual, can it?"

"Alright sir, let me add that investigating the purpose of a paper trail cover up is hard to prosecute."

"Is it possible to determine when a note was written?"

"Only when temperatures are vastly different when notes were added or adjusted. The best chance of getting proof is when an incarceration threat brings out an admission of guilt, from the person or persons under investigation. Is that helpful, General?"

"What about DNA left on files when handled?"

"Impossible sir, most have at least two samples. Having said that, a staff supervisor will be discounted and he or she would probably have to sign off on a file being permanently placed into an archival area to preserve it."

"Els, I will have to ask the General, next time we have a conversation on what type of gear was loaded on the plane. He did want me to ask if you were available to do some cleaning in Frankfurt."

"Yes, no classes for four days, some type of local holiday."

"Go to the airport, catch the next flight out leaving at1900 hours, you will be met at Frankfurt."

Lufthansa was immediately called to book her on their 1910 flight, before calling BEA for my flight out of Heathrow, one that would arrive close to Els's ETA. Both of these flights were electronically paid for by WW Holdings, Chanel Islands, because of the need for secrecy.

Lieutenant Els's flight was pulling up to the Frankfurt International gates a few minutes after I landed. This gave me time to wait for her to walk into the immigration halls. She came through spot on time, allowing us to go through the immigration officers' kiosk together, chatting to each other as we were quizzed. She was dressed like a typical college student, oversize sweater, tight blue jeans, ratty hair and carrying a denim purse.

Staring at her, thinking she didn't look like an American Air Force Officer, made her say, “What?”

“You look the part, Lieutenant.”

“And you don't?”

I have to shut this confrontation down, before we get into an argument on chauvinistic behavior. It's hard to be nice to a feral cat. My Lieutenant must have something in her past causing this animosity towards superiors.

She was booked into a luxury hotel in the center of Frankfurt, close to the Bahnhof(Train Station), instead of being a guest in my residence. At least we had a late dinner together, where the conversation was civil, discussing the States and upcoming Christmas Holiday travel.

Talking business needs to be left out until Els was rested and our slight set to at the airport was forgotten. Her attitude needed to change before we discussed anything pertaining to this investigation.

Over breakfast the next morning, she curiously asked, “When are you going to brief me on your troubles? This is quite an extreme way to carry on, we could have discussed it over the phone.”

“What troubles? Beside, the phone in the dorm hall was being listened to.”

How stupid, just saying this woke me up to where the British are getting their information.

No wonder they think a conspiracy was actually happening. Lord Chesterfield is aware of my plans. I would guess another British entity is stepping on another one's territory. MI5 against MI6, Sandbaggers against Spooks, British Intelligence in competition with our CIA and on it goes.

Another problem, complacency on my part was bordering on ineptness, with all of my attention on a pretty lady and not looking to see if we were being watched when we left the airport. This carelessness has to stop now, before my agenda is discovered.

"General you didn't answer me on the reason I had to fly to Frankfurt."

"I'm sorry Lieutenant a chill went up my spine, now knowing our group had been compromised. When you get back to Amman, get the other four together at a place where you will not be seen or hear."

"Give me a clue who would be watching us."

"Look for a British National and report back when you are certain someone is watching your team. Now what was it you wanted to know?"

"I understand you did not fly me first class and put me in a luxury suite to seduce me, you would have made me stay at your house if those were your intentions. Tell me what this trip is for."

"If I wanted to seduce you, you would have been taken while in an alcoholic state of euphoria, and we would have started this morning as lovers, instead of a team of two working on a major problem. We have to finish this conversation in my office. Now tell me, do you like living in Jordan with the rest of the team?"

"We are getting use to it, the other four members of your team, sorry, that was a slip. Yes, it is okay."

Over the rest of breakfast, we again talked about what we missed the most from the States.

Before leaving for my office, it was necessary to convey to her what is going on, "We are all in a precarious situation, where we could all be charged with sedition. Think about that for the rest of the day."

"Sir, that is quite unsettling."

Ignoring her statement because she needs to concentrate on what may be coming down the pipe.

Back in ASA Headquarters, I instructed my secretary, "Take the Bible from your desk drawer, then find an agent to witness Lieutenant Els being sworn in."

Finally with the four of us in my office, Els was sworn into the ASA, "Lieutenant Dannie Els, do you solemnly swear to abide by the code of our Military

Justice, have no allegiance, traitorous intentions foreign or domestic, so help me God."

"I do."

While the document was being witnessed I thought, *What would I say if she asked, why there was no mention of allegiance to the United States in her swearing in. That could be my undoing, we will have to wait and see. That oath would not stand up to any type of scrutiny in front of a U.S. Army court martial.*

With that stunt over we were in my office with Els being told, "Lieutenant, the paper trail is in files sitting on a table waiting to be examined inside Rhein Main Air Force Base. They are going to be opened today by a team out of Washington. This could be damaging if those files were found to be altered."

"Sir, did you tamper with the evidence? Do not answer that. Say if you did, no one can help the person who doctored the evidence. Saying that, the person may need to prove a timed sequence of events, like when he or she was officially notified files were to be seized."

"Lieutenant, you may want to think twice about helping with this investigation. Reason is, they could have you testify the purpose of your trip to Frankfurt. I would assume you would be truthful, which could be construed as helping in an ongoing inquiry. You could be charged with conspiring to thwart the course of justice if you kept any files from being studied."

Chapter 3

Felonious Bureaucrats

"General,why go through all of this, it doesn't make sense, to make enemies in Washington."

"This is needed to protect contacts behind the Iron Curtain and Western Europe, not to mention protecting myself and you guys in Jordan. Hypothesize a need to change course in the agencies, one who think future security threats are starting to metastasize in the Middle East."

"You are putting together a morph agency, aren't you sir. My ticket was paid by a WW Holdings, would that be your initials, sir? I do think you are skating on thin ice."

"Lieutenant that is your opinion. Back to the legal side of finding forensic evidence and your involvement. I take it you are considering staying for a few more days."

"Ycs sir. I am intrigucd by how you are going to work this out. It would be nice to know why

Washington needs to discredit you or the ASA. The question is, how many more are in this web. One last item sir, this new team is how large?"

"Not counting the Langley nine, who are being trained and schooled, there are another dozen."

"Would this inquiry be interested in knowing if anyone has been killed or imprisoned by knowing you? Have you unjustly killed for your safety?"

"Yes and Yes."

"I am still interested, comfort me in saying I am not going to be set up if push comes to shove, with someone going to prison or in front of a firing squad,like a scapegoat."

"No, you will not be sacrificed,no one knows your name Lieutenant, you are just another college student."

"Okay sir, why do you need a forensic major in this situation?"

"Plans from the start were to make you the kingpin of an agency monitoring Middle East attitudes, even uprisings. Your name and title would be control, or simply, C to deter outside interference. Forensics are going to be needed if and when an incursion is needed into the Middle East in the future, basically for justifying a mission if we are called on the proverbial carpet."

"My duties will be what, sir?"

"Control needs to have access to all financial records, with authorization to disburse checks to whoever needs paying. Once we agree on this, you will be as culpable as I am."

"That's quite enticing, sir. Am I going to be trusted with all strategies or on a need to know basis. In other words, are you going to divulge everything on your past missions and ongoing agenda."

"No. The past will not come to haunt me again. One last hurdle of foreign revenge will be dealt with. We are building something for our future. Whoever fills the seat of my command post, will have to coordinate activities around the Middle East. To do this job one person has to be in contact with all field agents, including a kill team used for extracting agents or assets, if they come into contact with hostile actions, that team has to be called in to keep our people safe."

"We are getting close, sir two more questions. When is this agency going to be functional?"

"In 21 months."

"Sir, what happened during the time you were notified of files being seized? Did you take precautions after the call?"

"Nothing provable, besides, original files were destroyed in a fire within hours. It was lucky copies were sent to Bad Aibling over the years. One thing you need to know before agreeing to be part of this caper is that the investigative team is being listened to by eaves dropping devices, planted by an anonymous Captain Smudgeholder, good looking fella."

"Yes General I am sure he is also probably smart."

"Oh, you know him too?"

"Very funny. I suppose you are in this for the long haul, meaning your thought process must be a meta-psychological one. I do not believe you would let another do an illegal act, like bugging an inquiry. One last thing, you are definitely in tune with physical elements around the Middle East."

"That is way too deep for me, lieutenant. You need to know my intentions are honorable."

"Where is this honor directed?"

"Els, towards our Country. Protecting an institution that is outdated, not to mention misdirected agency targets a waste of time chasing villains who are also outdated. I believe the Russians are finished they are both broke and corrupt. That assumption has come from many months of living in various Soviet Bloc Countries."

"Will you always be truthful in speaking your mind, or are you complacent in telling untruths to protect your interest, such as winning me over."

"I promise to tell C, who ever that may be, the truth

always. Winning you over is needed, if that person is you."

"Do I know too much to walk away?"

"My control will be told everything, and knowing I have the capacity to lance an infected boil when push comes to shove, he or she may want to think about taking the job. Dannie, take the rest of the morning to think about the offer get back to me at 1400 hours."

"I would like to work for you Will."

"Good, that is such a huge relief, your ability to adapt and ward off aggressive people are a must in keeping us all safe."

"You need to change your attire to a business suit. Take this envelope of money, purchase everything you need. Looking successful could be helpful if we need to pass you off as a lawyer."

"1000 marks sir, that's a lot of purchasing power."

"Your shoes have to look fashionable and functional, your hair, I want it in a bun. Ear rings should be silver or platinum, with a matching elegant necklace. See you this evening for dinner, say 2100 hours."

I couldn't wait to get her out of the way. To listen to the investigative team was now a priority. Being 10 am. they should be having their first briefing.

Back in the upstairs attic office, the recorder being voiced controlled was whirling, picking up a conversation.

Quietly listening, trying not to make any noise, a lady was heard, “That is the way it has to be.”

Not knowing what that meant was short lived when a male voice asked, “It is unethical to prove guilt when no evidence of a crime is found, Miss. Latta.”

“I disagree we know that he is a murderer, philanderer and a chauvinist pig. His fate has been decided, we are just going through the motions to make this procedure look legit.”

“Why was this trip necessary, so much agony to go through such a charade?”

“Listen for one last time we are here to prove the General is setting up his own shadow agency. The Brits are concerned and so are we. I want to be back in Washington before Thanksgiving.”

The same man put his dissatisfaction rather weakly in another way by saying, “How can we live with ourselves if General Wright isn't guilty of sedition?”

“We are going to find the proof needed to put him away, or my name isn't Linda Latta. All start again on the files from Bad Aibling. Do not open the other files until we have the proof needed. I have to make a call, you can start without me.”

Latta picked up the phone in her room after several minutes of leaving the conference room, starting another tape recorder to whirl away. A dial tone could barely be heard as it rang, probably an overseas call, since it took a long time for it to engage.

Some lady answered, saying, “Hello, Hello, Debra Schultz office.”

“Linda Latta here, are you settling in okay, I hope to be back soon and take over again. Is Debra in her office?”

“Yes mam, it will be good to see you again and I can get back to the West Wing. Wait a minute and let me see of Mrs. Schultz is available.”

The Communications director picked up her phone after a couple of minutes, saying, “Hi Linda, you have two minutes, the secretary of State is expecting me.”

“Thank you, mam. We have finally started the process of finding General Wright culpable in disloyal acts against our Government. We may have a problem, a team member has engaged in dissenting conversation.”

“That is not good. We have to deal with him when he returns. Now listen, insert the notes I gave you if you have to. Remember they are the ones with smaller numbers at the lower left on the back side, starting with the digit one. Sorry, darling, I have to go. Miss you and love you, goodbye.”

Hmm, *sounds like the male member is not long for*

this world. Deal with him is code for getting rid of a problem for good. How many problematic bodies are covered with concrete in Washington because of knowing too much? This could be my proverbial ace in the hole. It is difficult listening to one's own future being decided by exception. Have to do something different for a little while.

I left to go see if Els was enjoying her shopping, and to get a bite to eat while watching for her. Remembering across from her hotel was a large department store, with a cafeteria on the second floor, with views down the wide pedestrian shopping center.

After carefully parking in the hotel parking lot, I walked across to the restaurant and sat at a table where the window allowed me to see all of the stores, up and down the avenue, as well as across and towards the hotel forecourt.

A suspicious thin German looking guy pacing back and forth in front of this building, settling sometimes against a lamp post, gave every clue he was a gum shoe. His dirty tan trench coat, not exactly a suitable thing to wear, if one wanted to blend in as a shopper. On the other hand, this may be nothing, just a little paranoia creeping in.

Els crossed the street with several boxes dropping one by the stalker was happenstance. He picked it up with his left hand, responded to something she said. The man tipped his hat towards another man on the edge of the parking area, again with his left hand, who then followed Els. The gentleman was seen close up by Els, he had to drop out of sight and his backup take over.

When I left the store, the man with the tipping hat followed behind, until I went into the parking lot and drove away.

It was necessary to try and see if the man was able to follow me the few blocks back to the ASA Office. Making sure he wouldn't lose sight of me, I made sure to slow down enough to catch every red light. Even if he was on foot he could keep this vehicle in sight, all the way to headquarters.

Once inside the building, a window in the secretary pool was used to spy on the man who was spying on me. The man was again leaning against another light pole, this time he was on the other side of the street, outside this fenced in compound.

Now to find out who wanted a tail posted on this agency, or me. The conundrum was how to obtain information on the two detectives. Are they working for someone investigating my activities, or is there a third entity helping to gather damaging intelligence on this agency. None of the above must be a competing agency from another time.

A part time contractor was needed, one who is a seasoned retired German National, a paid informant for the old OSS after the war, was just the man to call.

Chapter 4

MI-5 & D.C. Nemesis

The ex OSS contractor, Otto Deiter, was called, and told, "This is Major General Wright, I need you to do a job, paid by the hour, cash, no pay checks. You probably do not know me and to get past that obstacle, we can pay you for 40 hours up front to start you off."

"I know of you, from what Thibby has said. You know he recruited me when he was only a Captain, and me a Private with the dreaded black uniformed brigade. I will agree to twenty five marks an hour, no less."

"Yes Major agreed."

"My ID will have Major beside my name?"

"Yes Major."

"It is agreed then. Tell me what has to be done, no killing, I am too old for those things. It will not look good on my resume when I am called up stairs."

"Herr Deiter, two men have followed me and another agent today. One man following my agent was dressed in a long tan trench coat, or London fog. He positioned himself across the big store down in the center of town."

"Any noticeable defects, physical or mannerisms?" When he picked up a package my agent dropped, he was switched, following me. Oh yes, the man is left handed."

"Wait a minute General, what does the left hand man following you look like?"

"Pale, pot marked face, a smoker, probably from this country. His associate was dressed in a dark blue quilted coat, which followed the other agent to the American hotel close by. I did not get a close view of him."

"I do not know them they may be employed locally for solicitors, usually on domestic disputes. When do I start?"

"Today, you can use my car."

"I have a rental Mercedes in the back by the dumpsters meet me in one hour, with one weeks pay and two hundred marks in bribe money. Your car will be known rent a car for one week."

The secretary was asked to find Dieters file and have an ID made with his new title, ASAP.

Just before the hour, a new Mercedes was parked in the back. His ID was ready with an old photo from the 50's.

Otto was already sitting behind the steering wheel, by the time I arrived in the alley. He motioned for me to get in the back seat where he was handed his money and ID.

He stared at his new ID, then me in the rear view mirror, saying, “This is a work of art. Happy to finally meet you Sir William.”

“Major Dieter, likewise, on meeting you. Your money, I take it is all there.”

“Count it later. Tell me Sir William, the funny papers they say you killed 50 Russians.”

“No sir, you can't trust the news. Meet me at the American Hotel bar, at 2030.”

“Too risky. Back here at 1930.”

He took off in a car fitting his persona, mysterious and cat like.

Back up stairs in the faux office, listening with no tapes humming, I was about to walk out when Latta came on, “Alright listen carefully. We need to break for an early dinner. Is there any objection to working late?”

A man's familiar voice asked, “Why, Miss. Latta. There is nothing here. So boring reading how Sergeant Wright was rude and obstinate to Captain Summerall. I suggest we go on to the next set of files.”

“No, we are here to finely go over Wright's past, all

of it. Be back at this table in one hour, I am going for a run."

Getting ready to lock up for the day, Latta was heard dialing the phone from her bedroom it made me stop and listen. No one answered she didn't leave a message, how rude.

Had to make sure I was early to meet Otto, hoping he would have some information on the two stalkers. Walking down to the real ASA office, a note was left saying Lieutenant Els called, reminding me, I had a dinner date at nine pm.

Otto pulled into the dark and drizzly cold alley, it made me stop and think, who framed the title of the cold war, must have been a romantic. He stopped the car leaned over and popped the passenger door open. He backed up to the main road, heading towards the train station.

Finally saying as he sped along, "The two private eyes are from Hamburg. As you know that sector is British."

We pulled along the curb of the main train station, watching passengers coming and going.

I asked, "Are we going to see a meet up here."

"Yes. As it happens tonight is payday."

While waiting for almost an hour, I learned that this old timer knew every crook and cranny in Frankfurt, where sleaze balls gravitate to, especially ex security men who belonged to the black uniformed SS brigade.

In the middle of a sentence, he thumped my arm, pointing towards a platform. A man dressed in a dark pin stripe wool suit, walked towards a Bratwurst stand.

While ordering a beer and hot dog he laid a briefcase on a tall stool around the corner of the small stand.

Otto said, "Let's go. I will order bratwurst and beer and start a conversation, you walk by and switch satchels, leave mine in its place."

Otto's briefcase was emptied onto the back seat and handed to me.

Ah the old bait and switch routine. Within three minutes Otto was talking to the British Spy, with probably a war story. I walked by quickly, did the switch and continued on towards an unlit area, then turning around and headed back to the car.

Quickly going through the briefcase, taking out a bundle of German Marks, a leather bound journal and German Luger.

I hurried back and made the switch again. The two guys were on their second beer, debating reasons for the Second World War

Back in the car, contents of that briefcase was stuffed into my overcoat, which was then rolled up and left on the back seat. Otto was back, amazed at the smooth double switch.

We watched and soon saw the two stalkers approached the British Agent, ordering beers and bratwurst before sitting next to the Brit.

Uh oh, here it goes he opened the briefcase, stared at it as if he may have forgotten to bring the money, looking around for the man who had talked to. Within minutes of seeing the spy was not able to pay them, he was thumped on his chest, with the two dicks leaving and shouting as they left.

The Brit walked while looking in all directions back inside the train station. Otto dropped me off at the hotel, where I found Els sitting at the bar with a half a glass of wine.

Having to apologize for being ten minutes late, I said, "Dannie, nice hair style. Sorry for being late, there was something I couldn't break away from. Have you read the menu?"

"No, I waited for you Will."

A waitress walking by was stopped and asked if we could sit at the back of the dining room.

She said in German, "Sorry sir, we are out of everything, except Wiener Schnitzel and vegetable soup."

Answering her in the same language, I said, "We would like to order two of each. Deliver them to Miss. Els room. Please put a bottle of Riesling and one of Chateauneuf du Pape on ice."

The waitress indignantly asked, "Sir. A red wine on ice, I do not understand."

"Yes, both on ice thank you."

Els asked, "Is there anything wrong?"

"They are taking no more orders. Room service is all we can get."

"That is fine with me Will."

The waitress walking by again, she asked, "Is it possible to have a rose on the tray."

"Yes sir. Our practice is to bring a small table for two from the dining room, and a extra chair delivered before your dinner is served, if this is good for sir."

"Thank you, Fraulein."

"It is set Lieutenant, shall we go."

Chapter 5

Training Els

Up in the room, she couldn't wait to try on her

outfit, to get my approval. Using a screen to undress and redress, she walked out with a stunning outfit showing her hour glass figure, sleek, looking like a successful business woman.

Dannie was behind the screen undressing, when room service was knocking on the door. She saw the funny side with them setting up a private dining area, and finally acting a little feminine. She was changing from a defensive demeanor to actually acting like a woman on a date.

Sitting down for our meal, with wine poured, and having our food, she wasn't aware this was going to be a training session, soon we were discussing spy tactics.

She was asked, "The man who picked up your package on the side walk, did he look out of place for the area?"

"Yes a little. Wait a minute, General Wright, how can you know a man helped me with picking up a parcel? Were you stalking me?"

"In a way I was. Back to the question."

"I admit he did not look like a shopper, kind of grungy."

"There were two Private Eyes, one following you, and after you saw the man watching you, another man switched with him. Your original stalker started tailing me. The new man kept you insight. Assuming they were carrying out orders, their employer has to be found, to see who wanted ASA Agents monitored. One possibility is, it may be our own government.

That idea changed when they both met a British Agent at the train station tonight, we think he came out of the British Sector, more specific, Hamburg. The Brit was either Army Security or British Intelligence. Either way, it seems someone is interested in the future plans of the ASA. You are in need of awareness training, so maybe we can work with you over the next 16 months."

"Well sir, I think maybe we both could use a little awareness schooling."

"We are going to ignore that last statement. While all of the other training is done, I also would like you to take a Russian language course, at the same time you are studying Arabic. That should still give you plenty of time to study when not attending classes."

"Where is this training going to take place? There isn't going to be any time for dating, is there General?"

"Around Muslim Holidays, would be useful. Your awareness training has to be diverse, visiting Frankfurt, Amman, London and Moscow. The exercises will be done one weekend a month, until you master the art of surveillance and evasion tactics."

"Enough business, Lieutenant, how is your schnitzel?"

"And your soup General? Are you a vegetarian?"

"No. Had to many brats yesterday, I thought a healthier meal would be better."

"May I have another glass of wine this food seems to be making me thirsty."

Dannie started to feel the alcohol before asking leading questions. Now she was flirting with her eyes and taking my hand asking if I had ever been married, or was I married now. After the meal she wanted to dance to the song moon river playing softly on the radio.

Without finishing the dance she collapsed, causing me to carry her to bed, taking off her shoes, and clothes, and hanging them up, before leaving to go to my place.

The next morning I was having breakfast when she walked in, looking a little pale, probably from too many glasses of wine. She sat down, waiting for me to tell her what happened last night, keeping quiet, to see what she was going to say was probably my only option.

Finally she asked, "Did we kiss last night?"

"No."

"Well, we must have done something, who took my clothes off?"

"I did. Put you to bed and left."

"You didn't want to make love to me?"

"Sure I did but not with you out of it, that's not

good."

"Lieutenant, you have nothing to apologize for, I should have spilled the wine to keep you from drinking too much. Anyway, your meal made you thirsty."

"Is that why you had soup, and I had something that would make me drink. Was that your plan? I find that so ungentlemanly."

Our waiter showed up to get her order, just in time to stop a discussion that would probably lead to a flare up. After he was gone, she started with the inquisition again.

"Alright, General if that is the way you want it, fine."

Now, to change her attitude from personal, to one of business.

"Listen Els, we have a lot of work to do today. What happened last night is inconsequential to our future together. You asked me last night if I was or had been married. Yes I was married, however my wife, working as a stewardess was on a plane that had a bomb planted on it, a few years back. I am engaged to a nice librarian, in South Florida. That is going to be all the personal stuff out of the way for now, do you agree?"

"Yes. Thank you sir for telling me, I feel more at ease knowing you are a man of principle."

"Okay Lieutenant. You need to meet me at

headquarters after you go upstairs to get ready. We have a lot of work and strategy to get through today."

Dannie went to her room while I left to get ready for what is going to be a training session on eaves dropping on a person of reputable morals, which would be Els. Of course I can't talk about being ethical, with this wire tap bordering on being illegal.

Dropping in on my secretary, I was told, "General Thibodeau will be calling at 10 this morning."

"Send Els on up when she arrives."

Turning on the two recorders to hear if any transmissions were coming in from, a briefing or Latta's room.

The tape recordings were backed up to hear any conversation initiated from Latta's devices. Several transmission spanning three hours last night, was somewhat disturbing because of the tapes content. Els arriving, causing me to wait until she had a pen and pad ready for taking down notes.

Els asked, "What am I supposed to hear?"

"Listen to the beginning of tape one, the one where Linda Latta instructed an associate to forget about Wright being the target of an illicit charge. You tell me who is the King pin after hearing the tapes."

After listening to ninety minutes of tapes from the briefing room and phone calls made to Washington, she said, "You are in trouble, General, I do not see a way out. There is something you should consider. What if one of your hidden agents talks to someone loosely over a beer or bragging about a new concept he or she may be involved with, their fears of a rogue agency being formed will be substantiated. Wait a minute, fear, where is that feeling generating from, it isn't the White House. What would they fear from the ASA or CIA branching into an area that could become incendiary? This doesn't make sense sir, who wants you out of the espionage business?"

"Spot on Lieutenant, when your ship is taking on water in a big ocean, a bucket for baling will not help. You have to jump or plug up the hole. We have to eradicate the problem, pay attention, you will see a minus made into a positive, in a few days of these recordings."

Chapter 6

From Training to Counter Intelligence

Now listening in on the conversation between Latta and her boss, "Schultzie where have you been, I am stuck in this fringe country, while you are out having a good time. Tell me you haven't been to the swinging parrot?"

Tapes playing, "For one drink, I promise. Alright darling Linda, close it down. Have you put in the evidence, the time line we both think should be enough to hand the pig?"

Still listening, "We may have a problem, mam. The

male members do not like inserting bogus evidence into a Generals dossier. They could prove to be damning to their careers, if we are found out."

"Do not worry that pretty head of yours we have ways of shutting up naysayers, if you know what I mean."

"Mam, have you been on the wine tonight, you sound quite aggressive."

The damning part, "I am always aggressive when chauvinist need to be exposed."

"What about the problem with our inquisitive team, we cannot trust them to stay quiet, if they are put under pressure."

"I am dealing with that as we speak. I have to ring off, early start tomorrow with that pig in the oval office. Bright eyed and bushy tail is a requirement for his staff, as he puts it, what a creep, I would like to do away with that ass. I need a night cap, love you darling, bye bye."

Els was shocked, saying, "General you had better jump ship. You will never be given access, or be heard by anyone in the White House."

"Lieutenant are you willing to go down with the ship, or do you feel like jumping?"

"General, are you confident in taking these people down in Washington?"

"No. Just two corrupt individuals. We have to

concentrate on intelligence gathering now."

Els was in this now, I *prefer to have her attitude less ambivalent. Before we finish she has to be on board one hundred percent, maybe a bail out situation can be set up for her if she needs to bail.*

We both listened to the rest of the conversations coming from the conference room, breaking at the same time they went for recess, and meals.

For their last session, lasting ninety minutes, Latta was a little too confident in her teams' agenda, in closing for the night she added, "Alright team, we have brought everyone up to date on our findings. We need to put this baby to bed. Tomorrow morning at ten we are going to file charges against General William Wright. A three judge panel will hear our request over in the I. G. Farben Building, under Wright's office, what irony. He will be brought to us in chains if he shows any trace of leaving this city. Any questions, no, good, let's celebrate at the officer's club. I'm buying."

Els stared towards me, asking, "What now sir?"

"Lieutenant, we are going to a party. We have a room booked next to Latta's room. I have to debug her room and the conference room. We will arrive at the officer's club at ten pm. just as the D. C. Team are getting inebriated, hoping these legless prey are easily snared."

“What does one wear to an officer's club?”

“Wear your new business suit. The elusive Captain Smudgeholder will show up once again. Remember he was the one who bugged the group's meeting area and Latta's bedroom.”

“Aren't you afraid she will recognize you?”

Els was right, it may be a little risky, but, if she was under the influence, no, I needed someone to help keep me hidden.

A plan was starting to ferment, having me say, “If you shield me from Miss Latta this could workout. Her cohorts were kept in the dark as to my identity. I need to find and listen to the two agents who are troubled about the frame up. When we hear their voices, we will know who the skeptics are. Els, do not forget your I.D. to get into the club, and as you are going to arrive on your own, see if Miss Latta, takes a shine to you. Is that okay with you Lieutenant?”

“Sir, after tonight everyone will know we are partners in your risky venture agency, in other words I will be exposed. This is quite uncomfortable for my career in the Air Force.”

“In that case, you may need an escape clause, let me come up with a solution.”

The Lieutenant eventually agreed to be the bait. She left to get ready, while I visited the base commander, who had proved to have been an understanding person on the last two occasions he was needed for a favor in using his base for meeting up with Frank's search and rescue team along with billeting.

Precautions are being prepared with the commander ordering two AP's to stand by, just in case an altercation resulted from intoxication or it was found out the group were upset on seeing General Wright at the club. He made it clear who ever is out of line on his base will be dealt with forthwith.

General Thibodeau was notified, regarding the Latta / Schultz tapes. His advice was to keep everything under wraps and report to Langley tomorrow, ahead of the investigatory team.

One more favor to ask. There are three Army Judges who had helped in getting a previous Kangaroo court setup quashed last year. A possible back up may be needed, if the hearing tomorrow is rigged against anyone in the ASA or CIA.

After getting in touch with the Army Inspector's General Office. He was given the names of the same three senior Judges who would be available. However they were not going to be cheap, since they needed to take a leave of absence. Three days had to be allocated in case a judgment was delayed. One day to study the evidence that is if an adjournment for twenty four hours was granted. It was agreed that the pay would be $750.00 per man for the three day stint.

When all of our arrangements were in place, Els and I were driven to Rhein Main AFB at 2130. On arrival, the noise of music was quite enticing, putting us into a lively party mood. The two AP's were sitting in a jeep outside the club, and were acknowledged with a tip of my hat, as they waited for a signal to do whatever was asked of them.

Quietly spoken instructions for the Lieutenant were clear by saying, "You go in first, when the attention is on you, I can quietly come in a few minutes later to see if Latta was actually in the club. The need to leave is more important for removing all listening devices. When I come back and see you are involved with Miss Latta, you will be asked to dance, hoping she will get upset, by you accepting a dance invitation from a man. It should cause a scene, especially if she has had a few drinks."

When Els was inside, it was necessary to give the two Military Police Officers strict orders to stop any type of rude behavior, especially by a civilian guest.

Just as suspected, Latta was in the club, feeling quite tipsy, allowing me to leave and retrieve my bugs.

Arriving back an hour later, Els was having to fend off an amorous Linda Latta, a wonderful opportunity to set this maleficent go between up.

Walking behind Miss Latta I whispered so she was the only one who could hear me, “She's mine tonight, go chase another skirt.”

Grabbing Els by the arm towards the dance floor, we started to slow dance, where my back was to the offending woman.”

I whispered, “Tell me when she starts over. If she starts anything, go outside and ask the two MP's sitting in a Jeep to come inside.”

At the start of our third dance, Els whispered into my ear, “Sir, she is coming.”

Latta came over, grabbed my right shoulder, attempting to pull me backwards with my jacket, I shrugged forwards, causing her to lose her balance and fall backwards. Everyone who witnessed her fall was now laughing, with one of her team helping her up and telling her she should go sleep it off.

She screamed, “Go to hell, all men are pigs, I am taking this lady back to my room.”

Els left to get the MP’s, having Latta follow her out side, where a real cat fight started, hair being pulled in all directions. Both policemen ended up being scratched by crazy Linda, who had to be cuffed and thrown into the back of their vehicle and carted off.

Lieutenant Els and I left when my own MP led us

to the car. He actually came up to see if Lieutenant Els was okay.

On the way back in the sedan, Els calmed down and asked, “Sir, how in hell did you know she would react like that?”

“If you remember her tone when talking to her team, and listening to the venomous rants of Mrs Schultz was a clue to her makeup. It is quite fortunate we now have a legal charge against Latta, her violent outburst is not going to be tolerated on an American Military Base, especially a SAC facility.

We didn't have time or opportunity to pull those two men aside, the two people we need to help expose this fraud.

Els and I returned the next morning, ready to take on the White House Teams unscrupulous agenda.

When we arrived in plenty of time to look around the place where the court was to be held. Latta, who was known as punctual, was nowhere to be seen. This time, showing up as a Major General, and addressing the remnants of the Washington team, I immediately had their attention, receiving some respect because of being a General.

The court started fifteen minutes late waiting for a missing accuser, who happened to be a kingpin in this inquisition.

The senior Judge struck his podium with a gavel, asking, “General have you a defense ready for charges of having unauthorized operatives outside your agency?”

“Your honors, I do not need notes to argue why this inquiry should be dismissed, with charges of conspiracy against this team of fraudsters. May I address the accusers?”

“Yes General you can.”

“You men are going to be charged with conspiring to prosecute a U. S. Army Soldier, by conjuring up false evidence, which is probably planted throughout all of these files on the table. Lieutenant Els has a PHD in forensic studies. She will find every piece of fraudulent evidence your team has manufactured. Speak up this morning, or prepare yourselves for what awaits you. My suggestion to each one of you is to lawyer up as soon as you get back to Washington. I see no hands so we will meet again in the States.”

A middle age man nervously climbed to his feet, with a fellow member trying to stop him speaking.” The senior man finally said, “I knew all along this was an unjust investigation. I tried to have Miss. Latta not manufacture evidence, I was sure we could come up with something the honest way but we couldn't find a shred of material in which to prosecute you General, so upsetting to be part of this crime. You were way to clever in covering your tracks for any of us to get away with prosecuting you General, we were told to manufacture damning evidence."

"Hold on sir, you think it was necessary for me to cover something up?"

"Yes General I do. We were warned by another agency of your ability to foretell the future. Saying that, anyone with half a brain can read between the lines to see how one such as you, could survive encounters against huge odds, I knew beforehand we were novices coming up against an astute survivor."

"You go pack your gear, take them to the hearing with you. The rest of you stay put until MP's can escort you from this installation, you have a cell waiting we have our witness."

One other member stood up and started to say something, prompting me to say, "You're too late. Take your seat."

The unknown person shouted out, "Please sir, give me another chance. I promise to also come clean. I saw where the directives were generated from."

"Where?"

"I want a deal."

"Sit down, no deals."

He suddenly changed his mind about a deal he was

now looking for leniency.

The man now talking in a subservient tone said "Mrs. Schultz received her orders by way of a junior Senator from Vermont a very important ways and means committee member.

"Hold on. Anything you say may be used against you, do you understand?"

"Yes sir, may I continue?"

"You can continue, let me give you a warning, If anything is left out, including the foreign agency who started this process, through Mrs. Schultz, you will no longer be allowed to speak. Make the best of it this is your only chance for anyone to take pity on you. Do you understand?"

"Yes sir, thank you sir. The heading of the request was Senator Shands, asking for a complete conviction of you General Wright.

"Mrs. Schultz does not have the authority to start this type of investigation. Last chance to tell us who was pushing this inquiry."

"British Intelligence had arranged for a dossier on your past to be delivered before we embarked on this assignment. We were told by Miss Latta that the British were willing to help to bring you to heel, their words not ours. Sir, may I ask, how did you know the British were pushing this inquiry?"

“Did you read the file?”

“No sir, however, we were shown the cover which was very strange in that it had a CIA watermark, no clue that it actually came from England.”

“Thank you, go pack your suitcase.”

“Good, I have one now to nail to the cross. A mere second later he also spilled his guts with knowing where the bodies were buried. He was told to follow the other two men.

Els whispered when I sat down, “Sir, I thought you were going to be hung, drawn and quartered, I was wrong to give up on you. One question, why didn't you use the courier incident?”

“We have bigger fish to fry after hearing there is a mole in the CIA.”

Chapter 7

Entrenched Moles

“The British courier and his material will be used later on.”

Latta was escorted in, looking all disheveled after spending the night in a cell, pale and hung over would fit a person held in a drunk tank.

When she zeroed in on the General's stars I was wearing she stridently asked, “Where are my people you fiendish lout?”

The two AP's who brought her in were asked to wait outside. Els was told to go with them and bring them back in ten minutes.

When the court settled down, Latta asked, “What is going on?”

Refusing to answer, her raging blood pressure had to be exacerbating a thumping great headache.

She let out a slew of profanity, causing the Judge to tell her, “Sit down Miss Latta. A gag will be applied if you shout or use profanity again. Do you understand?”

“Yes sir, sorry your honor.”

“General, you have the floor.”

“Thank you your honor. Miss Latta, we have two of your team willing to testify your involvement in a criminal conspiracy. Mam, do you have anything to say before the MP's come back in?”

“My name is not mam, it is Linda Latta. I do not care what those two weak men had to say, they are not telling the truth. It is my word against theirs. You will set me free today or pay the consequences when Washington hears what you all have done to me. We have witnesses on your iniquitous activities.”

“When we are in front of a stateside court, your defense team will be allowed to hear conversations you had with a Mrs. Schultz over the past week on how to insert damaging information by using a code of numbers given to you by your boss. This information was picked up by a British listening post at the Molesworth eaves dropping facility.”

“That is a bold face lie, the British would never divulge information to help your case they want you out of commission, now.”

Military Policemen entered on time, led in by Lieutenant Els. They handcuffed her again and started to take her away, stopping when she start to shout.

“Please can I stay at a hotel? That jail cell was so cold, please sir.”

The MP's were ordered to sit on both sides of her at the table.

“Miss. Latta, you have the right to an attorney, whatever you say may be brought up in evidence in a court of law. Having said that we are able to offer.”

Linda interrupted, stridently demanding, “I want to know what evidence you have against me, I insist on it.”

“You are going to find out in the States, please go with these two gentlemen. Transport will be arranged within two weeks.”

“Two weeks? Okay, okay, General please please

hear me out."

"Alright, Miss. Latta, you utter one wrong word and those two men are going to take care of you. No bargaining, listen, there are no terms for your outcome, on the other, hand after you do a complete mea culpa, we will take your admission of guilt to determine how you should be treated, understand?"

"Yes sir. Please let me say, I was coerced in many ways. Framing you and your agency was one of them."

Thinking to myself, *Els, the MP's and Linda are going to be shocked with my first question.*

"Miss Latta, how did Mrs. Schultz entice you into a relationship with her?"

First she was shocked, as were the others, then she started to cry while trying to say, "When I volunteered as a page."

"Were you in college?"

"No sir. The eleventh grade."

Linda was now too emotional to continue.

I took the two MP's outside, to let them know what they had to do, ordering them, "Wait in your Jeep until we come out and then take the three men and Miss. Latta to the I.G. Farben Building. Thank you men."

The ranking MP asked, "Sir, how did you know the young lady was coerced into a relationship?"

Simple deduction Sergeant, especially when Latta's

boss was overheard on several phone calls. What was said would make a French Madam blush."

When I got back inside, Miss. Latta was being consoled by Els and ready to continue with her ultimatum, even though she had no idea what she was going to be asked to do.

"This is going to test your resolve Miss Latta. Tell me the whole sordid story of how your relationship started with Mrs. Schultz."

"It started at the end of a summer farewell party. She was the White House supervisor for interns. I was given my first drink of alcohol spiked in fruit punch. Waking up the next morning in her bed, she was so sweet to me, telling me she was sorry for what happened. Her excuse was she had way too much to drink."

"You went back to school and did you go back after graduating from High School?"

"No sir. I told my mother what happened, causing her to send a registered letter to the President."

"What was the response from the President?"

"We assumed he was too busy to answer us, as we were ordinary citizens and it was just before the Tehran hostage situation. My mother waited and waited, a letter never came from the White House. I graduated from college four years later and was recruited to work for a

Senator from our state who introduced me to Mrs. Schultz who was his senior aide. She asked me to go out and start over again, of course I refused."

"When did the pictures start to appear?"

"The next morning an envelope was pushed under my door with photographs of me six years ago. Sir, that is all I want to say, you can guess the rest. I would do anything to keep this quiet."

"Okay Linda, you are going to go to another hearing today, then when in the States, you are going to give evidence to a tribunal, set up by me.

"When this is over, we have to iron out where my personal information was passed. Is that agreeable?"

"Yes sir. You need to also agree to help me. The photographs or negatives are going to surface sometime in the future, you need to deal with that."

She was playing hard ball now, I have to do this for her or she walks.

"Okay Miss Latta, the CIA will get those items, anything else?"

"Yes sir, you have to get them, I do not want anyone else seeing what happened, is that agreeable sir?"

"That's twice you have given me an ultimatum, I will keep it in mind. Yes. I alone will get the dirty pictures. Do you mind if I look at them?"

She laughed and said, "I'm sure you have seen

worse, sir."

That was quite hilarious, causing me to burst out laughing, saying, "Touché. When you are back in Washington, see a physician for symptoms of stress. Stay away from Schultz by taking three weeks off going home to see your parents."

"Back to business Linda. Your team members have given statements on Mrs. Schultz's orchestrated attempt to conspire with those she is in charge of using her power to hire and fire over all of your heads. All of those factors will be considered when prosecutors are faced with determining to prosecute the actors. You need to write a statement exonerating General Wright."

"Yes sir. I will do as you say. My mother will be pleased to see me knowing justice was half done. Telling her how I was a willing partner in this fraud would be the end of her. Thank you again General."

"You're welcome. When you are finished, the AP's are going to escort you and the team to a waiting plane. One last request. On another form write the names that were closely associated with Mrs. Schultz, not necessarily from the White House, everyone has to be named."

"Sir, even ones from the intelligence community?"

"Yes, everyone."

So much to do back in Washington. Starting to set

up a shadow group of informants if Latta agrees to be one of my informants on Capitol Hill.
Upcoming briefings with the CIA Director should be a lot easier we now stand on higher ground.

Chapter 8

Mole Trap

It was time to let the Lieutenant leave for Amman, Jordan.

She was told " Els go get packed, you are heading back to college. I will be in Jordan in a couple of weeks with your instructor in field surveillance tactics."

Dannie kissed and embraced me, whispering, "If it doesn't work out in Florida, I am available."

She started to blush and giggle. She was now back to being nice again, thankfully.

An official Court Martial was called the next day. Thankfully it started on time with the three original judges, who demanded I be put on the stand. Those were orders from the White House. We still had to go through the motions of an Official Army hearing on my conduct. My hope was to placate Schultz for at least two weeks.

One of the Judges, the senior one, stood up and asked, "Who exactly ordered this officer put on the stand?"

"And you are who?"

No one knew or expected a onetime high ranking Lawyer was going to vouch for me. An old friend was called in as a character witness, one past I.G.

The voucher slowly rose and answered the question, "NATO Supreme Inspector General, these are my colleagues beside me. We are here to ask why General Wright has been charged by a civilian while carrying out his duties as ASA Director."

The hearing was immediately adjourned, when an explanation was not forthcoming.

I was fortunate to catch the 2pm. flight to Washington, where Thibodeau was waiting in the arrivals lounge.

His first words were, "Wright you are again booked into the Hilton that is my first stop to get you signed in and order me a strong beverage."

Not, it is nice to see you again or you are looking great, no it was the Hilton Hotel Bar, typical, not to the Langley Farm or his office, but to his favorite bar.

He was mad as hell when he asked for a meeting in the morning and was told, "Sir, I need sleep and rest. It is almost midnight in Frankfurt."

I had things to do this evening, like turning into a cat burglar before a target arrives home.

When the General was gone, it was time to call my friend Clint and find Schultz's residence before she arrived home from work.

Her address was found to be in Columbia Heights, in an area of recently built upscale town homes.

Finding her place, Clint was told to leave the area he would be called later with a pickup place.

Easily entering though a back door where the bottom floor was used mostly for storage and garage. The first thing to do was to see if she had a partner or husband here. Luck was with me no one was using the spare bedroom or shared hers. A loaded snub nose pistol was in her bed side cabinet.

Taking the weapon for self preservation and placed into my back pocket for safe keeping, just in case she jumps me.. Four keys in bank sleeves, two pairs of deposit box keys at separate banks.

Downstairs looking through her sideboard, luck ran out, when no photographs were found and hearing the garage door opening, it was time to wait and hide.

Hurrying into the dining room and closing the door, listening as she set her keys down. She walked upstairs where water was heard being turned on a bath tub was being filled.

What an opportunity, keys were plunked on a small hall table. Alongside of her handbag were a few heavy brass keys on a separate ring with the initials of P. A. most likely code for Pennsylvania Avenue.

From her purse, a White House I. D. was taken along with all other Government documents, including two passports and a one way Swiss Air ticket to Zurich, in the name of Hilda Schneider, for this Sunday.

She's a freaking spy, but who for? I know she will not give up her foreign contact or contacts, and would probably keep her American informers secret, unless she was somehow persuaded with a nice little chit chat. No, medicine is what she needs, to obtain information from this wretched traitor.

Knowing this vile person, has to have sedatives somewhere for seducing acquaintances, ones she had used to get her way with young girls, according to Linda.

Barbiturates were found in her cocktail bar that makes sense, sleight of hand for spiking drinks. After fixing two scotch and sodas, I poured the powder into the scotch bottle, sloshed it around, until it was completely dissolved, then refilled the packet with powdered sugar, from her pantry.

Thinking she was taking a long time upstairs, she came down the stairs with a suitcase. Schultz was startled when she saw me by the bar.

After composing herself, she said, “Get out of my house. How did you get in?”

“Hilda, you must be civil, I fixed you a drink.”

Pulling her gun out and pointing at her I said, “Here drink.”

She clumsily knocked the glass over and fixed her own drink. It wasn't long before she had to sit down, feeling the effects of the drug. Halfway asleep, and still able to communicate, she started talking.

Slurring her words, she asked, “Arse shou ere ta takes me to ze airport? My prane to New York leaves soon.”

“Yes Hilda, my taxi is waiting. First you wanted me to join you in a drink.”

“I did? Of course I did, I always have a drink in the evening. You know, my flight leaves for Zurich in two days, very early. Comrade Gregory will be waiting at the airport, his American name is John Hamilton, isn't that hilarious, dumb Americans, heh heh.”

She fell asleep, after telling me she had a suitcase full of savings bonds.

Her case had two million dollars in certificate of deposits, not bonds.

General Thibodeau was called; he was not pleased at being disturbed, until he was aware of the situation. He knew John Hamilton and would have him arrested tomorrow morning. It seems Hamilton was an alias, who worked under the Carter administration, now assigned to the foreign office.

Two men in dark suits showed up within ten minutes to apprehend Schultz or whoever she was. Their ID's said they were with the Secret Service, hum, I thought, why would the White House Security be involved. Jeff walked in just as I was asked to go with them, refusing caused an immediate situation. I could be anyone and the security not knowing who I was, had them concerned. My identity had to be kept a secret for me to keep the two suit cases.

It was lucky Hank stepped in and said to the men, "You two take Schultz to the Marine Barracks at Andrews. Wright, sir, you come with me."

The two men looked as if they had seen a ghost, when Jeff told them, "You heard correctly, this is William Wright."

One G-Men said, "Sorry sir, we had no idea."
We were resigned now that discretion had flown out of the widow.

When the two men and Schultz were taken into custody, I asked Hank, "Please leave me to clean this up."

Two million dollars in C.D,'s for the new agency, not a bad days work. Just before leaving the house, the gas oven was turned up on high, along with the fire place. A scented candle in the bed room lit means it was time to quickly leave. A few minutes after the front door closed behind me and a loud blast was heard.

The next morning at a scheduled meeting with the CIA Director, General Thibodeau was asked, "Sir, I need to retrieve the contents of Schultz's deposit boxes. There are items used for black mailing a young lady that no one should see. This victim was coerced and then caught up in a web of extortion. Everything else will be handed over to you, except the photographs, is that agreeable sir?"

"Highly unusual Wright, yes it is agreed."

"Thank you sir, the young lady will be relieved. Schultz was flying out of JFK to Zurich on Sunday under the name of Schneider. That flight needs to be met to see who was going to meet her."

"Can you arrange it?"

"No Wright I cannot, that is your territory and you had better address me as sir or General next time you have something to say. Is that understood?"

"Sorry sir. Are you feeling alright?"

"You insolent ass, I'm a phone call away of having

you put in chains."

After he kicked me out of his office, laughter could be heard out in the foyer.

The next day General Thibodeau and I were asked to meet with the Vice President's secretary, even though she had to show up on a Saturday morning, where her attitude could show some annoyance.

After being picked up by the General at 0800, we arrived early for our 0900 meeting and escorted into the foyer of the Capitol Building by the same pair of secret service agents who showed up at Schultz's house. Hank was keeping a safe ten feet away which was smart; no one in this place needs to know of our association.

Within minutes we were escorted to a conference room next to the oval office. Three men already in the room and sitting around a table seemed to be expecting us. They rose showing a lot of respect for the CIA Director. Thibodeau was asked to introduce his associate.

As soon as we exchanged names and taking a seat, the crusty old General Thibodeau said, "The FBI Director will start this briefing. "

The man went straight for the jugular when he said, "General Wright, there are rumors of you heading a shadow CIA, funded through three off shore accounts. Is there any validity in this rumor?"

"No sir."

"You are a liar, General. Reports from a close ally has the proof."

"If there was anything to that charge, you would not need me to substantiate such a yarn. This session is over Mr. Brenisky."

I got up to leave, just before opening the door, General Thibodeau said, "Now you hold on Wright, sit down and show some respect."

Turning around at the door, purposely responding in a way to see what this group was made of by harshly saying, "That is a two way street, sir. Tell me later if anything was discussed worth listening to."

Another man asked, "Shall I call in the two men outside sir?"

"No sit down. They won't stop this man. We do not need a physical confrontation in this place."

Brenisky turned his attention towards me saying, "I should have known General Wright, my threats would be somewhat tame, compared to the treatment you have received in Eastern Europe. Tell us how you would improve a working relationship with the Bureau?"

"We can trade data without hurting some feelings, you first sir, Debra Schultz, was she being watched and are her British contacts under surveillance?"

The Bureau Chief rose to his feet and said, "Thank

you Gentlemen for your time. Wright, we may have to talk later."

"Looking forward to it Mr. Brenisky."

"On the way back to the Hilton, Thibodeau said, "Wright you have guts, I give you that. Do you know that man can have you disappear in a nano second?"

"Do not sell the CIA short sir. Brenisky knows that is also a two way street."

"I was going to take you for a drink but not now, you are radioactive and going to be watched, twenty four seven. He knows you were quietly threatening him."

"He knows better than to put a tail on a good CIA agent, sir."

"Ha ha ha that's a crock. Good day Wright, get out, we're at your hotel."

Thibodeau was still laughing when his sedan pulled away from the curb.

When the General's sedan was out of sight it was time to go back to the White House and have those two Security men empty a couple of safety deposit boxes since they have secret service authority to inspect all property. This still isn't over, the rat or in this case, the mole that passed on information about Nicola and I living and working out of TIA has to be ousted.

At the Capitol gates, one of the guards called Jeff to

come down to sign me in. He drove up with his two trusted confidants, who accompanied me before the banks closed at one pm. Hank walked back to his office so we could get going.

It was a breeze to inspect both trays with the G-Men insisting that the banks allow me to use the Schultz keys.

Going through the contents in a secure room, I took out close to 100 hundred photographs and the same amount of negatives plus two passports.

In the last safety deposit box were images of several your girls and women. If the names on the back of each picture wasn't bad enough, where and who they worked for could be useful for obtaining secrets.

When I returned to my hotel a request for using their copier was granted. Everything was copied, except the photographs; they had to be kept secret, in case Schultz was prosecuted. Thinking her brief will have a chance to have the evidence thrown out because of an illegal entry into a private residence.

That evening Jeff was called after a brain storm of wanting to see if Mrs. Schultz office was turned over by the security team. He was just sitting down to watch a Florida State football game and said he would see me Sunday morning after Mass.

While eating breakfast Sunday morning, Jeff walked

into the dining room, instead of coming over he got in the buffet line.

Jeff sat down and said, “Man o man what a selection of goodies, my wife would crucify me if she knew I was eating all of this fried bacon, hash browns and eggs. Now tell me what is the reason you need to know about the Communications Director office being looked into?”

“You do not need to know. Get me in and leave for ten minutes, while you make sure I am not disturbed.”

“Yea, maybe you're right. As soon as we finish here, I'll get you in. Wait, I don't have the keys to that office, that's strange isn't it, security not having access.”

“There’s a reason for that. Don't worry about keys I have a way of getting in.”

Fantastic news, security had no way to check out a possible spy's office. I wonder if Schultz could have been over confident, knowing no one had access to her files

He didn't need to respond to that last statement, keeping out of the loop is safer than having to answer questions.

When we got to the White House he left me alone, enough to plant a bogus passport, and to see if she had any more worthwhile documents or photographs.

After leaving the building we drove over to the CIA Directors office, to dump all of the documents on top of

Thibodeau's desk. The agency's code breakers are able to see who the villain passed documents to.

Jeff wanted to play golf over at the Greenbrier where he gets to play for free.

That evening after playing nine holes, we were having a drink in the club house, when he whispered, "There's the Vice President, do you want to meet him?"

"No. Already met him, we didn't exactly hit it off."

"Not many do from what I see. We'll just leave it at that I can't tell tales out of school, old boy."

Chapter 9

Ghost Protocol

I laughed, that was a code for the Veep and was from an Ivy League high society.

The next morning I was interrupted again at breakfast, when General Thibodeau walked in wearing his flashy uniform, the one used for special occasions. Silver buttons, silver stars and a gold braid that went from his left shoulder to his chest full of campaign medals.

He didn't get into the buffet line but waited for the waiter to take his order. Must have been the first time he couldn't load up on sausages, bacon and pan cakes.

It was seconds when the head waiter walker over asking, “General what would you like for breakfast?”

I quickly answered him, “He will have a bowl of oat meal and a side bowl of melon.”

Thibodeau turned red in the face, now in a rage he said, “You bring me that crap, I will have you fired. Bring me three eggs fried sunny side up a large bowl of grits, three rashers of bacon, three sausages and three biscuits with a side order of saw mill gravy. Got it?”

“Yes sir General takes about five minutes.”

The waiter was waved off now it was my turn to feel the old man's wrath, when he loudly said, “Private, you no good sonofabitch, I will have you in chains so fast your head'll swim. Don't you ever embarrass me like that again.”

By now everyone in the room was staring at us, to add to their entertainment, I replied, “I'm a General sir, anyway I was just looking out for your health, sir.”

“You ain't a general no more you insolent lying reprobate, I'll have you frog marched up Pennsylvania Avenue before the day is over.”

We both were laughing when the General's food arrived, having him stop momentarily from asking the question of, “My aid called this morning to say someone was in my office last night. Was that you Private

Wright?"

"It's General Wright, you must have amnesia sir. Yes sir it was me, they are the stuff out of Schulz's safety deposit boxes."

"I must have been crazy to suggest you should have your second star, anyway that is spilt milk. Be at my office Monday, no later than 1400."

"Yes sir. Is this meeting over?"

"No it isn't, you sit tight while I eat. Did you leave anything out of the dropped documents, like money?"

"If there was any money, it must be already in the place where she was running to."

"You find out, there must have been lots of payoffs, she seemed to be doing this sort of thing back when I was in the OSS. I have to go, maybe you are right, I will leave that last half biscuit. You say one word General Wright these people will see a show they won't forget."

"Yes sir. Would you send the results to Frankfurt from the papers? Sir, you need to know those files were taken with out permission."

"You never told me you broke into the White House for that purpose, are we clear on this. Where do you get your nerve from?"

"Yes sir. Those file were dumped anonymously on a weekend."

The old man finally finished his meal, leaving a little slower than when he entered. He was right any evidence taken without a Judge's permission would be deemed to be illegal.

Linda Latta was tracked down at her parent's house to go over a proposition for her becoming the new White House Communications Director.

We discussed who called her old boss, especially repeated conversations she had with foreign citizens and other Government employees. What was alarming was a close relationship with a CIA Secretary.

It was now important to be in the CIA Offices an hour early sitting in the waiting area down stairs, to see who entered the elevator to Thibodeau's office, . With me and everyone else knowing he would be back from his liquid lunch by noon, it was a safe bet if he had anyone scheduled they would be showing up before a meeting with me.

It was strange no one showed up before I had to stand and go up to see him however, two Brits came out of the elevator, just as I pushed the buttons.

Both in dark gray pin stripe wool suits, holding leather handled umbrellas, with one of them saying, "Do you think the man knows anything about Chesterfield's people, sharing secrets."

The other Brit answered, "Sir Giles, I'd rather not

say.”

“Alright ole bean, do you think she will be found out.”

They stopped in their tracks, knowing I was listening, with Sir Giles asking, “Have we met?”

“Don't think so, unless you have been to South Viet Nam.”

They left with the other man quietly saying, “An educated man doesn't say don’t, what is this world coming to, what.”

When I got to the big man's office, his secretary pressed her index finger across her lips, whispering, “He's on the phone to the V.P.”

“Whispering back to her, “Did I see Sir Giles come out of the building?”

“That has to be top secret stuff, with him and Sir Montague being called to Washington on such short notice. You know how hard it is to get their Civil Servants to agree to an inquiry, especially from the CIA.”

Something the Brit said, will she be found out. Was that Thibodeau's secretary, no other female was in the picture right now.

She interrupted my thoughts when I heard, “The General will see you sir.”

I was shown into Thibodeau's office, when invited

to sit down the secretary pulled out my chair before leaving. Instead of sitting down, I slightly opened his connecting door to witness his secretary turning on the intercom.

Gently closing the door, Thibodeau asked, "What in blazes is wrong with you Wright, sit down."

"Sorry sir got a charley horse in my right calf."

Not wanting to discuss anything now, I said, "Sorry General. I need a drink."

"Now you're talking my language. Put your coat back on, I've got just the place."

Hurrying back out and catching the secretary turning off the intercom, not before hearing the General say, "Where's that dam scarf."

She turned red in the face and said, "Can't seem to wipe all the dust off that machine."

"Your right, dust is everywhere. You want to join us for a drink?"

"A little soon in the day for me, thank you sir for asking."

We were driven back to the Hilton, where we found the lounge empty, a perfect place to have a debriefing.

Both of us ordering scotch and soda, the General asked, "Why did you not want to talk in my office?"

"No reason sir."

"It's my secretary, isn't it?"

"Why would you say that sir? Did your people find her name in Schultz's paperwork?"

"No. They are still being decoded. I do not think my secretary's name will be found. Look Wright, everything we needed exposing the threat to you, was heard in those tapes you gave us. We also came across a letter that was sent to Schultz from the Russian Embassy in Zurich, asking her to find out if you were alive and where you were. In that document was a statement asking her to find out if the rumors were correct. I know you suspected the leak was from my office, now knowing it wasn't, you have to get this behind us."

"Thank you sir for telling me, however, this isn't over by a long shot."

"You will be struck down General Wright if you go on another vengeful witch hunt. Do you understand?"

"Yes sir, may I go now."

"No you cannot young man, listen. The most damning document had the name of a first term Senator from Vermont, a known Communist sympathizer, giving your information to the White House Communications Director."

"Where would Schultz or the senator get addresses and employment details of Nicola and me if it didn't originate out of the CIA?"

The General's right hand fingers were tapping the

table many times, finally answering, "Um, I see, that is a problem. One other item Wright, did you turn everything over from the lady's residence?"

"Maybe I missed something, what is it you're looking for?"

"In the pile of papers were receipts from a purchase of $2,000,000.00 in C.D.'s. I take it those were burned?"

"I guess so sir."

"General Wright, how close did she come to exposing you?"

"In what way sir?"

"Get out of my office. Where are you going next?"

"Boca Grande to do some fishing."

"Isn't her father a banker?"

"Who's father sir?"

"Go on I wish I could go with you let Fran know mother and I were asking about her."

"Will do sir, thank you."

"Go on get out of here."

Thankfully the subject changed from almost being caught by the evil lady and Latta's investigation. Thanks to the fire, the shadow agency has working capital in funding a foreign operation, with high tech machinery.

Arriving in the late afternoon at Tampa International, I immediately went to my parents home, where I spent the night and brought my parents up to date on the few months on almost everything.

One of my brothers drove me to Everglades City to see Fran and to pick up my truck and I left immediately to get back before dark.

Business had to be done with Fran's father and give him the C.D.'s to add to my account. He was taken back at the amount, afraid to ask questions, he agreed to send the funds down to the Cayman's.

After our business was over, I walked into the high school library just as Fran was getting ready to leave. She pulled me down one of the isles, kissing me as if she couldn't wait any longer to be close to me.

I was barely able to say, “Let’s get out of here before we get into a situation neither one of us does not want to get out of.”

We drove to Marco Island in separate vehicles, where she stayed the night and left early to get back to school, before the bell rang.

Later that day, arriving on Boca Grande, my brother and I went fishing down on the old phosphate docks. We talked about how mom and dad were doing.

For the next few days we fished and caught up on friends and family. This was a relaxing time to be with one of my brothers, no time to think about what was going on in a world full of problems.

As soon as Fran arrived on Friday afternoon, my

brother left to go home. Fran and I spent the weekend talking about her coming to Frankfurt after Christmas for a week, only condition was that I did not leave her alone in London.

Fran and I left Sunday afternoon, she went back home, I went to drop off my truck at our farm and fly to London to rest up for a few days.

Tuesday afternoon Pierre met me at Birmingham Train Station, where we set up a time he could meet me in Amman. It was agreed we would meet this coming Friday, 7pm. in the Amman Airport Hilton lounge.

While in London I planned to see who was in the Russian Embassy KGB office. It doesn't hurt to keep up appearances, in case something was needed inside the KGB Director's office, in the way of military orders posting me to a part of the Middle East that I will be able to access. Russian officials are welcomed in many Arabian Countries where military arms are traded for oil.

Tuesday evening when most Russian Embassy staff were gone for the day turned out to be quite easy to access the building. What wasn't expected was hearing the KGB Chief talking to Moscow, with his back to the door, his feet propped up on the top of a filing cabinet.

Curious on whom he was talking to, I quietly sat down, listening to his conversation, assuming it was the

Kremlin he had on the phone, from the way he spoke in military jargon while perusing a telex.

He asked about one of my aliases, "Yes I know of a General Gennady Vagon, why do you ask? I see. Here in London, no he hasn't come by. Yes Comrade Petro, yes."

I was wrong, it was the KGB Director, wonder if Petro was looking for me, or needing to give out information.

I quietly left, leaving before he got off the phone. The Russians believe they have a General Vagon somewhere on holiday in Europe.

Getting to the flat at nine pm. Kenny was waiting on the curb.

He followed me through the door saying, "Evenen Guv, im in da big ouse wants a word, ben sommers, arrow I fancy."

"Russian house, not Harrow, cup of tea."

"Wouldn't say no guv. Did ya ear me."

"Yea, the whole building heard you. How did he know I was in town? You told him didn't you, and when does he want to see me."

"Not me Guv, e erd it on da tom tom. Morrow morning at eight bells, e said. I am to bring ya. Ow many commies ya killed since we last met."

Ignoring him, while making the tea, he was heard

muttering, “Fought so” chuckling at his own colloquialisms.”

“Here's your tea, any reds in the Russian safeway house?”

“Why, ya gonna turn it over, Guv?”

“I don't rob every Russian I see. Is there anyone living there?”

“Nah, just the same old Bakewell, Guv. (Cockney for tart, or whore).”

The next morning I was delivered to General Simpson, with Kenny making sure I went through the office door.

My driver told Simpson's secretary, “Ere e is love, I did me best, make sure e stays put, will ya.”

“Yes love. Leave him with me.”

“You two take the cake Miss. Peabody treating me like a teenager has to end one day.”

“We both know ya, love it. The General is on his way.”

“You know Miss Peabody, when you get finished talking to Kenny, you revert back to your Cockney colloquialisms.”

“My what?”

“Never mind,”

“Ya need to tell me what that collokisms is.”

“It is how some people talk.”

“Now I see thank you Will that wasn't hard to explain was it?”

General Simpson walked in and saved the day. He pointed towards his office for me to go in how rude.

Simpson asked, “Do you know a General Vagon a Russian KGB operative. Transmissions received a few months ago said he was living in London. No one knows what he looks like, how can a Russian General be incognito, with no dossier on him from the Brits or us.”

“He doesn't exist physically, only in files with the Kremlin, Prague Central Headquarters and the London Embassy. In other words he is a ghostly alias.”

“What are you talking about Wright? Have you been on the sauce this morning?”

“No sir. General Gennady Vagon was invented, a stealthy operator, hiding in the shadows, spying on all Soviet clandestine operations. Reason being is, my past aliases are somewhat old and dubious being named after real Russian Colonels could be dangerous. I thought that a General, who no one knows or what he looks like, could be beneficial in infiltrating foreign Embassy's, especially Russian Embassy's, consulates and getting through foreign immigrations and borders in the Middle East.”

“You're insane. One day you are going to go to far,

maybe cause a conflict that cannot be taken care of diplomatically, conflicts aren't always on a battle field. Do you really enjoy living on the edge, God help us if you get caught."

"My wish is to stop a larger conflict which may encompass many Middle Eastern nations. One where ideologies are now working to undermine and infiltrate Western societies, through mass migration. Vitriolic preaching brings turmoil, where tribal peoples want to avenge whatever they are told to avenge. Countries can cause unrest keeping their people in the dark."

Chapter 10

Forwarding My Agenda

"Look General Wright, the Crusades are in the past."

Sir, I believe we are an unwilling protector in a movement that started many centuries ago. Someone inside an organization like ours has to stop this gathering threat."

"Get out Wright, for now, you need to stay close by until we figure out what you think is going to happen in your lunacy and delusional fantasy world. Where will you be for the next week?"

"Frankfurt and Amman."

"Why Amman? Don't answer that. We will call you in Frankfurt you may need to be looked at by one of our shrinks."

"You think I am delusional, sir?"

"Get out call me every day I need to know where you are at all times."

Imagining me staying in touch, don't think so, then responding with, "Yes sir."

Leaving Simpson shaking his head, probably knowing, fat chance he is going to be kept up to date on my activities. Kenny was waiting downstairs to take me to wherever I needed to go. On the way down the stairs, instead of taking an elevator to give me a few minutes to think on what Simpson said and his thought process.

Simpson was saying something, as if he wasn't through with me. Having second thoughts on letting Simpson in on some of my plans. The main reason was, the General doesn't assimilate information the way I do. The need to get out of London and to Frankfurt is an instant priority now, because if Simpson would want to know more of an advancing agenda. He can't help sending Kenny to fetch me when he needs to clear up a problem.

Out on the curb, Kenny was half asleep in his taxi, and opening his back door startled him, saying, Rhoit Guv where we headed?"

"Let's go get a cup of tea, and while I pack for a trip, you can do the honors."

"Tah Guv, appy ta make the tea, Guv."

Two hours later, I was standing in line at a BEA ticket counter, my mind still on Simpson, asking myself, was the General given too much information.

Jolted out of a cerebral haze by a question from a pretty lady in a posh accent," Do you require a ticket sir?"

"Yes, sorry miss, I need to purchase a first class ticket to Frankfurt."

"May I have your passport please?"

Searching my pockets, I found my documents and enough cash to get me to West Germany.

"Any luggage sir?"

"Oh yeah, one carry on."

Not aware Kenny was still behind me and turning to go, he scared the stuffing out of me as he was inches from my face causing me to say, "What are you doing I thought you was on your way back to London.".

"Sorry Guv, looks like ya could use a nice cup of tea you have an hour, Guv."

Kenny sat me in a booth, then left to get our tea.

When he got back to the booth he stared, waiting for me to say something.

My mind was buzzing working out what to do about unraveling the message Simpson was just given. Finally coming to the conclusion that nothing can be done, now the proverbial cat was well and truly out of the bag. Why did I mention Amman?

I heard him say, "Your tea's getting cold, Guv."

"Thank you. I may have done it this time Kenny. My words may come back to haunt me, what I said to Jerald, probably sounded a little strange. Enough so, he certainly will be on the blower to Thibby."

"E always does Guv, after one of your visits. And e wooden like ya calling im Thibby"

"Sorry, what was that?"

"Well Guv, after e see's you for a spell, e gits in me cab just a mumbling. Something bout wot e told that geezer in Washington, bout you Guv."

I had to laugh. Kenny was right, why go over what may or may not happen. They were calling my flight, I had to leave.

After saying so long, my body started moving towards the gates. After getting to Frankfurt I took a cab to ASA Headquarters, thinking it was necessary to go through the swag that was taken from the MI5 or MI6 Agent, I totally forgot which branch it was.

No one was in the office. *I was wondering if it was a weekend or why has everyone left for the day. No it has to be Tuesday, drat, it's Wednesday, so much to do. What's needed for me to get my mind back on track is to get away, maybe a camping trip on the Czech Border.*

First things first, contraband lifted from a British Intel satchel had to be examined thoroughly.

First items brought out were two British Home Office Passports, in different names. However, the same photograph of the British Agent who was carrying this MI-5 cache was in them.

Names of Lord Cravenhall and Nigel Naise' Smyth were inside the front flaps. Those two people were once moles ex Soviet double agents, killed years ago by an unknown foreign agent, which Whitehall thought was, William Wright.

Each passport's origination date was the same, meaning these may be from a standard batch, were a dozen are usually printed by her Majesty's Printers. This find may help in shifting my agenda forward into a higher gear.

Starting with reading travel logs, going by entry dates and exit stamps on these travel documents from airports and ferry ports when entering and exiting the U.K. and Western Europe. Have to remember that these were aliases, hoping the man's real identity is in with the other documents. All of these are connected with finding out where a shadow agency is operating from and who is running a rogue agency.

A military I.D., drivers license with no photograph, on a Major Montague Marlborough. A list of names working for MI5 throughout the Middle East and Europe, with the signature of an initial"M", where each person was stationed and moved to. Evidently he was working on that document while on the train.

Cravenhall	Nigel M
Cairo-June, July, Oct.	*Moscow- May, Aug. Sept.*
Back = = =	*back in UK = = =*
3 day trips	*5 day trips*

British Army postings for Marlborough

Moleshill-	*1965-1970*
Stoney Cross-	*1970- 1975*
Cypress-	*1975- 1980*
Hamburg-	1980-present- Centcom Europe

TDY-NATO British Liaison Officer- Brussels

Marlborough looks old enough to have been in the intelligence game during the halcyon days of the OSS, I wonder if he, noThibodeau wouldn't ally the CIA with an adversarial agency, not now. Back during post war Germany it was different to it what it is today, with the Soviets trying to steal high tech information, especially on missile delivery systems and a new program covering

GPS.

This man was no ordinary courier; he was either calling the shots in Germany, or receiving his orders directly from the Prime Minister's Office. Now to figure out where the map is leading to.

Finding the Brits objective or purpose will give me useful answers. One other document was in code, a mixture of numbers and letters.

Have to start with places, then dates where one was repeated with a digit or a member of the alphabet. This British made conundrum could use an enigma decoder to digest its content and spit out something that makes sense of these digits and letters. Wait, who would have the answer sheet, where was this document heading or was it sent here.

Time was slowly going by for two days without any hope of breaking the code, realizing it was time to fly to Amman to meet with Pierre and Els. Still wishing it was the woods I was headed to for a week, oh well, this meeting has to be done to get Els trained.

Pierre was in the hotel lounge when I arrived, seeing me he said, "Check in and meet me here in thirty minutes, I have to see an old friend, who lives close by."

Up in my room, I called Els to see if she could have dinner with us tonight.

She eventually came to the phone, sounding tired,

and after hearing my voice, she perked up, gladly accepting the invitation.

Pierre and I were having a drink when Lieutenant Els came in, dressed in her outfit from Frankfurt. Pierre was stunned by her beauty and grace, he was all eyes.

Starting the evening off with introductions, "Dannie meet Pierre. He is going to instruct you how to blend in, in a Muslim Country."

Pierre replied, "It is important to find this young lady the attire where she will be able to mix in with other ladies."

Lieutenant Els wanted to know, "Pierre, why not dress me up like a man, a small frail man."

"Non, bon ami, you are to much a lady. The way you walk, throw your hips, thees weel be no good, non."

Watching these two getting their logistics in order was entertaining. We ordered our meals through all of discussions on what was going to happen tomorrow.

Relaxing while we ate, gave me the impetus to include these two agents in helping me tonight to solve the MI6 conundrum.

When we left to have coffee in the back of the lounge, I showed the coded document to them.

The two of them hashed over a few ideas on what could be the unraveling of the enigmatic array of numbers and letters on each line.

That was until Els excitedly said, “I've got it.”

Pierre looking bemused said, “Mon Cherie, yees, what is it you have found?”

“Think about this you two. M is number 26 in the alphabet, A is 12-the clue is 12 along with I=5, along with e- flip the e and you get 6- flip the upside G- you get 9.

Pierre and I were thoroughly confused, making me ask, “Well Els is there a message?”

“Yes, can't you see it now?”

“No I can't.”

“Okay, look at the multiple numbers and letters. Put them in your mind and space them like they are spaced in the text. Do you see it now?”

“No.”

“When we get to your room, I will draw it out.”

“What do you mean, to my room?”

“I can't go back to the dorm at this time of night, you're not a prude, are you sir?” Pierre was looking on in a way of saying, are you telling her no.

In my bedroom, Els put the conundrum of codes on the bed, Pierre pulled up two chairs and a luggage rack to sit on, while the sheet of paper was placed strategically for us all to see.

Waiting for someone to say something, she was told, “Okay Els, tell us the jest of the message?”

“The Brits want your agenda. To tell you the truth sir, no one knows what your plans are. Not even your closest allies, even the CIA Director is discussing this with the British. My summation is, keeping these agencies in the dark will create theories of a possible overthrow of an agency. Pierre, do you know why we are in this group?”

“Non, bon ami.”

The look of consternation on Pierre's face was like a road map, having him say, “Will, Els has said something I was wondering myself. Why are you, we doing this? Where is the profit?”

“You two think about it for a few minutes. If the Brits are investigating our little association, so are the Soviets and the Arabs. This is why plans have not been divulged, so no one can get information on our agenda.”

Pausing for room service delivering desert and coffee, I continued with, “When an investigation team was sent to Frankfurt to find evidence of a conspiracy, not once but twice and coming up dry, they had to try and manufacture the proof, but failed. And for them to put a tainted report in front of the President was an act of desperation, which should stop or slow down any other investigations.”

Els asked, “Who would gain from this attempt?”

Humm, *her and Pierre nailed it. Where was the*

impetus generating from. It had to have an American initiator, who else would try and stop a CIA or ASA agenda.

Sock Puppet's files, either in the Senate office or at home could help in finding out who are the culprits. Maybe a copy of a letter could be in a Kremlin file cabinet collecting dust. I wonder if our planted mole in the KGB, Petro could send it to me.

Getting back from what could be described as a brain meltdown or day dreaming, I had to say, "Sorry about that, Els struck a nerve let's continue. Take this into account, a junior Socialist Senator, who resembles a white hair sock puppet, who wanted me deposed, or hold on a minute."

Rudely interrupted by Els, determined to stall this conversation, by saying, "Sir, you accuse someone with no proof is irresponsible. Besides, it may be General Thibodeau who is the target."

"By golly you're right; it is the CIA on the rack, that's it. We must remember, the communist Senator took his wife to Moscow on their honeymoon, a candidate for being a Soviet spy. I bet my bottom dollar on it. That is why some colleagues call him the sock puppet, they know of his leftist views."

Pierre spoke up on his concerns, "My friend, if this goes tits up, what is to become of your co-conspirators.

Are willing associates going to be prosecuted?"

"Yes, sure hope they are. Also knowing there are always opposing forces with obstacles by legal means or at the point of a gun from a foreign entity. We have to break this off for now. Pierre is going to train the group in how to blend into an Islamic Society. He will need to train you in pairs, with Els being trained alone, that is because she may be in control overseas. I will see you all in a month."

After we finished, Aeroflot was phoned, to purchase a reservation to Moscow. A plane was leaving in ninety minutes, where a first class ticket was booked.

My ticket was bought using the name of Gora Demyan, which was taking somewhat of a chance if an alert was put out a decade ago on that name being used in covert operations. All of my Russian uniforms were back in Frankfurt, along with matching passports but not Demyan's passport; it was always kept in the lining of my garment bag.

Pierre and Els were back down stairs, seeing me checking out, they both came over wanting to know what was going on.

Els asked, "You have an emergency, General?"

I whispered to them, "My name is Gora."

The large French man said, "Oh bon ami, one day you will be keeled by the red rooster, no?

"No. You two train the others, I will test your work in four weeks. Goodbye my taxi is waiting. One more thing Els, take this money and get the appropriate attire."

Aeroflot was late as usual; their planes are notorious for breaking down or crashing. It was way past midnight when I arrived at the flat where Isla and Petro live the property that used to be my resident when in Moscow.

Petro let me in, and going back to bed I sent a message that we all needed our sleep.

Later that morning Isla opened the bedroom door, holding a cup of coffee, causing me to ask, "Don't you knock before going into a man's bedroom?"

"Billy, you have nothing I haven't seen before, do you have something new?"

"No, I mean yes. Oh hell, what would Petro say?"

"Slide over, I am cold."

"Isla, you are a tease. Petro must have gone in to work. Why would he on a Saturday?"

"He got a call from security, Gora Demyan has surfaced."

"Great. Now how do I get back to Germany?"

"You will figure out a way. We see a friend of yours from time to time. Natasha asks about you, always. So do the three girls in your other apartment, how many girls do you have Billy?"

"I need to get into the Kremlin today."

"Not today. Petro said every ranking officer will be meeting to set up a dragnet, as you Americans call it."

"Has he ever been suspected in being my agent?"

"No. Petro is the most careful person on the planet."

"Can you take him a message?"

"Yes, when I take his lunch over. Do not write it, tell me."

"Have the KGB send a message to an American Senator through the Russian Embassy in New York, copy to their Consulate in Washington and through the KGB office inside the U.N. Building. The letter has to say something about an ASA agent setting up a ghost agency. No names in the text. Include the British Consulate here in Moscow."

"Billy, one of these days you are going to be caught, why do you do this."

"I really have no idea, yes I do. I love doing this type of work."

"Is it so America can be more powerful than the Soviets?"

"No. There is no explanation for it my life is full of excitement, because of this cloak and dagger stuff."

"Alright my darling Will. I have to go take Petro his lunch. Are you going to be here when I get back?"

"Probably not."

As soon as she was gone, I went to the other flat to see the girls, and to watch this place from the end of the living room over there. If the airport taxi told the police I was dropped off in this area, I will have to lie low, until I can get out of the city. When I arrived, my Gypsy minder was parked across the street.

That was a pleasant surprise; I forgot his wages were paid in advance. He had to be told the chance of police asking questions this afternoon was quite likely.

It was almost noon the girls were just getting up, running around in their nighties. They sat me down by the window I always liked to look out of and made me tea and scones.

I fell asleep on the couch, until a knock was heard at the door. My blood pressure was climbing with anticipation if it was the police. It was too late to run, so composing myself was the next best thing. Just before a girl called Catia opened the door, Isla called out to see if anyone was home.

Isla came in to see the girls in their silk shorts and sheer tops, she said. "Billy, how many girls do you have?"

They all found that very funny with giggles from all four of them.

Before I could say anything, Isla said, "Here is the

document. Then whispered, Petro said you must leave now, go Billy, I do miss you."

Hurrying down stairs while shoving the paper into my trouser pockets, I had the big taxi driver take me to the Gypsy flea market, on the edge of Moscow. On the way we saw four police cars entering the area

Chapter 11

British MI-5 Memorandum

One Army transport truck across the motorway was barreling towards us, no doubt they were going to close down several streets.

At the market, a motorcycle was bought from one of the clan members who deals in used bicycles and and motor bikes. I had to leave ASAP to get to a Leipzig safe house before midnight and spend the night there making sure one young arrogant British agent hasn't burned that bridge.

Drat, my old motorcycle was leaning against the garden shed, this means Graham Makepeace must be in the flat. I have had reservations recently on the MI5 agent being able to work in Eastern Europe, without messing up my old CIA network.

The old couple, caretakers must have heard the noise when I pulled in. It wasn't long before we were hugging and kissing, when Graham came down stairs. He sarcastically asked, where are you staying tonight?"

"In my bed."

"It isn't your place anymore old boy, remember I am leasing this hovel, what?"

His sense of humor bordered on rudeness. The couple invited us in to have a bite to eat and a glass of vodka.

When Graham and I got up stairs after a saying good night to the old couple, he couldn't wait to tell me, "Wright, I was summoned to London ten days ago to see the man in charge of MI5. Do you know him?"

"Do not play games; you know I do, what was it he wanted?"

"Come on mate, work your clairvoyant magic, you tell me."

"Makepeace, you are the most annoying butt I had the displeasure to listen to. Anyway it isn't true they have the wrong bloke this time."

"You're not exactly Mr. amiable yourself yank. Listen carefully, you have something they want, Lord Chesterfield wants to make a deal on what your ASA clan are up to in the Middle East, not to mention a large sum of stolen money. Question is Wright, have you squandered all of our reliable contacts in the desert?"

"Now tell me, how in the hell could he know I would be seeing you again."

"It's in your dossier old stick, every move you have made in the last twelve years, he knows you better than anyone. One can tell he thinks a lot of you Wright; he is worried someone is going to stop you. Give him the list of names back, along with the five million quid. He could be persuaded to let you off the hook and forget about you having to report to London."

Report to London, what an ass Graham is, that group are the last ones who will have information handed over.

Back to answering the man, "Alright Graham, how is the network of safe house working out for you?"

"Bloody marvelous, thank you, however I feel there is another one you do not want me to know about."

"You have any petrol in the shed?"

"Yes mate, two Jerry cans, help yourself, leave the money on the table when you leave."

I was able to leave at four am.without waking the Brit up, and pulled into the Hotel Botanika three hours later.

Leila ran out when I drove up to the front door, to greet me. I ate breakfast and left for the Austrian border, and being a Sunday no road blocks were set up.

Passing the Cheb cut off, an Army truck was just pulling onto the high way, honking his horn and flashing his lights, for me to stop.

Flipping him off, and gunning the machine, an hour and a half later I pulled off the road, onto the trail that was used before to walk to the border. Another hour later I stopped on the edge of the forest, gazing across an expansive clearing on both sides of the single fenced zone, watching for any signs of troops or guards.

Nothing was seen, however helicopters were heard about ten miles away. Quickly crossing under an iron bar, I made it to the line of trees on the Austrian side, when choppers were seen coming in at tree top level. I hurriedly pushed the bike until I could safely get on my way.

That was a close call, thinking now about stopping at the Passau Guest Haus to rest up.

Walking into the Inn, Elke came out of the kitchen to see who had walked in. After a long embrace we went into the bar area, hand in hand.

Sitting in the lounge having a freshly drawn draft pilsner, I read the document Isla handed me back in Moscow, while Elke went back to her kitchen to prepare lunch.

It read; Comrade Senator, re- your last offer to shed

some light on BTK (Billy the Kid), his memorandum to CIA, D.C. Stop him he seems to be delving into uncharted territory, ie. Middle Eastern Affairs, see transmission dated 22 Nov. ASA Frankfurt. We order you, M D, PW stop at all cost. Consequences no more cash in Baghdad.

Comrade Brezhnev.

Have to deal with this later; first MI5 has to be dealt with.

Calling Chesterfield at home, he answered having been informed it was a long distance call, saying, "I need to see you in the morning, where are you?"

"Germany."

"Bloody liar, you are in Austria."

Wonderful info, he must have been told by an operator from Whitehall, where this call originated from. That meant all of David's calls are listened to.

"I take it Graham has been in touch."

"He doesn't call on weekends. By your question, I take it you saw him?"

"Yes. He gave me your message, how about 0900?"

"Meet me for lunch, a pass will be at the door, how is noon sounding."

"See you then."

As soon as I hung the phone up, Alke walked in and asked, "When are you coming back to see me?"

"Sorry Alke, I have to go, see you in a couple of months."

"Next time you drop by the phone will be out of order."

That was funny she was upset, even more when watching me walk out the door.

After filling up with gas I stopped at Bad Aibling to make reservations for flying to London on the BEA ten pm. flight. An MP showed up to drive me to Frankfurt, where we arrived an hour before the flight left.

Arriving at my London residence at almost midnight it was essential to get as much sleep as possible, for the purpose of being ready to grill Lord David on his firms meddling into CIA or ASA affairs.

It felt good to settle into bed imagining a scenario of sitting across from Chesterfield in the House of Lords restaurant, asking my first question, something like, David we need to air out our grievances. Sleep soon overtook this processing session for dealing with British Intelligence, actually dreaming I was in the middle of a tense partisan interrogation.

That nightmare was sobering to say the least. An unnecessary MI5 agenda wanting to find something nefarious with American Agents in Amman as possible sleeper cells. This Home Office meeting is wasting my time for forwarding a much more important agenda than sitting in a musty old House of Lords dining room.

If I can switch this luncheon into an ASA fact finding operation by carefully worded questions, then, this could be time well spent.

Must stop this inherit dreaming, have to get to the House of Lords a good hour early, for canvassing inside the building and its interworking.

Miraculously, Kenny pulled up to the curb just as I closed the downstairs door, still thinking about that dream, wondering if it was a scent of clairvoyance.

Once in his taxi, he said, "Morning Guv, ung oer are ya. Ang about, afore I forget, the bloke in da compound needen ta see ya."

"Morning Kenny. I was in the middle of thinking about an appointment at David's office. If there is time to see Simpson after that, the General can have what is left of my rear end. Do you have anything to do this afternoon?"

"Wot ya needen Guv?"

"Park in the Lords back parking lot to see who drives off between 1300 and 1400 hours."

"Ya mean like da last time ya ad me follow some posh geezer? Ya gonna ave ta git me one of dose passes ya know no ordinary Tom, Dick an 'arry can park their motor in there.""

"Yes, and don't worry it has been arranged."

Thirty minutes later, I was dropped off in front of Whitehall, with Kenny driving around to the other side of the building, after he was handed a voucher for going through the parking lot check point.

Upstairs where Chesterfield's and other top echelon offices were located, it would be easy to scope out other offices, even with all of their doors closed. Main reason is, once a person was inside, no one would question their credentials.

Also assuming the group would be huddled together going over the reports from Amman and Makepeace, discussing what to say for obtaining ASA plans for the immediate future.

It's coming to me they want to know if documents from the Frankfurt heist was compromised, not to mention the five million quid that is still missing.

Upstairs and seeing Lord Montague's closed door, I quietly knocked twice, waiting for someone to answer the knock, I opened the door after thirty seconds, walked in to see no one, and quietly closing the door behind me, I hurried to the Lord's desk to see if any notes or documents were around. Eureka, one was on the very top, with a heading of CIA Operatives.

Quickly photocopying the files, stuffing them into my jacket pocket, I left to meet David.

A few minutes early for the appointment, I sat on a

hall seat reading the copied file. A mole in the CIA Headquarters was evident; no one would know any of this except a few Generals. It was telling when thumbing through the years of gathered data, a notation about a missing CIA Agent West was brought to the attention of MI6 "C" some twelve years ago.

If they had access to the firm back then, what about when Nicola was murdered. Nothing was in the file during that time, in fact, six months of logs were ripped out, on both sides of the Pan Am crash and no wonder this file was so thin.

David walked up while reading the dossier, making me jump, causing him to ask, "How long have you been in the building, Will?"

"An hour, I wasn't sure if we were meeting for brunch or lunch."

"Will, you forget. What do you have there?"

"You can have it, I'm finished reading it."

"How could you. There cannot be a meeting now, let's go, Kenny can take us to Victoria station. We need to keep quiet until we are in the Station's Pub."

Kenny was taken back when we climbed in his taxi, and putting a finger across my lips for him to drive and not say anything, arriving at Victoria with nothing said between the three of us.

In the pub and after getting two pints of beer, David

asked, "Why would you break into a fellow Lord's office, stealing his files? This outcome may have you banned from visiting me again in the House."

"You're kidding."

"I am serious William, you have lost all of your credibility with me. If you were found riffling through Montague's files, I would have to forfeit everything."

"Tell the truth, it isn't about dishonoring our special association; it is about an investigation into MI5 not warning me about my wife's murder."

"When are you going to get over that? You dealt with the all of the conspirators?"

"Not all. There's another shoe that has to drop you may not know when, you do know where that is going to happen."

"Wait a minute, our food is arriving."

Before he could say anything, I asked my old friend, "Did you read the memorandum your eaves droppers passed on. The one from Moscow KGB, with my name in it?"

"This morning. I knew it had to be a set up. KGB never spells out anyone's name. That was clever, now you suspect where transmissions were probably seen or at least interrupted when the Pan Am thing was being planned. Alright Will, if our interest goes away concerning your so called secret agenda, will you stop your inquiry into MI5 involvement? We are willing to handover Russian and the Egyptian transmissions on their involvement?"

"You were confided in about my wishes on stopping Middle Eastern uprisings, how can I trust what you are telling me. You may be playing a shell game, on top of your firm revisiting a fearsome fantasy."

"That is rubbish, it isn't a fear, it is what you admitted to the last time you were in my home and yes I did relay that confidential information onwards."

"Nothing on paper, David. It never happened. Forget about how Nicola could be alive if I was warned by you scoundrels, never. That would be hard to do, not impossible, but hard."

David was just given an opening.

"Be realistic Wright, it was going to happen one day, sure it was deplorable, but what could we do with out giving up our informers in those areas. Having said that, I will never discuss your conversations again, they will be confidential, unless you tell me to leak them. We do not want a war with the ASA or CIA when you move into General Thibodeau's chair."

"You can't erase Nicola's memory from my head. We need to leave this for now. Why did you cancel this morning's meeting?"

Lords Montague and Smyth were advised to do this.

You had to much time to plan out some type of reversal. What are we going to do about the five million and did you review documents from our courier?"

Five million pounds doesn't start to pay for my wife's passing. Second question, you know the answer. You tell those involved I know where they sleep."

"Alright Will, we knew this was not going to be easy. I wished many times Nicola wasn't on that flight."

Chapter 12

The Sock Puppet

Lord Chesterfield must know our agreement isn't going to be set in concrete, with him so wrapped up in keeping his family's name unsoiled, not to mention his title. At least a reprieve for my agenda is going to allow some latitude for now. One more item to take care of before the ink on this agreement is dry, even though it was verbal. Whatever happens, Nicola's memory will be with me forever.

That was it then. A trip to Vermont to ski and hunt next weekend. No time for a camping trip because of this new information. Once this walking scourge is taken care of, time may be available for a little personal activity.

Early the next morning I left London for Frankfurt, and Bad Aibling to see my old friend Buck, and lay out his duties.

The next afternoon, deciding Frankfurt had to be by passed, except for taking a taxi to get a motor bike out of the ASA headquarters parking lot to drive to Bavaria.

Inside the Bavarian Base and before getting off my bike, Buck was out the door shouting, Don't turn it off sir."

Ignoring him, I brushed past to go to my old office and see what was on the desk, in case our group picked up any chatter on Gora Demyan.

Buck stepped in and said, "Sir, General Thibodeau is in Frankfurt. He is furious, that you got your bike and rode away, you needed to greet him. He said he was going to have me busted if I didn't tell him where you were going. Wright, the General did not believe me when I told him I really didn't know."

"Oh shut up, I need to go through the logs for the last thirty days. You take the first two weeks of November, hand me anything that came in from Russian High Command."

Shouting out for my attache to hear, "I got it Buck, a ham radio operator from Nome, relayed a message from, Moose Breath, who relayed a message from New

Newfoundland, who relayed a message from Burlington. Who in the hell would live in a place called Moose Breath? Has to be a tree kisser, or some left wing goof ball. Find anything Buck? Look good around the 14th

"Nothing Sir, unless you need to know about a sock puppet."

"That's it, who is it from?"

"Sir, from the White House Communications Director, to a Vermont Senator."

"Book me on the first flight to New York, out of Frankfurt."

"What about General Thibodeau?"

"Tell him you haven't seen me."

"I can't do that sir, it's easy for you to lie, not me, I get nervous, they will find out."

"Alright Buck, I am leaving for Headquarters now. Book me in first class, see you later."

He was muttering when I left, something like, "Who's going to pay for the ticket, what the hell. It was an order from my Commanding Officer. Who cares anyway?"

Arriving in Frankfurt with Thibodeau hot on my heels, walking into my office, he slamed the door and said, "Pour me a scotch, forget about the soda. Where have you been? We had reports you were seen in

Jordan, London and Moscow Airport in the last three days
What are you working on? The agency has no orders on you going covert anywhere."

"You heard about Schultz, she seems to be buddies with a connected Junior Senator who is possibly a Russian informant. I obtained evidence from the Kremlin dispatches. That is why I was in Moscow."

"I was told by Simpson you are working in the shadows, is he correct?"

"Yes sir."

"Mrs. Shultz has filed charges against you for sedition."

"How could she from jail sir? Anyway, she does not have the authority to charge anyone."

"She was released on her own recognizance two days ago. She has a politician doing her dirty laundry."

"She is probably in Moscow by now."

"I do not think so, Wright, she has too much to lose, like her job and husband."

"She is a spy for the Russians and the GDR, where she was born, in East Germany."

"Say you are correct, her charges are pending. Anyway, why were you in Amman last Friday?"

I need to get him off the Middle East, since Russia is his bugaboo, I may be able to sidetrack him with a daunting question pitting Russian against a country who wants to see their main nemesis dealt with

"Sir, the Russians are determined to bring down the CIA, with assistance from some members of congress who are leftist, by creating a scenario of a rogue ghost agency being formed by an intel General. That is there ploy, if it works, the Brits and other allies will have an excuse to work with us, even if it is only suspicious."

"That's preposperous, no one is going to believe that crap. Oh, I get it now Wright, you planted that little scenario in Simpsons mind a long time ago, he responded by telexing me, in turn the Brits and Russians picked it up.

"That's a stretch, sir."

"Bull crap, anyway, it was very clever of you, if I say so myself. I have to get some rest now and leave on the first MATS plane in the morning, good evening General Wright."

"Sir."

That was a close one. How did he think it was a plan, clever one at that? He must have thought it was a way to get the competition going in another direction. I have to see a Senator about a dog, and then track down Schultz before she is grilled on my whereabouts. If she can have me assassinated, her tenure would still be intact, in Washington if she is still there.

My trip to New York has to be postponed until Friday morning. It was important to track down Schultz after a dispatch was intercepted disclosing a DS agent was flown to Moscow to visit a terminal sick mother.

It doesn't take much imagination to put two and two together, who D. S. was. Clumsy to use her initials, must have been a quick extraction.

After calling Buck he said he would change my ticket and book me on the morning flight to Moscow. He was told to book it under the name of General Gennady Vagon on Aeroflot.

At noon the next day I walked into the KGB Directors Office inside the Kremlin. Petro wasn't in, which allowed me to rake through his files to see if any notes were pertaining to Schultz. He never closes his door because of sending a message he may be up to something secret, meaning I had to be very careful.

Very strange, nothing was in recent Russian mail or department dispatches. Now what, maybe she is resting in her former digs in East Germany, one place to check on who would know, the Stasi in East Berlin, in Herr Wolf's office. Calling from KGB Headquarters would hopefully relax my would be informant into telling me where she is at this moment.

Hoping lady luck was on my right shoulder I called Wolf's office.

His secretary answered saying, “Moscow, how can I assist you.”

“Herr Wolf, bitte.”

“He is on a trip, could I assist you.”

“Frau Schultz, is she now safe and secure?”

“Yes, she is safe here in Berlin. At her mother’s new apartment by the airport.”

“I hope you are treating her as a true German Hero.”

“Yes, we are having her friends come to her party tonight inside the new wing at the airport, can you be there.”

“No, I am very busy. What if I send a Russian delegation headed by General Vagon.”

“Wonderful, we are having problems contacting enough comrades for a good showing.”

“Will Herr Wolf be there?”

“Nein, his daughter will be here instead.”

“What time should the General be there?”

“1900 hours. His invitation will be held at the door.”

“Thank you.”

A flight for Schonefeld, East Berlin was leaving at three pm, plenty of time to get to a hotel and the party. Arriving in Berlin, a chauffeur was seen outside the arrivals hall, holding up a paper sign with Gen. Vagon on it.

The driver talked incessantly about how Americans and British destroyed his once beautiful city. This was strange since the majority of Eastern Europeans never discussed anything, fearing an informant may overhear a misspoken word.

I forgot about being a Russian General, he was buttering me up, validated when he asked, “Please let Herr Wolf know I am always alert here on the streets.”

Did he ever thnk this city needs more refurbishing from the war almost forty years ago, my driver doesn't realize that the Russians use resources from here.

The man started up his rant again when he informed me, “It seems that old repairs need a little more refurbishing, what can one do with so little money. The wealthy Americans should help us, they have become rich from their bombs. Oh yes, Herr Wolf's daughter is staying at your hotel sir, and also the master spy, Frau Schultz. We are so fortunate to have the loyal and brave stay here in Berlin.”

When we arrived, the chauffeur accepted a quite generous tip, and said, “General Vagon, my super said I was told to wait out on the curb and to take you where you needed to go, like the brothel for beautiful women or to view our wall that keeps unauthorized intruders out.”

This man may be useful if an escape was needed. How does one become so brainwashed.

After registering I went up to unpack my bags and throw a little water on my face. Quickly back down stairs, going out a rear service door to avoid prying eyes a call box was spotted down the street.

It was essential to call the hotel's front desk, to see what room Frau Schultz was in. Drat, the phone was busted and the call box smelled like a urinal.

Entering the hotel again from the rear, I went into the lounge for a beer and to see if a pay phone was on the wall.

Not seeing a phone the barman was willing to let me use his phone for inter hotel service. Luck was with me as the front desk was visible and asking if Frau Schultz was in, he looked in a block of key boxes where a key was pulled out and placed back in. Before he turned to pick up the phone again, I hung up.

It was necessary to go to the desk to see what room she was assigned, 421, on my floor. Back in the hotel foyer, I sat down and waited for Schultz to show up. In Europe, it was customary to hand room keys over when leaving a hotel. Within the hour she walked in with a couple of bags from a department store.

Waiting for her to get to her room and a few minutes to powder her nose, I walked over to the stair case, and walked up stairs, because the lift wasn't working, I knocked on Schultz's door.

She asked, “What do you need.”

“A package from Herr Wolf.”

She opened the door with a towel over her wet hair, not seeing me I pushed her back in. She started to yell, causing me to shoot her in the forehead. Going through her papers, I found recently written notes on her activities leading up to her arrest, most of it pertaining to Miss Latta.

The notes and other paperwork from my room were put inside my coat. Back downstairs, the driver was told to take me to where the women are. He left me at the front of post war high rise, to go back to the airport to pick up another VIP. Once he was gone I went to find an old address that could be useful in fleeing the East.

Remembering an address where a tunnel was to the West, the call sign did escape me. I had to stop and think what the word or words were.

Finally remembering the call sign, I was given access through the door leading to the tunnel, and under the wall.

Hailing a taxi, for the air port, I spent the night at the West Berlin Templehof Airport hotel and flew out the next day to Frankfurt, where I spent the night in the ASA directors residence, before flying on to New York, connecting to a Vermont flight, in hopes of finding and hunting down a puppet.

Friday afternoon I arrived in Burlington, which was colder than Moscow, no wonder Socialist love to live here it is similar to their prized mother land.

A car rented from the airport was registered to me as Ivan Azarov, with a Ukrainian address, which caused no curiosity in this state.

Sock puppets house was conveniently located next to a large house with boarded up windows, probably belonging to snow birds who had gone to Florida for the winter. No signs of security made it easy to break into the vacant house's garage, stowing the car, and going out back to view the target's house.

Confident that there was no one around since it was dark and no lights were turned on, I settled down in this place for a time to move over next door. The heat was turned up here as far as it would go, just in case my stay was extended. Mail pushed through the letter box was in a pile on the mat, finding the name of the owners may be helpful if a neighbor dropped by.

The phone was still on, which gave me the idea of finding the Senator's name in the white pages or blue government listings. Calling his number was beneficial to find out if he was getting his messages, meaning he could come back on weekends.

Have to go, darkness was covering my movements to the back of the targets house, where breaking in through a back door could be potentially dangerous if the house was monitored.

My estimation was that the man should be arriving home from Washington before midnight, if he stayed until the final gavel was struck; it was possible he could have ducked out earlier.

What was striking about his house, no children, wife or domestics were seen or heard. His house was not watched by secret service however an alarm company's sticker was on the back door's glass.

Putting on gloves and climbing up a tree, a window on the second floor was not wired. Pulling the window open was easy as the wood was rotten around the latch.

Once inside, making my way to the kitchen to study family photographs on the fridge door.

No pictures, no milk in the fridge, no leftover food. The guy must live alone. One more place to investigate, his study, more precise, his desk.

Nothing, no evidence of a family. I know he was married, now where is her stuff, maybe in the bathroom. Nope, nothing, no lipstick, no bubble bath, and no cotton swabs.

I lay on his bed with my shoes on and dozed off, awakened hearing the front door opening downstairs and him saying, "Thank you officer, see you Sunday afternoon."

He came up stairs, seeing me he calmly said, "I have no money here, except a hundred dollars in my wallet."

"It isn't money it's your ties to Russian agents in this country?"

"I have seen your face in a dossier you are here to kill me. First let me ask you a question, Why me?"

"Does the name William Wright ring a bell."

"Yes General. Let me say in my defense, all of my pontificating on your activities over seas was innocently portrayed as a threat, that is all, no substance to it. Please let me hang my coat up."

"The alarm is disabled, throw it on the sofa and sit down."

"Are you going to shoot me?"

"Who are the Russian informants in Washington?"

"There are no informants, you are mistaken. Let me say, if you leave now, this will be forgotten and you will have a free hand in whatever you want to do, I give you my word."

Can't help thinking about this weak worm in front of me. He cannot be trusted, words to him are a tool to ply his evil intentions, meaning he is not needed to further the safety security of this great nation. However he does have some information that will substantiate what is already known.

While screwing on a silencer to my revolver, I asked, “Senator, General Thibodeau's secretary and Debra Schultz, are they moles?”

He was given plenty of time to answer.

Leaving his house, knowing America was a safer place without him was comforting.

Chapter 13

The Way Forward

Driving across the Canadian border towards Montreal was a breeze; a rural road bypassing a border crossing was too easy. For a half hour I was expecting to see a Canadian Mounty in my rear mirror, fortunately it never happened.

Spending the rest of the night and next day in the Montreal Airport Marriott, resting up before an evening flight to London was exactly what was needed to give space from time spent in Burlington.

Arriving in the Hyde Park flat I had a few days to weigh up the state of affairs in forwarding an agenda.

My five students have finished their two year

course in Amman, with high marks for language, skills in discussions while assimilating into an Islamic community. The kill teams 5 are now operating off a carrier in the Persian Gulf we are almost ready.

New Langley trainee graduates are now in Jordan on the same two year language course. Pierre held weekend field trips in Amman, Cairo and Riyadh for all agents attending the American University in Amman. General Simpson called to say the New Years briefing on Boca Grande was going on as as planned with Thibodeau, in two weeks. Two nights in Harrow and flying to Florida on Christmas Eve proved to be quite hectic, but highly enjoyable.

After spending Christmas day with my family and traveling to Fran's in Monroe County it was a case of over eating and to much indulging in egg nog.

Getting to the barrier island ahead of the two Generals, Fran and I enjoyed two blissful days alone, lying on a sun bleached white sandy beach. When they did arrive, Fran and I had to act as host and hostess.

During our first early breakfast overlooking the Gulf and with the ladies still in their rooms, Thibodeau started our impromptu meeting with a startling announcement of another covert action.

General Thibodeau said, "Wright, you are aware our President's re-election was a success. Having said that, our ex Director, the Vice President is starting to get the ball rolling for him to succeed his boss in four years. This Contra thing, he thinks will be brought back up by the democrats, to besmirch this agency and himself. We need you to pay Havana and Nicaragua a visit."

"Sir, it may not be possible to enter those two countries the same way again, especially through Nicaragua,s main airport. They must have some type of alert on me showing up again."

"Before you go back to where ever you need to go. Is there any thing you need us to do or provide for this to work?"

"General Thibodeau, are you aware a poster may be hanging in the Immigration's hall at Managua Airport."

Our ex director needs this done. You will be briefed on the plane."

"When is the plane picking me up?"

Simpson half sounding indignant when he said, "Do you think we would order a flight without you saying you would do the job?"

"When, sir?"

"Three days Marco field."

Having to laugh at his insincere statement, I thought for less than a minute and said, "You two sirs really take the cake. I was almost up on charges of sedition and now the Vice President wants me to do a job."

Thibodeau started laughing while saying, “What do you mean almost? You are still going to be treated like Benedict Arnold, you traitorous SOB.”

“General Thibodeau, are you going to be on the plane?”

“You impertinent traitor, the last time I tried to help you, I was kicked off the flight in Miami, no I am not.”

“Good. Before I get to the nuts and bolts, my request is for the Vice President to drop any type of investigation on me now or in the future.”

“He won't go for that Wright, you must be out of your mind, asking for a cart blanche on your illegal activities.”

“Maybe the VP will go for it, say in three years, call him to see if he will do it, before we go any farther.”

After a few choice expletives Thibodeau had a phone brought out to the veranda. Good thing the VP was an early riser, he agreed to a clean passage for one General Wright, as long as he is a Veep or President.

Simpson stated, “Alright you got what you wanted General. How about your tools?”

“Have Buck send me the same stuff he packaged up for the last South American assignment. Have $100,000 in fifty dollar bundles stuffed in an Army duffle bag.”

Thibodeau protested, “You're mad, the VP won't go for that, how about half that in fifties?”

“Sorry sir, I made mistake, $200,000.”

“Who in the hell do you think you are? Holding us hostage for more money.”

“Sir, you have crossed the Rubicon, there is no negotiation when my life may have to be ransomed off.”

“Alright. One hundred thousand and not one penny more. Every unused dollar is to be brought back, is that understood? You may be brought up on charges of extortion if you fail.”

“I think the VP was giving me immunity from any future charges.”

“He may have Wright, I didn't promise anything, except a possible firing squad. Heh heh, heh. Put that in your pipe and smoke it.”

His laughing seemed a little immature for someone his age.

However I am looking forward to seeing if this can be done, through the Russian Embassy in Havana or Managua. I will need assistance in having Loupe act as my body guard and an extra pair of eyes.

One last item sir, I need a Cuban passport in the name of Loupe Delgado, 5'2”, born 1952, brown hair, black eyes. Residence 4230 San Pedro, Havana, Cuba.”

“When do you expect to be back, and where do you want the plane to take you?”

“Panama will be the best place, sir. It may take six

months to erase all CIA activities in Nicaragua and Havana."

"We will set up an interpreter for you, out of Miami."

"No thank you sir, I am fluent in Spanish, and would like no transmissions or radio chatter concerning Loupe, me or this mission. What happened to the last interpreter?"

"He is in Leavenworth, isolated for his own safety. Did you really have the back door opened with him dangling over the edge at 30,000 feet?"

"No sir. It was 29,000 feet; you know how those types of people like to exaggerate."

"Heh heh heh, we are done. The ladies are here, let's make room. Tomorrow morning Wright same time, we will have our last briefing on this matter."

Thibodeau's laugh is the most unusual, more like the leghorn cartoon character. Fran's chair was pulled out so she could shield me from Thibodeau, with Simpson's wife Prissy sitting on my other side. Now no more Generals casting aspersions with their grimaces or finger pointing.

Fran whispered, "Were you guys telling jokes?"

"No. Tell you later, let's finish and go to the beach."

We quickly finished eating, and were given permission to leave by our elders, however that didn't stop me from telling Thibodeau, “Sir, you ought to put that pancake down and grab that apple on the center piece instead.”

General Thibodeau now in a rage forgot ladies were at the table, when he said, while spitting pancake out, “You son of a bitch, I'll have you in front of a court martial for your insolence, and frog marched down Pennsylvania Avenue to the White House steps.”

His wife had to warn him, saying, “Now Thibby, remember your heart isn't what it use to be, anyway you like that boy, you shouldn't treat him so harshly.”

“I never have liked that upstart, heh heh heh.”

Prissy Simpson said, “You two better leave while you can.”

On the way to our room to put on swim suits, Fran said, “You shouldn't talk to the General like you do, it's disrespectful.”

“There's a purpose for my behavior. I can't let those two consider me as an equal, because of needing certain favors, having to reciprocate would not be good. It is hard to explain the full reason.”

We avoided the rest of that group all day, and saw them briefly for drinks at sunset.

The next morning the Generals were enjoying a pre breakfast breakfast, in other words the Generals ate all of the fried stuff before the wives joined them. Our briefing went over what was said yesterday, except for rehashing the funds needed.

Fran and I drove to Marco Island that Sunday, where we spent the night and waited for the C-130 to land the next morning. While sitting on the truck's tail gate, we saw the plane landing, making us quickly talk about getting together during spring break.

On the way to Homestead Air Force Base to fuel up, gave me time to look through the suitcase from Bad Aibling, along with counting bundles of 50 dollar notes in the heavy canvas duffle bag. Two Russian Army uniforms were in a before bag, with a passport, a pair of Colonel insignia and two stars for each shoulder.

Landing in Panama I asked the three pilots to wait ninety minutes, in case I couldn't catch my next flight.

If I had a problem carrying my luggage through customs, I had a back up. The three Air Force Pilots thought it shouldn't be a problem, if Military Air Command granted the request. I was given one hour to find Loupe and ask the airlines if it was possible to take my luggage on board.

Loupe was waiting as planned, at the ticket counter. Seeing me again we quickly caught up on our hello's and news. The ticket agent said I had to buy an extra seat for the large duffle bag in first class, saying there were plenty of seats to choose from.

It was a little disconcerting to see the C-130 trundling down the taxi way, knowing there goes a safe ride back to the States. Loupe and I settled in for the long ride to Managua, where she caught me up on her studies and the area she had moved to, a block from the university.

I was thinking about Phil, (Hills) and Alison while Loupe talked non stop. Hills should be in Jordan starting their two year course, after completing the CIA training. The name Hills, with out an apostrophe, will be their call sign from now on.

Something interesting Loupe asking, “Will, are we going to try and find the Sandinista leader, Che? Or maybe something else you have in mind with me.”

She let out a little school girl laugh, while turning a darker shade of pale.

“To tell you the truth, Loupe I do not know where to start. If the job cannot be done here, we may have to go to Cuba where the Russian staging area is.”

“As you have seen in your last visit, Che's men do not have the tools to engage loyalist in long fights. I think they may be finished soon, our Army is too many and with helicopters, they are too quick in getting into a skirmish and out of hostile situations. What can we do to help the American backed Junta?”

We need to get out, and let the people decide on

which poison they would like to continue with."

"That would be good news for the Communist."

"Maybe not. The Catholic Church wields a lot of power, do they not?"

"Oh I see. You maybe want to have a takeover by the Church, a third interested group in which both sides have to deal with, very ingenious. The Russians will keep pouring money and goods into the rebels, the Americans can leave, knowing a quiet revolution by a third army may be successful."

"Yes Loupe, that is the best scenario, why not have three groups working for their people."

"One thing you forget Will, the church has hardly any money, poor people can give pennies, where foreigners can give much more."

"Where is the headquarters of the Catholic Church, and is there a bank to change dollars."

"It is risky for Americans to be seen changing money. The Priest may know where the marketeers are who trade for dollars, on the black market. The rate of exchange should give many more funds, where the poor could be helped in having food bank shelves stocked up and material, for making clothes."

She was right it was a stroke of accidental genius to have a third entity included in restructuring a corrupt government and an even more corruptible Communist take over. The poor are always the ones who have to be persuaded, since they are majority in this country.

Just before landing, it was necessary to change into a Russian Army Uniform with General Vagon's clothes.

Getting back to my seat, Loupe said, “If you get caught they will kill you for being a spy. Especially if they find out you are an American.”

“I know it is risky, that's a chance we have to take. The Communist having jobs of power in your country, this uniform may get us in unsearched or more important, the luggage. You may have to act out a diversion, if customs pull us over. What could that be?”

“Let me think. It has to be convincing. Maybe, you should request a wheel chair Will. I will tell our attendant my aunt is in the back needing help.”

That may work. While Loupe explained to the stewardess I had to pretend to be asleep, not exactly accompanying her into Managua. Holding the duffle bag of money, while Loupe pushed me in the chair, would hopefully get us into the short immigration lines the airline crews used to gain access through the immigration process quicker. A porter may be the best route, since they would know how to get around the line.

Okay, a bribe has to be ready one $50 bill should do the trick.

We heard the pilot radio his operation center for a

wheel chair to be brought to the ramp. When we landed a porter was waiting for us, hobbling down the steps, I sat down.

The porter asked Loupe about a lady he was waiting to help. She told him that the attendant got it wrong, the chair was for this man, a General, not a senorita.

Loupe and I were led under the terminal towards an elevator. The duffle bag was covering my upper body, shielding me from two police officials watching to make sure no one deviated from going up stairs.

Once inside the terminal, we somehow ended up in the area outside customs.

The wheel chair was about to be pushed through a set of double doors, when Loupe started waving and saying papa wait for us, she left us.

Our porter chasing after her, saying loudly. She had to go through immigration. I turned around and pushed a $50 dollar bill into his hand. That made him smile and turn the chair around, slowing down to follow her. He had to have seen it was a large amount of money, more than he could make in weeks for him to act so quickly.

She stopped to speak to an elderly man, causing him to push me to a row of seats. After helping me out of the chair and onto a stationary seat, our porter left to go through the two doors, alone. I couldn't believe we were past all potential hurdles.

Just like that, a relief came over me. Loupe came back over, helped me get to my feet, just in case cameras had picked up our antics.

She whispered, “We are lucky, no.”

Was she ever right? Still pretending to be handicap, Loupe helped me into a taxi. We arrived at her apartment thirty minutes later, struggling to get up the stairs with all of our gear. Once inside we got back to acting normal, with a degree of relief we embraced, where she took the liberty of a full kiss on the lips.

Chapter 14

The Stratagem

Her pressing was way to long for it to be just a friendly nice to see you kiss.

I couldn't get out of my mind she was once a sort of call girl for one of Che's commanders. That had a lot to do with not pursuing her romantically and Fran in my thoughts provided a firewall of sorts.

We rested and talked about Loupe working full time for me in the Middle East. Her course in Islamic studies is over in May, where she will be able to travel to Jordan to hone her linguistic skills in an Arabic country.

While I was sleeping, Loupe left to get something for dinner and breakfast. When she got back I was awakened by the front door shutting.

She went into the only bedroom in the apartment where I was sleeping, giving me a bag of material, she said, “Try these clothes on.”

White cotton trousers, matching plain tee shirt, peasant clothing, this should help me blend, if it was,'t for my short blond hair.

She was told, “This isn't going to work, too white.”

She laughed at me trying to look like a Nicaraguan farm helper, saying, do not leave; I will be back soon, with the rest of your outfit.”

It wasn't long before Loupe was back with a straw sombrero. Looking in a mirror to see if this getup would fool anyone, I thought yea, not bad.

The next morning we arrived at a Catholic Church just after Mass was finished. The Priest standing on the steps looked more like a Bishop than a regular Priest, quite impressive.

Loupe seeing the flowing robe said, “Luck is with us again Will, he is in charge of all Catholic Churches in Nicaragua. Do you see how most of the people are dressed plain cotton clothes for the few men who go to Mass.?”

She led the way up the long array of steps, with the Priest looking at two peasants making their way to see him, while parishioners were still leaving. He was reticent at first in letting us have a private audience, however when he heard my accent he asked us to follow him.

He was shown $90,000 in the duffle bag, and asked, “Is it possible your Imminence, we could make many friends with such a donation.”

His reply was calculated as he slowly responded with, “To capture the hearts and minds of my people would be possible with such a generous contribution. It is possible maybe we can give a gift to another large parish on the opposite side of Nicaragua, where your name will be mentioned in a Sunday service and on a monthly leaflet for the rest of the year. The name you would like to use please.”

“Miss Loupe, American, Nicaraguan food stores. Please give $40,000 to the parish of La Cruz De Rio Grande, with my associate Miss Loupe accompanying the gift. Sell the dollars to a black market dealer for a much better exchange rate, lastly, send a letter to the White House, attention Senoir Presidenta, saying all is forgiven.”

“It is possible it will be as you wish. I know of Loupe and her family, they will be pleased she is back with the flock, I must go now, please do excuse me, the dispatch to your President will be sent to the Vatican and then to your White House, thank you both.

Loupe and I headed back to her place where I gave her the remaining money to hand out to various charities hoping they will also send thank you notes to friends in Washington.

Over a wonderful home cooked dinner prepared by the attractive agent, we talked about how Loupe was to travel to Amman, stopping off in London, where she would stay at my flat for two weeks, to rest up and get accustomed to the vast time difference.

The next morning it was necessary to fly to Havana in the name of General Vagon, check in with the station KGB Director inside his country's Embassy, as an alibi, which may be needed in a future Kremlin briefing.

Arriving in Havana, a taxi was taken from the airport, eventually checking in at an old run down hotel in the center of the city, similar to a hotel I stayed in several years back.

This quiet part of the city was walking distance to the USSR Embassy and waterfront where I hoped to spend the afternoons relaxing, dozing on a bench watching fishing boats coming in to unload their catch.

When it was starting to get dark the next evening, I left this peaceful seaside setting for the Russian

Embassy, where I found the KGB Director in his office.

Introducing myself to him, saying, "Comrade Director, my name is General Vagon it is good to see you here in such a warm friendly climate."

"Thank you, call me Comrade Levy."

His name seems Hungarian and Jewish, humm, I wonder if he is truly a staunch Soviet supporter. He had to have come up through the ranks during the years surrounding Khrushchev, which meant he was possibly involved in the Hungarian winter of discontent, as a Soviet.

"General Vagon, are you alright."

"Yes, please excuse me, my mind was still in the Nicaraguan Jungle."

"I was told a Soviet General had arrived. Is there a reason you waited twenty four hours to check in."

He was probably alerted by the police at Havana Airport or by immigration officials. That may mean all Russians are tracked while here.

"Stationed in a jungle was arduous and being subjected to various diseases takes it toll, especially when mosquito carrying malaria are always a risk."

"General you need rest, come back on Monday."

"Thank you Comrade Levy, I'd rather talk to you now, I haven't talked to a fellow Soviet in a long time."

"If you are sure the strain isn't too much. We were

not notified a Russian General was coming in this week. Havana Immigration wanted to know if you were cleared to visit."

"What did you tell them?"

"I was incensed they thought of not allowing one of our Generals in this backward country."

"Thank you sir, no one knows I am here, getting away from the Sandinista Rebels for a holiday, was quickly planned by only me."

"General you stay and make phone calls back home I have to leave to get changed for a restaurant reservation overlooking the docks. Please join me in one hour if you have time."

"Thank you Levy, I will see you there. What is the name and address?"

"He laughed and said, "What else could it be, than Fidel's, 1961 Castro Avenue."

When Levy was seen walking across the street in front of the building, I started typing orders that would have me sent to Cairo in three months.

Typing several orders was taking a lot of time, especially with separate orders, for serving a successful six months in South America, with copies stuffed inside a Russian interdepartmental mail bag.

A Government dossier on Leonid Miska, was on top of a file cabinet, for what reason? It is somewhat peculiar to read a file, and leave it exposed.

This could be Comrade Levy's, yes, it was his own file and he lied about his name. Especially one with a lot of abbreviations and jargon pertaining to past assignments. Wait, that's it, where was this man's first posting, which could be a vulnerable time, if he was a teenager. His first assignment was as a guard in London, 1953 to 1959, as an Embassy Guard. I better hurry. I do not need to have the man agitated by a late dinner guest.

Very fortunate to arrive in time to order the Director a large vodka with a side glass of water with ice, just before he walked in. When he saw his drink already ordered, he let slip a little smile.

The service was slow enough for him to drink three large vodkas before we ate. Looking at a moonlit harbor and seeing one or two boats coming and going, thinking who would go fishing this time of night. This may be a good time to ask Levy a few off the record questions.

Starting with, “Comrade Levy, did you say you had a dinner reservation?”

“Yes, for me each evening at this time. I must say it is nice to talk to someone over dinner. These people do not like to be seen collaborating with foreigners, bloody ingrates."

"That is the way the world over, no one cares if Russians dine alone, unless trading for arms are asked for."

"You're right Vagon."

"Comrade Levy, America is such a short distance across that water in front of us, do you ever think about going to see what the interest is."

"Yes, I always have wondered, is it really as good as the Yanks brag about."

"I can't imagine such a place, can you?"

"Yes, I can. London was a place one could travel in the 50's. The English did not know they were blessed, they were so unaware."

"Comrade Levy, do you have friends in England?"

"Yes of course, my wife is there with our two children, she left Havana last year after getting a terrible reaction to a mosquito bite in a remote area where we were camping."

"When is your replacement arriving?"

"You are my successor, are you not?"

"No Levy, I am a man looking for a place to rest."

"General, we need to take a walk, are you ready?"

"Yes, let me have the honor of paying for our drinks and dinner."

"No need General, the Embassy takes care of these

things, anyway it is a small amount, a few Rubles."

We walked for several minutes before the KGB Chief stopped to gaze at a fisherman working on his vessel.

He sighed and said, "I wish these people spoke Russian or Chechnya."

"Is there something you want me to ask them?"

"You can speak Cuban?"

"Yes. Let's go back to the restaurant and get another drink. No, we go to my place no one will hear us there."

He had a fantastic home not far away overlooking the water. He poured our drinks while I opened the door to a balcony.

Joining me, he said, "Every night the boats are moored with one leaving every Saturday after midnight. Maybe he is a liberator, for money. I often wondered why these Cubans would risk their lives to go to a place called Florida, in very dangerous waters."

"Levy, these waters are calm in winter, summer is when storms are dangerous."

"The radio blasts out all year, storms are in the Gulf and Caribbean sea."

"They are wrong. You wish to talk to the boat Captain about fleeing?"

"No, betray my Government, never."

"Why did you use the Jewish name Levy?"

"How do you know my name is not Levy."

"It may be Levy. Why would you use Leonid Miska, is it so close to your atonement period?"

"You are quite astute my young General in your summing up of people. What is to happen with me?"

"What do you want to happen?"

"You know the answer."

"That is good, Levy. I need top secret files on Cuban military bases, number of Russian advisers in South America. This information will afford you to negotiate a price from the Americans when you arrive in Washington D.C."

"Nyet, I do not wish to betray Russia."

"Would you work for an organization being formed in London, one that spies on Islamist fundamentalist throughout the Middle East, the Caucasus and Western Europe?"

"Who are you? Not Russian, speaking like this. No one has talked of this problem, not even the Americans. Please give me your means of information."

"That will never happen Levy. Do you want to go to London or is it Moscow you yearn for."

"Before we leave, my successor may arrive to thwart your plans."

I took that as a yes. Now to make sure our getaway

is set up and the man's replacement doesn't upset the proverbial apple cart. Studying the Gruff KGB Agent, I still needed to be cautious.

"Mr. Levy is the name you will use from now on, no more comrade introductions. The name of the boat that leaves on Saturday is what?"

"Aqua Vista. When will I know that you have actually secured our passage."

"You may have one hour to leave, that means your one bag has to be packed by this Thursday. One last item, how and when will your replacement arrive in Cuba?"

"Thursday is tomorrow, that is impossible."

"There isn't a choice, be ready. The chance of the boat not booked is remote. I need to know about the new KGB man coming in. It is evident I am not your replacement."

"You could be trying to trick me into a decision."

"A decision is made assurance is what you're after."

"How do you know this?"

"Miska, this is no trick, you know too much, I had no choice to try and move you soon and it was me who was taking a chance. You could report me to the Cuban Authorities and have me carted off. That will not happen there are consequences with this conversation, for both of us."

“He will arrive by Aeroflot next Friday, maybe this weekend, no one really knows. The reason for this flexibility, only one flight per week is scheduled from Moscow. I will pack tomorrow then with the files, I will be ready.”

After leaving the Directors house, I walked by the wharf to find the Aqua Vista. Locating the boat, noticing the vessel had an inboard motor, which concerned me a lot. Traveling over ninety miles of open water in a fishing boat sure would be nice to have a spare motor. Well, one can't always have an assurance policy in all circumstances.

During this scouting for a vessel and looking back at Miska's building hoping not to see police show up, was unnerving. I was caught between a body of water and a skittish KGB agent, if this went south, there is nowhere to run.

Noticing a small thin young man in a khaki uniform with bloused boots, starting to cross the road about fifty yards to my left. It was time to go back to the hotel.

Back in my room, there were signs of someone snooping into my stuff. Good thing my money, pistols and papers were on me.

Early the next morning I sat on the docks waiting for the Captain of the Aqua Vista. He must have been a late sleeper or he was storing up rest for a trip tonight.

My bet is, he is making a run after midnight.

Tired of waiting I left to get some more sleep, in case we had to move out in less than twelve hours. On the way up to my room, the maid at the hotel was heard discussing with a taxi driver in Spanish about a Government Detective wanting to know if the Russian slept in his bed last night.

After a long siesta I went back to see if the boat Captain was there. His vessel had the engine cover off, lying on the dock. From a few feet away he was seen bent over pouring oil into the motor.

Watching him for a few minutes, he asked, “May I help you senor?”

“Yes Captain you can. My friend and I would like to go on an overnight fishing trip tonight.”

Chapter 15

Fleeing Castro's Cuba

“No senor, my boat is in need of repair.”

“Would 500 Yankee Dollars get it fixed?”

“Si Senor. Would you mind if my uncle goes with you and your friend.”

“Here take the money. What time should we be

here?"

"Sometimes between midnight and 0100, do not be late."

I went to a small shop, sparsely stocked up on dry goods. Fruit juice is what we need for the trip, with having no luck at acquiring this, another store had to be found.

Rethinking the liquid situation, the restaurant was the only place to find something to store water. After pulling several empty bottles from the trash cans, I went back to my room, to get a little more rest, and fill the bottles from the bath tub tap.

Waiting in my room until, 11pm I went to get Levy, who was sound asleep. His bag was packed, lying under his bed.

Shaking the man, saying, "Get up Levy, we are leaving in one hour."

"It is impossible, I cannot do it, have to take my chances in Moscow."

"You have no choice, get dressed or they will find you dead in the morning. Hurry, we do not have time to discuss this."

"Sure, leave while I get dressed."

"No chance Miska, get dressed."

Fifteen minutes later we walked to the sea front, by hiding in the the dark shadows, towards the back of his building, making sure it was clear to continue walking towards the tied up boats.

Fortunately when we showed up, the vessels Captain seemed to be taking off early. That meant the man can't be trusted, or he was warned about the time he should leave.

Once on the boat the Captain took off slowly, maneuvering his way in the dark out into the open waters. The boat was traveling about twenty miles an hour and seeing the lights getting fainter as we headed due east it was a fantastic feeling when the lights could no longer be seen. It meant we were now past the twelve mile Cuban waters.

Looking towards the door leading down to the hull or galley, wondering when the other passenger was going to surface was causing a little angst.

The Captain turned on his ship to shore radio to pick up radio chatter. That was when the stowaway came out from hiding. He started to say something, when the Captain shouted, not now.

Who was this man, who was well fed, unlike most Cubans? Describing him as portly, around fifty, needing a shave and clean clothes, could mean he had been waiting awhile to leave for Florida.

Our passenger went back down the few steps to where he appeared from.

Three hours later we were over halfway to Key West, a radio transmission coming from an American Coast guard cutter interrupting the still night of looking for lights towards the East. Another American accent answered, saying he was sitting off the Tortugas. Thinking he was probably from the same Coast Guard unit.

I loudly asked the Captain, “Cut your engine to an idle.”

This was allowing us to barely move forward, with us looking in front, trying to pick up ship's lights.

Not having to look back because of being so far away from Cuba, helped us to concentrate towards Florida. After an hour, the other passenger came up to ask what was going on, speaking in Spanish.

Chatter started up again, causing the mystery man to say, “El Capatain, I must not be found and sent back by the Americano's.”

He nervously answered, “That man speaks our language, be quiet.”

Staring towards me in the moonlit semi darkness, the stowaway asked, “Who are you, a liberator?”

With our vessel Captain waiting for me to say something, ignoring the question and him, I said, “Keep your eyes towards Florida, one more set of eyes could be useful.”

That wasn't going to suffice, the Captain reached towards a glove box, thinking a gun could be in there, I took out my weapon, pointed it at his head, made him stop reaching.

He said, “I need the charts.”

“In the dark, let me help you.”

He had a pistol that looked like it should be in a museum, not used as a weapon. No bullets in the chamber, what a risk he was taking.

This was starting to go bad with the boat captain bluffing a stranger, one who could have been anyone, like a hired assassin.

He asked, “What now?”

“Nothing is going to stop us getting to Florida.”

“Senor, our path is blocked; we are going to run out of fuel if we do not get up speed.”

“Head due north quickly, we should bypass the patrol boat just ahead, and the other one blocking our route to Key West.”

“I do not know any other way to Florida we could run aground when we try to make a run for shore.”

“Do not worry. Is there enough petrol to go for six hours?”

“Si, only because we are burning diesel, not petrol. You know these waters.”

“I know them a hundred miles north of here.

Continue at half throttle, the coast guards are at least ten miles away, or else we would be seeing their beacon."

"Who are you, will we be turned in?"

"Up to you. Why is that man running away from his country?"

"No senor, you first. Who are you and your compadre?"

"He is KGB, running away from his country."

"That must mean you are CIA, no."

"Your turn. Who is the fat man?"

"Miqueal Estrada."

Estrada was immediately asked, "When did you last see the chemist."

He was caught off guard, struggling to say, "You are CIA Spy. Only CIA would know Alberto Jimenez, who tortured and murdered Che to have that information taken from him."

"Are you willing to talk to the CIA?"

"What is in it for me?"

"Retirement or prison."

"Okay Joe, retirement is what it will be. Now your name please."

Ignoring his question, and after several hours the Captain was instructed to angle towards the East for a while, until we see lights on the West Coast of Florida. Less than two hours later we entered Boca Grande Pass.

During the entire trip Levy was sea sick, keeping his head down.

When we were in the Gasparilla Sound seeing markers leading towards marina lights the Captain asked, “We go into the Marina.”

“No, the Sheriff stores his boat there. Go under the bridge and keep to the channel towards the island on our left, point the boat towards 190 degrees, do not stray or we will be grounded.”

Twenty minutes later we landed at dock 88, where we could land and use a telephone from one of the vacant holiday homes. We also needed to rest while the marina water taxi came for us. I handed the Captain another $100 to fill up over at the big Marina. He was delighted to be leaving with another hundred dollars, that is until he finds out what the marina charges for fuel.

Our Cuban Captain sailed back across Gasparilla Sound, and I now have two stowaways, one well connected Cuban and a Russian Spy.

A house next to the dock had a key under a door mat, where we entered to use the phone and bathroom, thinking there is two ways to handle this predicament. Have the Sheriff pick us up and have Thibodeau send a plane for us into Punta Gorda Airport.

After calling the General at home, I was told,

"Good job Wright. You get those two men to PGI, no wait; A Deputy will drive you to that airport. See you in two hours at Punta Gorda."

Eldred's Marina water taxi was called, asking for a pickup, having them tell me, we would be picked up within ten minutes, the water taxi was at a dock South of where we were.

When we arrived at the marina, two sheriffs' cars with four deputies were waiting.

Estrada, Levy and I waited inside two sheriffs cars until Thibodeau's plane landed at PGI.

When we were driven out to the tarmac, and waiting for the rear ramp to lower, Estrada said, "Who ever you are, I am impressed how this has been done."

This prompted me to ask him, "Would you like to work for the U.S. Government?"

He did say it was possible in a few months.

I could see General Thibodeau at the top of the ramp waving for us to quickly board. Evidently he wanted to get back to Washington in time for drinks at five. They had to put on fuel, so why the hurry.

When we got on board, he said great news, "The man in the Vatican held a news conference announcing that American involvement in arms for hostages was a hoax percolated out of the DNC. You did it boy, the Veep wants to see you this evening, over dinner at his place."

Starting the intro, I said, "General meet Mr. Levy, you may know him as Leonid Miska and Alberto Jimenez, a confidant of the chemist."

"Dam Wright, you never cease to amaze me. Gora is on board."

Acknowledging Gora, I said, "Hello Gora, good to see you again sir. Levy this is Gora Demyan, as you know an ex KGB Operative,"

Speaking Russian, Levy said, "Agent Demyan, we thought you were killed by BTK, somewhere in a swamp in Florida."

Gora speaking back in Russian, said to Levy, "Do you know this man here, the one who brought you over?"

"Yes, of course, he is General Gennady Vagon."

"His birth name is William Wright."

"Billy? No, you mean to say when he asked last night I had a decision to make he wouldn't be playing a game."

"Let me say Levy, you made the right choice, you are now free to go where ever you want to go."

We were in the air, when General Thibodeau said, "First you have to be debriefed in Washington, then you are free to go."

Chapter 16

Havana KGB Director to go underground

Gora interpreted for Levy to what the General said, and then replied in Russian, "Tell him I am not going to betray my country for money."

Demyan didn't know what to say as he looked at me for help. This prompted me to negotiate for Levy on selling the files he brought with him to the CIA. This attempt had to be worth 100 G's and stern enough not to have Levy taken into custody when we landed at Andrews.

"General, these files are filled with information on Soviet Agents serving in all of the America's. His price is $100,000, not negotiable; those files are to be sold to you or me. He is requesting that no one knows he is in America. To make sure the request is granted, he will fly with me tonight to London. His family is there they should be reunited and left alone for at least three months. Would this be agreeable to the CIA?"

"Don't like this arrangement, he needs to answer some questions on missing American agents, dissidents and prisoners from the Bay of Pigs debacle."

His information can be relayed through Simpson's

office in three months."

"Alright, he can vanish for now, however will you be able to work him after his three months are up if he gets cold feet?"

"You can count on it, sir. Now about his fee."

"Pay him in English Pounds, Simpson will reimburse you."

"Thank you sir."

Levy handed over his two files.

He did ask one question, "Billy, you really killed over 50 Soviet Agents and Soldiers?"

Not answering him, Gora stepped in to help me out by saying, "Levy, he has helped a thousand times that over the last 12 years."

That was a bit of an exaggeration but by the look on Levy's face, he believed the yarn.

Thibodeau and I talked while the other two were conversing in their native tongue. The General quietly asked what was it they were saying? I relayed most of their conversation until when it got to how Demyan was injured and what happened to the other Russian Agent deep in the Everglades. Gora may have exaggerated the gory stuff.

Levy was shaken from what he heard while staring at me in a way of saying you must be mad.

The General finally told me, after suspecting for

several months he was ill, saying, “General Wright, I am going through a series of treatments at Walter Reed and had been for several months. These two captives may be my crowning glory from many years in the service of this country. Thank you.”

He was almost getting friendly or personal, however he pulled back when he caught himself saying, our working together has made his life interesting again.

I couldn't say anything so I let him ramble on and on. His health was a concern for some time. He showed in the past a discomfort making him irritable was inconsequential now, unimportant.

After landing at the Air force Base close to D.C., we were taken to the Hilton for a late lunch, and to get a couple hours of sleep before flying out of Dulles on the Pan Am Delta interchange into Heathrow. Unbeknownst to me or Levy, Thibodeau's secretary was setting up our travel arrangements in London on our arrival. Getting a rain check for dinner at the V P's house was fortunate. The only thing that felt uncomfortable was the secretary knowing about Miska.

We were lucky to be flown in a Delta DC-8, where the front of first class had a large table where we could sit. Miska talked all the way, even though I drifted off to sleep in the middle of his conversation. Waking up a couple of hours later, a stewardess, who was part of the

Pan Am crew, came and sat next to me bringing a scotch and water with her.

She asked, “Do you still drink scotch?”

“Yes, how did you know?”

“We met on a trip to San Juan when I was one of the crew. Nicola and I started at the same time we went through stewardess training together in Miami.”

“How wonderful to speak to you, I do miss her and our life with the airlines.”

“Billy, I was hurt when I heard she was in that plane. We heard you were too and then were told you’d missed your connection. I took a double take when I saw you in the departure lounge.”

She left to answer a call button and when she returned she sat down and said, “We tried to find out what happened to you Billy, we were told you vanished off the face of the earth. What have you been doing?”

“It's a long story too much to tell you in the time we have before landing.”

“You can tell me tonight the crew are staying at the Hilton on Edgeware Road, are you able to have dinner with us or me?”

“That would be nice, thank you. It's Jeanie isn't it?”

“You remember, how nice, see you at seven then.”

Racking my brain, it was no use; I didn't remember who she was. Luckily, her name was mentioned by a fellow crew member when she had to get ready to take off, back in Washington. If it wasn't for that happenstance her name would have been unknown.

Levy or Miska, woke up in time to see his breakfast being served.

Miska a little groggy and disheveled with his hair looking like a birds nest he needed to be told, "Go comb your locks."

He let out a laugh from the toilet, promptly closing the door behind him.

When we walked out to the arrivals area, Levy's family rushed up to welcome him to London.

Kenny was standing in the back waving and saying, "Guv, over ere."

Our crew walked by just as I started talking to Levy in Russian, making Jeanie slowdown to hear what we were saying.

Miska's instructions were, "Call me the first day of each month, to find out where we can meet up. When we do meet you have to take precautions you are not followed. Is that clear?"

"Yes sir. Thank you so very much, you can see how thrilled my family are to have their papa with them again."

Jeanie hurried to catch up with her work mates, looking over her right shoulder, smiling with a slight wave. Thinking it would be nice to have her tell me about Nicola's work and her friends.

Allowing Kenny to come over to be introduced to a future agent, he said, “That ostess looked like she knows ya, Guv.”

“From a long time ago Kenny, she worked with Nicola.”

“Right Guv, I'm to take tha Russian and 'is family, to 'is wife's 'ouse, orders from the big cheese, da big cheese wots in the Yank's compound, ketch me drift, Guv.”

I made my way to the flat on the underground. In a way that was a good thing not having to entertain him over a cup of tea. Since sleep was needed more that talking in catching up the happenings here in London.

Nothing like entering a cold damp apartment with the lure of lying under a heavy duvet.

Waking up a couple of hours later, when Kenny let the bottom door slam shut making me sit up in bed, and hearing him say, “Putten da kettle on Guv, cup o tea den.”

He was talking to someone, I thought oh no, it must be General Simpson. I stumbled out with nothing on but a robe, to see the General staring towards me.

Thinking to my self, next time when sleep was needed, I am definitely going to Nicola's parents' house.

The General sitting down to a hot cup of tea, started in with, “What's your plans for the next two weeks, Wright?”

I did not like the sound of this, as he continued on talking after taking a sip and describing what this impromptu briefing is, having him sup tea at my kitchen table.

“Look Wright, your trip was a success, doesn't mean you have time to rest. We need you to solidify our relationship with the Soviets. A transmission picked up from the Russians on a missing Leonid Miska, from the Russian Embassy in Havana, that wouldn't be our new defector, would it?”

Chapter 16

Assignment Moscow

“Yes sir, Miska, has decided to come over.”

“Wright, if the Russians find out we took a high ranking KGB agent, it may be hard to repair the damaged you have done.”

“Sir, the man was ready to bolt we were lucky to get him before the Brits.”

“Please, hold your fire, “You know the President is

working on what the Russians call perestroika, which now may include turning Miska over to the KGB."

General Simpson, "For now they may assume he made it to London on his own, however we need to continue on as if we do not have him."

"Alright, say hypothetically, they do find out the CIA was involved, when can you be in Moscow?"

"I need to go to Frankfurt and clear my desk. A few days is needed in Garmisch to relax while setting up a plan of action. Lastly, $10,000 in cash is what it will take to gain access to the right departments inside the Kremlin. If we get lucky by greasing a few palms, this may blow over."

"Okay, you have to negotiate to repair damage done by this unfortunate defection and when you are finished, I need a report on my desk on the outcome, plus a name would be helpful for future correspondence. You remember the President is counting on the Soviets to come to the table and discuss all of our future plans with the Soviets."

"Alright sir, I'll go. Before that happens, I need to get Miska's payoff to him."

"I will have it ready tomorrow afternoon, I take it cash will suffice?"

"Yes sir. Now if you two will excuse me, it is necessary to get some sleep. One last item, do not radio, write or transmit the name of Miska, or Levy anywhere. When you call Washington do it from a phone booth away from the Embassy."

Simpson and Kenny left, talking as they went down the stairs.

Now, back in bed, I went over how to pacify the Soviets if it is needed, slowly drifting off to sleep.

That evening I arrived at the hotel where Jeanie was staying and being a little early and walking down to where the restaurant was, I saw her in a souvenir shop. When she noticed someone was watching her, she smiled and asked, "Where are we dining?"

Seeing her dressed casual I suggested a pub. We ended up at Flanagan's where we sang along, from our music sheet of old songs.

During a break in the singing, Jeanie asked, "Billy, are you over Nicola?"

Jeanie, I can't think of a time when that will happen. Having said that I do enjoy company from attractive ladies especially stewardesses. Also traveling and seeing old friends, meaning, life is good maybe that is why I need to keep busy."

"What about you, did you ever marry that dashing young pilot?"

"No Billy, he called it off. As it happened I was better off not marrying him. My mother became ill and needing my help it left little time to socialize outside of work."

"Are you still with Delta?"

"I resigned the day Nicola died. A place to hide was all I wanted where no one knew me. I needed to get back onto a path of going forward. Looking for anything to hang onto, revenge was keeping me focused; I needed to get the people that caused the crash."

"Billy, revenge is not a good way to live, where does one go to hide from a tragedy?"

"A dark dismal place where pain is meted out through physical and mental drills, mainly fitness regiments at various Army training centers and Ranger School. Jeanie for me to go forward was to get in shape to deal with some very bad villains. A two year training program full of pain was a way to think about something other than missing my wife. I'm sorry Jeanie, I must seem self centered, are you enjoying flying the London route?"

"Billy, you must need to talk this out. Yes, Nicola and I both loved going to London anytime we could. We did use your flat several times when you had to stay in Tampa. It is unbelievable you went back into the Army. What if you wanted to back out when your heart started to mend, it would be too late the Army would not let you quit. That was a bit drastic, wasn't it?"

"It worked Jeanie. I was able to get the guys who brought the plane down, and go on assignments that took my mind away from thinking about the past. These jobs were often in turbulent areas, mainly overseas, where the landscape did not remind me of our life in Tampa."

"You may not know, Nicola and I were close enough to talk about personal things. She did not like your line of work before you were married, are you again doing similar jobs."

"Yes, now I am happy doing it again. It is hard to explain to good people who are sheltered from evil foreign destroyers. What I do now is for national security."

It was good to have Jeanie for company, instead of being alone. She was not only intelligent, but quite attractive and interesting. We could become close, if my occupation wasn't such a hurdle and of course Fran was still in my heart.

Back at her hotel she asked, "Billy, can we get together again? I am based in Atlanta if you ever are in need of a place to stay or just passing through, please give me a call."

We parted as friends, where I left to walk back to my flat, thinking if she viewed my occupation, one built on malice, it was distasteful. Oh well I must continue on my own path.

The next morning while packing to fly to Frankfurt Kenny and General Simpson brazenly walked up the stairs and into the living room.

Simpson said, "We have a problem, General Wright. White House communications Director said the Russian Leader has canceled a visit to Washington next month, citing it was necessary for him to travel to Cairo."

"Sir, I would assume at worst they are stalling or trying to get some type of a bargaining advantage on their detente."

"Wright, I do not care about your assumptions you know the new Director, I believe. She went on to say, in the same correspondence that the Soviets alliance with the Egyptians was a higher priority at this time. Miss Latta said you have to get to Moscow today and fix this rift. She expects to hear this is solved by the end of next week."

"What do we give them?"

"Wright, you may have to hand over Miska."

Oh, so naive, the USSR needs cash, they are broke.

It was necessary to be contrite, by replying in a low key manner "Alright General, I will be in Moscow tomorrow afternoon. Go with me to Heathrow to catch my plane to Frankfurt and tell me why we have to bow down to a dinosaur. Kenny go warm up your motor, we leave in five minutes."

"Right Guv."

In the back of Kenny's taxi, Simpson asked, "What are your chances of patching up this rift?"

"Sir, I would think it is fifty, fifty."

"Okay, say you patch things up, when will you come and get Miska."

"I hope it doesn't come to that, sir. My word is at stake."

"Dam your word, Wright. Your reputation isn't under scrutiny, our security is at stake. How are you going to get this done?"

"I need the $10,000 in my hands by tomorrow morning, sir. I will try to buy some influence with one of the Kremlin Generals. You know my word won't be worth spit to future defectors if I hand over Levy."

General Simpson put his hand inside his jacket and pulled out two bundles of $100.00 Bills, saying, "Take care of this, and bring it back if whoever you try to bribe doesn't take it."

"Yes sir."

Kenny pulled up at Terminal One leaving as soon as I had my carry on walking inside the double doors, without looking back. All I could think of was getting on the plane and going through KGB dispatches to see if

I was going to be identified.

Finally reading what was on my desk inside ASA Headquarters from an airplane seat. One interesting intercepted dispatch, directed to London KGB office from Moscow read;

Comrade Sergei

Forward recent activity reports to KGB, Moscow, on Col's Azarov, Rasstoff, General Vagon, Comrade Demyan, also BTK/CIA Agent Wright.

RGRDS

P. Apostolic

P. Apostolic desk only:

Reply, via London, KGB

No information on BTK, Azarov- visits- twice, past two weeks. General Vagon, seen on Hyde Park Corner, with unidentified Soviet Agent, could be Vagon?

Sergei

Now the KGB are manufacturing false narratives engaged in sending false reports. This means London wants their bosses to think they are on the job twenty four seven.

One could assume that Sergei is into bird watching in Hyde Park not the flying types, rather the ones with mini skirts who stop to eat a packed lunch.

Another weakness has been exposed inside the

Soviet Intelligence Agencies, in having to post inaccurate reports back to Moscow. No one in Washington believes the days of the Iron Curtain are slowly closing.

Call it a clairvoyant gift or maybe a brazen game of chance, either way I could be in front of a court martial if my hunches are wrong.

Why take this chance, when I could take a seat behind a desk, and wait for the CIA Directorship to be handed to me. It is tough not to welcome adrenalin rushing through your veins, anticipating the next covert mission.

The next afternoon and on my way to Moscow, with the 10 grand stuffed into a diplomatic bag, along with a hand gun and silencer hidden in a garment bag. This is the type of activity that causes one's blood to rush through your veins. Planning on changing into the uniform of General Vagon once we were airborne in order to bypass the Russian Authorities at Moscow Airport was necessary.

My double agent Petro Apostolic was phoned just before boarding the Aeroflot Flight in the hopes of having a driver meet the flight on arrival, solely for the purpose of gaining entrance to the Kremlin fortress by having my ride waved through.

The plan went smoothly, and seeing Petro waiting

on the steps validated the successful entry. He had the driver stand by to take us to his house within the hour.

He whispered, “Do not say anything until we are in the apartment. We need to go upstairs to grab my case and a few papers for you to peruse and hang around for a while to see if you are looked at suspiciously,”

When we arrived at his place, his wife an ex agent of mine said, “Billy, how wonderful, I hope you are staying for a long time this time, you still look so young, how do you do it?”

“Isla, I can stay two nights, maybe three. Thank you for inviting me to stay.”

“Billy, it is still your place, thank you for paying our rent.”

Now this KGB director, myself and Isla an ordinary ASA Agent was about to have a clandestine meeting, one where the two agencies were about to come together. Petro and I were excused to go into the spare bedroom to talk, while Isla made a pot of coffee.

Petro started ripping into me, saying, “Will, are you insane? Arriving in Moscow as a General. What would you do when and if immigration pulled you over, well it could be the end of you, and possibly me and Isla.”

“What's gotten into you, making up Soviet orders has never been a problem.”

“Your fake orders are full of errors the Kremlin has

changed its forms, with abbreviations having two letters instead of three. Isla and I had to retype the ones you sent from London through our Embassy."

"Darn, thank you. When was the new format started?"

"Two months past. Reason being, they suspected a foreign agent gaining access to the Soviet Bloc and the Kremlin. It's not easy anymore lots of procedures had to be changed."

"Petro, as you know, there's two storms brewing, one from Washington with a larger front coming from Russia. All of this over Leonid Miska who seems to be missing from Cuba. However this is a tempest in a tea cup compared to the gathering storm coming out of the Middle East."

"So that is your plan. My superiors were wondering why you gave up safe houses in Eastern Europe. You have traded those assets for similar properties in the Arabian Peninsula with British complicity. You must have known those places were being monitored because of indifferent activity."

"There are several foreign entities on alert to ASA activities, allies and adversaries. You have known for some time I have a strong feeling the Arabian Peninsula is where our security will be compromised. Another opinion is the Russians are broke at least that is what I think. Now Miska could be a problem that is why General Thibodeau has ordered me to quell any threats or retaliation emanating out of the Politburo."

"Look Will, the Premier is going all out for blood on this. Miska knows where the bodies are buried in South America a walking time bomb that has to be returned or taken out. The directives are being planned, with a round the clock surveillance of his wife's residence in London. Now tell me Will, you are not involved in his disappearance."

Miska is in a safe house in Arizona. I want a meeting with the one who is planning the Miska action. The answer to your question is Miska was taken out of Cuba by an American Agent. He was not abducted, that is important."

"Get your coat, we need to go back to work, the President will be having a drink with his minister of Soviet Security at this time of day. Change into a Soviet Colonel's uniform, a general is way too presumptuous."

Chapter 18

Our Russian Partners

On the way over to the fortress, *Petro went over a*

scenario, one that had me acting grateful, with hat in hand when the President would ask me into his office.

I had another idea, one that required a gun tucked into a holster across my chest.

We entered the office of the Russian President by passing through metal detectors. Metal buttons on the jacket were seen and causing us to be waved through. Inside we were handed a glass of vodka, no it wasn't cocktail hour in Moscow most people drink vodka during the day.

Petro introduced me to President Gorbachev, a gracious man with knowledge of world events and of course of his predicament with the Soviet Territories.

The Soviet Leader asked, “Colonel Azarov, what can we help you with.”

“Comrade President, a British Agent working as an intermediary for the Americans was asked by the CIA to begin bargaining for Comrade Miska's release as soon as possible.”

He choked while taking a drink, Petro beginning to look uncomfortable raised his eyes toward the ceiling.

Waiting for his reply, he wiped his chin before saying, “How could that be Colonel? Our secret service doesn't know where Miska is. It seems you have started drinking early. Castro cannot find the traitor he has combed his Island and the waters around the tiny country. No debris or signs of suicide, for that matter, no American Chatter has been heard."

Umm, what is going on, the ASA and CIA have intercepted radio transmissions from KGB Moscow, or was it? It was now crucial to reply in a way to quell a possible fire storm.

"Sir, Miska wants to be with his family, he is not going to betray his country unless his country betrays him."

"What insolence. How can you prove what you say is the truth?"

"The Americans sent their ace William Wright to take him out of Havana. They arrived in South Florida on a speed boat sent from Miami."

"Why is it not possible to eradicate that vermin, Billy, once and for all? Yes, Azarov, that seems plausible. Do you know the terms of this bargaining?"

The PM was beginning to calm down; waiting for something he could live with.

"Yes sir. The CIA needs someone to keep an eye on the Chechnyan rebels, along with a group of Islamist, organizing a separatist movement in Georgia, Lithuania and other Balkan states. They want Miska to help the Soviets keep an eye on extremist and their Imam's. One stipulation he has the freedom to travel to see his family in London, and to relay the same intelligence to the

CIA."

The President excused himself, heading towards the rest room, with Petro following close behind.

When the door closed behind them and I was left alone I stuck a listening device under the man's desk and one on a coat rack.

The President sent my friend back in probably catching a case of paranoia.

When Gorbachev came back in, he told Petro to go to the washroom he would like to talk to Azarov alone.

He said, "This is an unfortunate time for you Colonel or whoever you are. My minders are on their way up to escort you to a detention center. I have to be sure you are actually a Russian Colonel, do you understand why this has to be done?"

"Yes sir, I would probably do the same thing if I was entrenched in an old antiquated agenda. However, you are on the verge of losing an agent who knows about Soviet atrocities in Prague and Budapest, along with interment facilities in Leipzig, East Berlin, Pilzen, Cheb plus another dozen cities. Not to mention his knowledge of places illegal Russian armaments were delivered to in South America. The man is in a safe house in the USA, waiting for me to pass on your answer. He has given the Kremlin 36 hours to send a response of yea or nay. Russian credibility is at stake here tonight."

"Colonel, you have nerve, I give you that."

A knock at the door, made the leader stare through me, waiting for a reaction, or contemplating to have me taken away, a mental game of Russian roulette.

Having to stay calm with my right hand inching towards the inside my coat and fingers now firmly wrapped around the pistol's handle, with one on it's trigger, kind of gave me an escape route.

He got up and opened the door, telling the two guards to go home he would see them tomorrow morning. He then called Petro in to witness what was going to be said.

The Russian leader asked, "You give me your word, Miska will not divulge Russian secrets."

"Yes sir. All the Americans want, is a way to spy on Imams, nothing else."

"That is good. We would also like this, come lets drink to our agreement. Would you have used your weapon, Billy?"

"Yes sir."

"Where are the listening devises?"

"Under your center desk drawer and on top of your coat rack."

He laughed, with Petro looking and wondering did the leader think he knew he was BTK, and himself fooled or maybe associated with the American Spy who had wrecked havoc against the Soviet Bloc for years.

The leader asked, "I would like to know how you were going to leave this country if you were threatened with an arrest. Would you have murdered my guards so you could flee to where ever you came from?"

"Mr. President, your guards, yourself and the KGB Director would not be able to say what happened here tonight. You would have the murder weapon in your hands when all of you were found in the morning. Your other question sir."

"Where is your escape route?"

"Prime Minister, as you well know, leaving Russia is difficult without appropriate documents. There are ways around this that has to be kept confidential for my own safety."

"Agent Wright, we like to have order in this country even if it means having restrictions placed on our citizens."

"Sir that is the reason your people are restricted on traveling to the West. I know why you deny your fellow country men and women the freedom of flight it would be catastrophic if your people could see how Western European countries are enjoying living in freedom."

"That is enough we are not debating our differences. It is hard to believe you have the levity to work with Miska."

Having espoused my intentions, including Petro in the slaying of these two gentlemen, eased my mole's concerns; it showed on his face, he was relieved. Thinking now how to alleviate the Presidents fears, he has to be sure that his country's dirty laundry will not be mentioned to the U.N.

"Mr. President, Miska will be available to meet with you at anytime."

"When is this firt meeting?"

"The ASA's weekly planner will hold open a week each month, for me to travel and meet with you Mikhail; Nothing must stop Russia and the ASA coalescing to stop the Islamist extremist movement."

"Give me time to consider this."

"You have one minute to decide."

After 59 seconds he said, "Ya, for one year, we may try this your way."

"No Mr. President five years, a pattern needs to be logged and mapped in actions or extremist preaching are espoused through Muslim Imam's in the Caucasus's."

"We are willing to compromise, three years that is my last offer."

"We agree to your terms sir. One stipulation, our agreement is too sensitive to mention outside this room. The White House does not need to get involved, for obvious reasons, understand?"

"Ya, we were told you are setting up a separate division General? This would be a problem, if that is your agenda."

"Your intelligence information seems to be up to date. How could one man set up such a system, I am not that astute in intelligence operations, sir."

"Nyet. You know more than most, our system is not anywhere close to what it used to be, that is why you were able to access this city and my office. When did this plan of yours begin? We knew the day you were made a one star General, and now you have another star, not intelligent, please Wright, you have many skills, we here in Russia need. Answer my question, please."

"Several years ago, I happened on to a group targeting Western passenger flights, with your KGB funding and advice on how to plant undetectable plastic Czech made C-5 explosives on commercial jetliners."

"Both of our countries, will do whatever it takes to obtain an advantage, human collateral damage is an unfortunate by-product of some actions. Before we are off the proverbial track, please give me the schedule Miska is to give us a report."

"In approximately three months, Miska and I will travel to Chechnya to set up a safe house. Two weeks after our arrival we will then travel back to London, where he will take a two week break. We both will travel back to his country after he has rested, after another two weeks in Chechnya, I will travel to Moscow with his report."

Chapter 19

Shadow Agency

"General Wright, you should leave us now and be out of Moscow in the morning. I am expecting to see you in two months."

"It is important sir to let my President know the rift between out countries is over, without mentioning our arrangement. To explain what I am doing in the Middle East is to stop innocent families being blown out of the skies by Islamist extremest, this is driving an agenda. Not one the CIA believes is necessary."

"Thank you General. You may go."

Taking the stairs instead of an elevator, a way to avoid guards in the Presidential Palace, and thinking how close I came to assassinating the Russian Supreme Leader. How different things could have been, just under an hour ago. Having a partner instead of having to flee is a definite plus in continuing a program to go after hateful zealots.

Arriving at the apartment, Isla was in the kitchen, shouting out, “How did it go Petro?”

“He is with the President they needed me to leave so they could have a discussion without anyone hearing what was being said.”

“Want a drink, or a cup of tea?”

“Tea please.”

Sipping the tea and talking to Isla, I couldn't stop thinking about how my agenda was slowly coming together.

Before the cup was empty, Agent Apostolic was now in the kitchen, having a vodka poured for him.

He said to his wife, “Isla, you will not believe what this crazy man was going to do.”

“Remember Petro, Billy and I go back many years, I am never surprised by his actions. Let me guess, he threatened the President, and then got his way.”

“Exactly darling. Threatened him with a pistol he never showed if he actually was carrying a weapon. Do you have a gun inside your jacket Will?”

“Sure I do.”

“You are one crazy man, Will. Would you have shot the President?”

“If he was in the way of getting out of his office, I

would have had no choice. Having done the deed, I would have sabotaged anyone's ability to track me escaping.”

“Alright, lets drop the what if's. The Russian Leader likes you, because of your straight forwardness, and the way you handle yourself. The question is, can you deliver?”

“Sure I can, delivering information from Chechnya on extremist elements I’m going to give it a shot. Hopefully Miska is going to be bored after three months of doing jobs for his wife, and ready to escape domestic chores like gardening and odd jobs.”

“How can you know she is that type of woman?”

“Let’s see, if you were under Isla's toes, every day, every hour for three months, what would she be having you do?”

Apostolic laughed and said, “I see what you mean, Miska may appreciate his freedom.”

Isla had to respond in a way that showed her annoyance grouping all women into one category, saying, “Alright you two, continue your chauvinistic opinions in the lounge, I will call you when the meal is on the table.”

The next morning I caught a flight to Frankfurt, where messages from Washington were waiting to be taken care of or more precisely messages from one person, General Thibodeau.

Several notes were left by the secretary for me to call him ASAP. Finally making the call, and holding I hung up after thirty minutes and started going through reports from this station and Bad Aibling.

Ready to go home, I grabbed my overcoat and headed for the door, when the phone rang.

Contemplating not answering, I chickened out, thinking it could be Fran or Els. No such luck, it was Thibodeau, from his home on the edge of D.C.

He loudly said, “Jolly good show, Wright, I'm proud of you my boy.”

I could hear him take a sip of his drink. He sounded as if he had too many already, prompting me reply in a rude way.

“Sir, I believe we should hold off discussing company business until tomorrow.”

He was now in a rage, saying, “You think I'm uncapable to talk, is it because you think I have had to many cocktails?”

“Sir, the word is incapable.”

“General Wright I can still have you up in front of a court martial, don yu fink I can't.”

“Sorry sir, have to go, a British General is waiting to see me, sorry sir, goodbye.”

The next morning my secretary pointed to the

phone, miming it's the General. Shaking my head no and miming back, I'm not here, made her get up and walk toward my office.

The darn secretary hurried to move in front of me, picked up the phone, then handing it to me.

I heard, “General Wright, you there yet?”

“Sorry sir, I am in a bit of a rush this morning.”

“You listen to me my young General, Simpson is meeting me at crooked waters tomorrow morning he is going to board my plane. You be at Rhein Main in the morning at 0900 hours to meet us, you understand me? We are going to get some things straighten out, post haste.”

“Yes sir. It is called Bentwaters, RAF Bentwaters.”

“I don't care if it's called Timbuktu, you ingrate, just be at Rhein Main.”

“Have a nice flight, sir. See you at 0900.”

Oh brother now what is provoking this visit, post haste, what was that all about? He sounded as if he was at the bar, can't be, it's three pm. should be at work.

This day is going to be used to have my secretary help set up the conference room, plus sketch a map of the Russian Caucasus.

Asking for such a large area of Russia to be drawn was not received happily. The secretary abruptly left for the Frankfurt Library.

It was up to me to set up the room for the briefing, after asking the sketch be at least 4' by 4', so aging Generals could see how Muslim Enclaves were steadily expanding. Turkey and Armenia bordering the targeted Soviet States are predominantly Muslim, so why wouldn't they continue their Caliphate?”

Detailed sketch of the Caucasus areas

The secretary did not return by 1700 hours, and as it turned out, it was fortunate, since she was not in a good mood leaving for home right on time.

When everyone had gone for the day, it was time to get busy preparing the conference room, by placing a secondary tape recorder in a sideboard with the main machine on top. If asked to stop the recording for off the record discussions, the second device would continue on recording, this is an insurance policy, in case a nefarious covert action was ordered and if it went South, the two Generals would leave me hanging.

Early the next morning arriving at headquarters, the secretary was seen hanging the map and muttering what a slave driver her boss was. Luckily I left to pick up the guest at Rhein Main, before being discovered by a wet hen.

Waiting for the Generals plane to land, the Base Commander joined me for a cup of coffee in his Flight control's break room.

He curiously asked, “Tell me General Wright, why are two Army Generals having their plane stay here on a parking pad for three days, then requiring that a flight plan be filed to Moscow?”

“Colonel, it is to do with a program called Detente or Perestroika. That information does not leave this room, understand?”

“Yes General Wright. I will leave you sir, since you are meeting the two men. You three Generals have been here more times than any high ranking officers in the past ten years. Why is that?"

"Long story, thank you for your hospitality."

When the Commander left, I took my coffee outside to think, why a trip to Moscow was necessary for a CIA Director and alert his ASA Director. This all has to be because of sharing Miska what else could it be, hopefully not for another job. Flying on a MATS HOP isn't the most comfortable way to fly, especially overnight across the pond. Whatever, it is has got to be with Congress or receiving the President's blessing.

Finally, the C-130 was seen banking north of the city, lining up on a runway provided for military traffic. Not long now before the rubber hits the tarmac.

With the back ramp of this large cargo freighter lowered two Generals walking down the ramp looked disheveled. The closer they got it was clear they were needing sleep with blood shot eyes and unshaven faces. They need to get some sleep before we discuss anything.

The MP drivers were told to take the Generals to their hotel with Thibodeau objecting, saying, "Look here Wright, we do not have time to rest."

"General you are on my turf now, I will not discuss important matters to two jet lagged Directors. We can start at 1500 hours, that will be 0900 Washington time."

"Alright Wright, this may be your turf, however I am still your superior, do not forget that, you had better be on time."

"Yes sir, see you two in the conference room."

Now that was over with, it is time to get a late breakfast and prepare for a long evening. Everything was in place by noon, allowing me to get an hour's sleep with my office door closed.

After a short respite the secretary was told to phone the mess hall and have coffee, hot tea and sweet rolls delivered here at precisely 1700.

A lot of commotion heard downstairs meant the two old bears were in the house. General Thibodeau leading General Simpson into the room, rubbing his hands, looking refreshed and clean shaven pointing to an open window, motioning with his right index finger for it to be closed. He then arranged new seating positions.

He opened the briefing saying, "Don't tell me you believe in all that fresh air stuff. Turn the heat up, we are cold. Two things you need to do, order your secretary to go back to her desk, we are not to be disturbed, and turn off that blasted tape recorder."

General Thibodeau had taken over this briefing, he was now officially in charge, a relief if a new mission was ordered and had to be scuttled.

When everything was done he seemed to be

pondering what or how to start this briefing.

After a couple minutes, he said, "Thank you for having Gerald and me take a nap. We are anxious to get this nasty business over with. This meeting is not happening. There will be no notes taken, no recordings of our conversation, no correspondence on our mission. Absolutely no follow up after we leave Frankfurt. Do you understand, Wright?"

"Yes General I do. Who ordered you to have this briefing deemed never have taken place? ASA has a practice to record all meetings."

"General Wright, clean out your ears, Gerald and I are not here, do you now understand? No more questions, you listen and only then can you ask about your mission, nothing else, comprende."

The General is feeling his oats, saying comprende, as if he was used to a point of wanting a confrontation. I wonder if his trip here was logged out of Andrews. Rhein Main must have been alerted by someone, since the Base Commander was there to meet the plane. It will be necessary to find out what this is all about, especially if I was going to be the goat.

The two Generals must have some type of paper trail, but where, and in what form. Surely, funds had to be signed for this trip.

My thinking was interrupted with Thibodeau

shouting, "Wright, wake up, what are you planning, I know that look. You are not allowed to anticipate or use any of your weird clairvoyant crap. Do you understand?"

"Sorry sir, I must be tired."

"Tired my ass, your secretary said you had a nap. Gerald your turn. Tell this abrasive young General what is in store for him."

"Wright, there is some unfinished business with the perpetrators involved in the Marine Barracks Bombing. As you know, 241 Marines and Sailors were murdered while sleeping. The President wants this nasty business behind him, before he leaves office."

Chapter 20

Black Ops Briefing

"Sir I have to protest this action, as you know that area is now a wasteland, surrounded by a flock of crazies."

Thibodeau jumped out of his chair, shouting, "You have no say in this matter. You will do as you are ordered. General Simpson, finish up."

"Yes sir. Wright, one other matter, after you discuss

this first assignment with us, the conversation stays in this room. Now General Thibodeau wants to ask you a few questions on Leonid Miska. First, what do you think about going into the desert again?"

"You are talking as if you have rehearsed your lines. This is insane those guys are long gone, probably laying on a beach somewhere. What happens if a CIA or ASA Agent gets caught inside Arabia?"

Thibodeau quickly responded, "We are not in school rehearsing you insolent SOB. You are going in as a Russian General. After you finish the job, we will meet in South Florida. Any questions?"

"Yes sir. What is the mission?"

We were interrupted with a knock on our door. Coffee and pastries were pushed into the room, prompting the General to mime, be quiet.

While picking up a honey bun, Thibodeau sternly spouted, "Give the evil doers a hand in seeing their seventy two virgins sooner than later. We have information your targets are joining Hezbollah and the PLO in an Arab Summit next month, either in Beirut or Sheikh El Sheikh, on the Egyptian Coast. My bet would be the bombed out area in Lebanon. Before we go any further, any questions?"

"Yes sir. Funding of $100,000 will be needed. This is not negotiable."

"Where are we going to get that much cash in such a short time?"

"You have half of that with you, the other $50,000 can be obtained by wire from USAEUR."

"You impertinent ass, trying to extort money from our Government. Okay, the money will be in your office tomorrow morning. For that money we also want Miska handed over, the same day."

"Miska will cost you one million dollars, non negotiable."

They would never go for a million, thankfully.

"I have the authority to have you hauled in front of a Court Martial, for extortion, you insolent ass. We are not giving you any money for Miska."

"I believe you sir, forget about Miska."

General Simpson was called out side, Thibodeau was fuming as he stridently walked out the door. The General knew I was holding him and the President of the United States for ransom. If this mission had any chance of succeeding, people had to be bribed in Lebanon. The summit had better be in a place where innocent people were not close by. Sharm El Sheikh would cause a huge problem, where an airstrike could not be used. Where did T get the place as Sheikh El Sheikh? Like past missions left over funds are used for financing the stealth team.

General Thibodeau walked in and immediately said, "Alright Wright, you keep Miska be it on your own head if he goes back to Russia. We need to meet up in Florida one month from today."

"Yes General. We have more coffee on the way do you want some more sweet rolls?"

"Enjoy them Wright, I need a drink. Get someone to take Gerald and myself to our hotel. We will see you tomorrow morning at 0900."

"What about the three of us having diner together this evening?"

"No way Hozay, we have had enough of your company. Simpson and I will talk over tonight how your assignment is to be conducted."

Hozay! He is on a roll with Mexican names and meanings. What worries me is how could they know where my mission's direction is going, until an agent was actually on the ground in a volatile area.

With the two superiors now out of the way I can gather needed arms for a short or lengthy assignment, not to mention planning for an escape. A dangerous thought of me being found out by the extremist is on the forefront of my thinking. Working out what to do and where to escape to was necessary in helping in my preparations. My motto has always been "Prepare for the worst, anything else will be a bonus"

Going to sleep while plotting my entry into Beirut was a sort of a sleeping aide, after a short period of time of thinking on who could be my interpreter I must have dozed off.

Waking up, I had the person in mind. Pierre Farouk is the man. Even though he was Jewish, he looked Arabian at least to me he seemed to fit the part.

Pierre answering my call in England, it was necessary to say delicately, “Pierre, my good friend, we need an interpreter for possible traveling to the Middle East are you available to do a job this week?”

“Yes, one provision, Paul Combs will be relieved in Astara, Azerbaijan in four weeks by another, allowing me to spend time with my family.”

“Combs will be notified today, and if he cannot stay on an agent will be sent to take your post for four to six weeks, let me know closer how much time you will need off. Pierre, pack your bags we may have to leave tomorrow, thank you for volunteering.”

Thibodeau and Simpson walked into the briefing room with Frankfurt's Cathedral clock striking nine. A tape had been replaced in the hidden machine ready for recording conversations that superiors do not want used for my defense, much less out in public.

The CIA Director started by saying, “You listen Wright, we have to get a few things straight. First, this meeting never happened second, we are not going to write anything down, or for that matter, we are not going to correspond in writing, by phone, teletype or any other way. Do you understand?"

"Yes sir. Same as yesterday nothing ever changes."

"What do you mean by that remark?"

"It seems when ever a situation comes up in a place we need to tread lightly old muggins here has to do the dirty, while my trusted Generals cover their rear ends. Can I assume we are having a follow up briefing, somewhere in Florida?"

"Precisely, my soon to be demoted young General. Easter, on the phosphate docks. Will that fit into your schedule or do you need a towel to wipe away those tears?"

"No tears sir, just concerns, if I'm served up as the sacrificial goat. General, may I ask who has sanctioned this action?"

"No, you may not. Your assignments are, one to pinpoint where the Hezbollah and PLO summit is being held. Two, find where Gaddifi is going to be in early April. That's it; this meeting is over see you in Florida, Private. Heh heh heh."

He knows I couldn't give a toss about wearing two stars, or four, he wants me to understand he is always going to be my superior. Thibodeau in the past had let it slip, a successor should come from the Agency, one who had been though all facets of the ASA, and experience in running a sub agency.

This is not the only secretive mission assigned to William Wright; ninety nine percent of them had been without written orders. I have known that if caught in a foreign country spying, there would be no one coming to help, maybe a trade, never a rescue attempt.

The two Generals were on the way to Rhein Main to board their flight to D.C. when I called Pierre to confirm he will be in Frankfurt tomorrow morning.

Farouk forgot he had to attend the Bar Mitzvah at his Synagogue this Saturday. He agreed to be in Cairo Sunday morning.

Leaving for Cairo alone the next morning with half of the money and two revolvers stuffed into two Russian Diplomatic bags was risky, but should prove useful. A garment bag filled with three Russian uniforms, two Arabic Thawbs - which are ankle length garments- and two fifths of vodka.

Egyptian Immigration was without incident after arriving as a Russian Colonel, where masquerading as a General may have been a little precarious, since no warning would have been issued and most Generals have military transport in which they travel, not to mention, ground transportation provided for a curb side pickup.

After hailing a taxi and being dropped off at the Russian Embassy guest barracks, it was now essential to change into the uniform of General Vagon, before walking across to the Embassy.

As I headed upstairs to the KGB office, I was stopped just before entering the foyer, by a young, quite attractive blond lady, telling me the Director had gone to Moscow.

Staring at her face and asking, "Who are you?"

She smiled and said, "I have been assigned to Cairo for the purpose of helping my comrades in a special investigation."

Oh my, this girl was either naive or dangerous, having assets that would make the most hard nose criminal melt. Love at first sight is a weakness for many young guys, the question is, how do I play her?"

Still thinking, not responding quickly, caused her to say, "General, are you alright?"

"Yes, thank you. I was wondering how such an attractive young lady could become a KGB Operator, fresh out of high school."

She laughed and said, "I was also wondering, how an attractive young man, could be come a General, who looks like he is fresh out of Military School."

She's good and quick, maybe too good. How many

men has she caught in her web where this blond beauty would conspire to trap an unsuspecting adversary.

We both laughed and exchange names. She is called Olga from the Georgian border, looked more Scandinavian than a white Russian, which had me wondering how her hair was almost platinum, with having dark brown eye brows.

She interrupted my thinking again by asking, "General, were you ever close to an explosion, and would you join me for lunch?"

"Sorry, I may have symptoms of shell shock, but that isn't the reason my response seems slow. I would like to join you, where do you suggest we go."

"There is a small bistro by the museum. We can take the Embassy taxi they will wait while we dine."

"Good, are you ready?"

"Not exactly, I have to freshen up. You men are all alike. Give me twenty minutes."

While Olga was in the restroom, I rifled through the Director's files. That was just the time needed to find the file on this female agent called Olga Prada. Perusing quickly, discovering she was used in the past for coercing politicians to her bed.

A note typed on Politburo's stationary, asked that she be used to seduce and photograph as many top Egyptian officials as possible, even the President.

That is out of the same play book used by the soviets for decades, for black mailing anyone who is needed for different scenarios.

That correspondence originated two weeks ago, meaning it was probably delivered after she was already here. A small wonder Petro's name was not on it or his initials, which meant he is being kept in the dark. But why? Just maybe she is helping someone's black OPS from the KGB or Kremlin.

Olga was heard coming down the hall, giving me time to make sure the filing cabinet was closed and secure.

She leaned against the door in a suggestive manner, saying, "My General, are you ready to take me?"

That had to be the quickest invite I had ever had the pleasure of receiving.

Helping Olga with her full white fur coat, covering a white tight dress, made me wonder, who she was working for. This polished call girl had all of the right mannerisms, feminine and classy, as if she went to finishing school. That's it, she was groomed for this.

Chapter 21

Alluring KGB Asset

It was fortunate, the restaurant was not the same one the Russian Ambassador and I frequented several years ago. After a lengthy lunch with consuming a bottle of vodka between us, we decided, it may be better to stay away from work this afternoon.

Arriving at a Cairo Airport Hotel with the Embassy taxi dropping us off, we checked into the Cairo Grand. Booking separate rooms confused the concierge, especially when we had no luggage for someone who was either flying out later or who had a late connecting flight.

His facial expression was one who showed instantly disapproval, especially when we were seen getting out of a shared taxi. We have to remember what the rules are in this predominant Muslim country.

After explaining our luggage did not arrive and we were put into the same taxi by an Air Egypt arrivals agent, the concierge still had of look of disapproval.

He wasn't buying it, causing him to ask, “You two do not know each other?”

What business was it of his, unless he was a part time ethics policeman. No, he has to be an Egyptian plant or a paid informant, with his ideology getting in the way of welcoming guests.

Majority of concierge's I had met wanted two

items, approval of their hotel and cash. This man showed his disdain of two supposed lovers together without the female having a parent or overseer with her, making sure nothing untoward happens. Either way he may be useful.

Being pressured for one of us to answer, I took the bait, saying, "We met at the airport for the first time, and continued to get to know each other in the cab."

"Is good understood. Come, you will follow me to your rooms."

After showing Olga to her room, he escorted me to the next floor where I was to stay.

Once in my room, the porter stridently asked after the door was closed, "Your new friend is a working lady?"

Acting innocently, I replied, "She seems really nice. If she is, my reputation is at stake what do I do?"

He finally smiled while saying, "You do nothing we are capable of dealing with loose single women."

Within minutes after the prude was gone, Olga was knocking on my door, and asking out loud, "Gennady please open the door I need to talk to you."

As soon as she was let in, a person in a tan western style suit was seen opening and closing the fire escape door. If it wasn't for the exit door being opened on the opposite wall, the eavesdropper could have been considered, someone wanting to get a little exercise, by walking down to the lobby, instead of taking an elevator.

It was essential to obtain information from this tipsy lady before we have hotel police show up. There is little time to do this.

Olga was overly aggressive, and with me stepping back she asked, “You are not in the mood Gennady?”

To get her ready for exiting this room,I kissed her and acted as if my mood was now in a semi desirous rage.

Slowly taking my jacket off I asked without turning around looking at her, “When are you due back in Moscow?”

“Please Gennady, no talking now, we will have time to talk business later. I want you like I have never wanted a man so much.”

“Olga, straighten up. We are leaving I want you to follow me without saying one word.”

“My clothes are off, it's your turn wait General, I will help.”

“No Olga, you do not understand. It will be too late if you do not get dressed, now.”

“You are to cautious, no one knows we are here alone.”

“That is the problem, the religious police will have

been told by now we are using this room for what they call sinful purposes."

By the time I had my jacket back on, the door opened with the concierge and two men in uniform and the tanned man in the Savil Row suit.

Olga was hauled out of the bed with her underwear showing, ferociously kicking her feet to get free. She was harshly flipped over and handcuffed, screaming, let me go you animals.

When she was gone, the plain clothes policeman asked in English, "Please General, I cannot talk your language, please speak English."

" This lady is an employee at the Russian Embassy, who may or may not be a prostitute. I need to talk with her to see what she actually does in the Embassy. Where will she be taken and how long will it take to process her?"

"The criminal is going to Cairo Central. Paperwork most times takes one or two hours. Shall we release her in your custody?"

"In the morning please, thank you officer. It is important to first obtain her file from the Embassy, and present them to your supervisor."

"All prisoners in holding cells, have to go before a Judge, however if your lady is picked up by 0800, then she can go with you."

"How is 0700 then?"

"That will be fine."

"Is it possible to see her alone when I arrive?"

"Yes. remember, the prisoner has to be out of the building by 0800."

Thank you again. My driver and I will be there around 0630."

When I left my room, I was a little paranoid about his men watching for me, making me wait thirty minutes before calling the elevator up. Punching the second floor button, to send it back down, and before gaining entrance to a room several doors down and on the opposite side of the corridor, I, waited and watched through a one half inch opening in the door to see if anyone was alerted.

Within ten minutes, four men came out of the fire escape. Two knocked loudly on my door, waited for a few seconds and unlocked it.

When they left and taking the elevator this time, I ran down the stairs to get to the bottom floor before them. On exiting through a service door, it was possible to work my away around the hotel, using the building to shield my escape towards the airport.

Just before getting to the main terminal, a taxi was hailed going into the airport, to take me to the Embassy barracks.

Back in my room, it was necessary to change into a Colonel's uniform again for gaining access to KGB files and head to the Embassy to check on Olga's orders, their origination and past assignments.

While walking across a wide parade ground, thinking now it may be advantageous to show up tomorrow morning as General Vagon, since Olga assumes that is my rank and name. What is needed is a driver and the KGB Station's sedan for impressing what should be the midnight shift's junior prison crew.

At the Embassy entrance, two guards holding doors open, were asked, “Have your commander call the KGB office in ten minutes.”

By the time my call came in, three months reports were on the desk, with the guards' commander saying, “Colonel, you wanted me to call you?”

“Yes, thank you. My superior General Vagon needs a car and driver tomorrow morning at precisely 0600 in front of the Embassy Barracks.”

“Will there be an order cut for this job?”

“You can come over in two hours, they will be ready.”

“Please Colonel give them to the driver my shift will be over by that time.”

This was anticipated; knowing the graveyard shift crew are ready to get some sleep, and the chances the driver would be embarrassed to ask for orders giving a General permission to use a staff car.

Informative dispatches on comrade Olga Sokolov. That name brought back memories of almost two decades ago. I wonder if there is a correlation with a nasty Major Sokolov who had become an obstacle in a mission to North Vietnam aboard a freighter out of Gdansk. She is twenty one, so if he was her father, her age when he disappeared should be about eight or nine, a fragile time in a young adolescence's life, who thinks of a father figure as her protector.

A two and a half month old introductory letter from one Russian Colonel, an Adjutant with an occupational Polish Third Army, read,

"Comrade Chairman,

Comrade Olga Sokolov is in need of a foreign posting. Her assets are convincing male competitors and enemies to change course or discourse.

Comrade Sokolov analyzes from our Military Hospital Psychological Unit at the age of sixteen, found she was in need of strong male suitors.

Using her skills of attracting males could be an asset in procuring contracts with Egyptian Cabinet members for the purpose of procuring armaments for oil.

Regrds

Comrade
Yuri Alagov

Alagov was liquidated by an American Agent over ten years ago. Okay, the letter was written by someone who does not want to be associated with Olga's past. If that's the case, her behavior is an act, in need of mature male acceptance. It may be abhorrent to take advantage of a vulnerable young lady but not if it is going to help her.

Time is running out to get everything read before the cleaning crew shows up.

Barely got through copying all of the dispatches and heading for the barracks when the cleaners were seen getting out of their van.

Sleep overtook my plans to get through all of the dispatches with Olga's name in them.

On the way to Cairo's Central Police station the next morning, I was able to read the remainder of Olga's info from Moscow. She was used to a point where it was shameful, running a prostitution service to acquire Intel.

We arrived at the jail a little after oh six hundred catching many of it's wardens dealing with way too many prisoners who were needing to be served a breakfast of weevil infested bread and weak coffee before appearing in court.

My arrival caused a security situation, enough concern for the head of police to be notified. A junior officer who was in charge of the night shift led me into a small room that was probably used for interrogations, since a large mirror, was on a wall behind a desk.

It was obvious this mirror was used for viewing and listening to prisoners, which might be a useful tool in turning Olga.

Twenty minutes after arriving, the prisoner was escorted into the room, looking like someone who needed lots of sleep. Her hair resembled a birds nest, and seeing herself in the large mirror, she started crying, mumbling in Russian, collapsing onto a heavy metal chair.

While seated with her head buried in two dirty hands, she cried out, "Please Gennady Help me."

Wanting Olga to see how her predicament could elevate her she was asked, "Miss Sokolov, were your rights violated during your stay?"

"My body was violated by two guards. Please let Moscow know the animals they want to ally themselves with."

When the door opened and seeing two guards and the Commander entered, the plan worked.

Guards were instantly issued an order, grabbing the prisoner by both of her arms, causing me to stand and harshly shout in English, “Let her stay. Commander I am General Vagon, special envoy, representing my country's interest in Egypt. Please have a chair brought in for you to witness my interrogation.”

He replied in broken English, “Yees, good, thankful Geeneeral.”

When a chair was brought in and the door closed, I asked, “Olga can you speak and understand English?”

“Yes.”

“Charges of prostitution are going to be brought against you. If you cooperate with Egyptian authorities, they may be lenient and have your sentence reduced or possibly have you turned over to our own military officials.”

The Prison Commander nodded, adding, “My men they done nothing, you agree?”

Olga started to say something causing a quick reply from me with, “Thank you Commander. Miss Sokolov will sign a release, knowing this charge will not go away, only delayed, if your prisoner changes her ways.”

When the commander left to have the release forms filled out, Olga whispered, “I will not go along with this.”

“Comrade Sokolov in ten years when your sentence is up, you will be lucky to have any teeth left in your mouth and instead of looking thirty, you will look seventy. You want me to leave you here?"

"Please get me out, please."

"Good you are in my care from now on."

Twenty long minutes went by when the prison commander came in, standing by the open door, he said, "Geeneeral, how you say, a spanner was thrown in works."

Anticipating a snafu in a country known for fowl ups, it was necessary to quickly say, "That is fine sir. Book us two hotel rooms across the street. We are willing to wait."

"May be not possible, have to get okay from politicians."

"No, we will not allow a Russian citizen to be hurt any further. Release her to me or lose the backing of the Russian Government."

"One moment General."

Another twenty minutes went by before he came back in and said, "You have two rooms in my name. My guard will take you now."

We were led across the wide avenue into an old concrete fortress called Hotel Cairo. Booked into rooms down the hall from each other on the second floor, it was essential for me to take the room next to a fire exit. Our guard was stationed outside Olga's room, where he stood at attention for a few hours. Thinking he has to go to the bathroom sometime, I will make a move then.

The guard walked quickly to the elevator, giving me the chance to go get Olga. She was fast asleep and had to be carried to my room. When she was put to bed, with a manky old green blanket covering her, I went to see if the guard was back.

Finally, the man was back standing at attention, gave me an idea of going to see if he would say something if I attempted to enter the guarded room. When I got close, he waved me off in a way to say that room was off limits.

Satisfied, the guard doesn't know Olga was gone, and getting back I laid next to Olga, gently shaking her, whispering, “Wake up, be quiet, we need to go.”

“I must not get into trouble Gennady. The authorities had told me they would send me to a work camp in Russia, if I wasn't a good girl.”

“Shush, they will not find us if we keep quiet and do not move around. You must get in the linen closet and cover yourself it is going to be some time before we can leave.”

An hour later I heard foot steps, the people could be seen through a crack in the slightly open door. The man in the tan suit, looking around from the other area, was heard speaking to the guard.

After waiting another two hours, Olga said, “I must visit the latrine.”

“Listen Olga, do not flush the commode, do not turn any water on, we will get a drink when we exit the building.”

Over by the window, a small bus was seen pulling up to the hotel it was an Army crew, arriving to stay the night.

I told Olga, “It is time to go.”

I managed to get the bus driver to take us to the airport after a sizable bribe was handed to him. In the hotel lobby everyone was busy taking care of getting the men signed in and escorted up to their rooms.

From the airport we took a taxi to the Embassy Barracks. Once inside Olga had to have a large drink of water, followed by a large vodka. I had to forego the water for a glass of club soda.

She did not stop and think about how dangerous drinking public water in Egypt was. To late now, she is going to have one big problem in the morning a problem I do not want to be around for her sake and mine, it is going to be quite embarrassing for her.

Olga asked, “Why treat ordinary people as if we are

some type of enemy?"

"Egypt is the birthplace of a following, called, Qutbism, an extremist form of Islamic ethics. If they had found you in bed with me and we are not married, you most likely would have been prosecuted. As for me, I would have been fined or slightly disciplined. We have to be careful this is not Moscow, Cairo could be quite restricted to young lovers."

We talked for a few hours before she passed out from lack of food and to much vodka, this allowed me to call my old friend the Coptic Taxi driver.

We were taken to the Cairo Mubarak Hospital, where they pumped her stomach out after paying the emergency room doctor a sizable bribe, to have her seen right away and to stay the night without any paper work.

I was taken back to the barracks, where the driver was asked to be back Sunday morning, for a ride to the Coptic Church Service.

Arriving at St. Marks the next morning, walking in past the Bishop greeting his flock, who gave me the nod to see him after the service. There were two suspicious looking Egyptians sitting in the rear of the Cathedral, who looked out of place. Their attempts to keep up with the proceedings substantiated my suspicions.

Services over and waiting for the Church to empty, it was necessary to kneel down and pray, as if I had a ton of sins to be forgiven, which I probably did.

When it was safe, the Bishop slid onto the pew and asked, "Are you more than halfway through confessing your sins."

"No your Imminence, I need the rest of the day for that."

He laughed and said, "You will have to confess in stages, God does get tired too. The two men are gone, it is safe to talk."

In his office, I handed over two bundles of dollars, then saying, "This is from Thibodeau."

"That is another sin you have to confess to. Lying to a Bishop, Thibby may buy a drink, however he does not give manna freely."

We were both laughing just as the door opened with a sidesman carrying coffee and a stack of Jaffa cakes.

After a friendly chat, the Bishop asked, "Now then my young spy, what is the reason for this visit."

"I am going on a long and dangerous journey, one that requires information on how deep the waters are going to be, off the coast of Babylon and Mesopotamia. My mission is to slow down a reaching intifada."

"My son, it is too late. This, what you speak of, started one thousand years ago, where it was slowed down, instead of quashing the scourge, the army went back to their home lands. There is a rumor, a caravan of travelers are on their way to Libya, where they will be camped for three days out side Tripoli. Another group left Lebanon several months past, hoping to arrive before the summit begins. These Gypsies are vastly diverse however they all have one thing in common, their own language. It is possible for you to join them, if your schedule is flexible. One last item, Coptic Christians make up a good percentage of the group."

"Thank you Bishop. Is it possible to purchase a wagon and oxen or horse, to pull the cart?"

"I know of no one who will be willing to sell you the gear needed. However there is an old man, a sideman in the Church, who wants to go on his last trip. I am sure he will be agreeable to having you go with him if you agree to do all the work."

"Bishop there will be two of us, please arrange with the old man, where we need to meet him and see his rig."

"Be here tomorrow at morning Mass."

"Yes sir, we will be here."

I had enough time to go see Olga and meet Pierre at the airport after visiting the hospital.

Olga was staring through me when I entered her room, asking as I got closer to her bed, "General, what did you do to me last night how did I end up in this awful place?"

"You drank the water from a tap in your hotel room. On top of your alcohol consumption, it could have been your undoing."

"You're right, I remember being so thirsty. Thank you for having my stomach pumped, now get me out of here."

"Come on lets go we do not have time to fill out any papers."

"I need my clothes, and ID."

"Come on, you were admitted without documentation."

Olga was taken to her room in the barracks guest women's quarter.

She pleaded, "Please Gennady, stay and listen to the reason for me joining the KGB. You must know I want out."

"Sorry Olga, have to go. I promise to be back later today. Stay here until we can discuss your future."

Chapter 22

Alluring Double Agent

Pierre was walking through Egyptian Immigration and Customs exit doors, when I walked into the arrivals hall.

Seeing me he waved and when we started walking, he whispered, "These people are insane, what are we doing here. This is a huge mistake, being in this country."

"Alright Pierre, take the next flight to London. Take over for Combs as soon as possible. A caravan of travelers will be entering Azerbaijan in three months, pin point their travels with the Astara Inn Keeper. Have him arrange me to join the travelers, before they get to Lebanon. See you in Astara or Baku in June."

"Sorry for letting you down."

"You are not letting me down, Pierre. Thank you for telling me of your fears, that confession has probably saved both of our lives. By the way, I couldn't get a hold of Paul, this was meant to be. Thanks again."

I was back with Olga sooner than expected. This was fortunate she was just pouring a large vodka.

"How do you feel, Olga.?"

"I'm good, hard to keep food down, maybe this will help."

"No, that will hurt your stomach, not help it. Throw it away we need to go get you a few bottles of tonic and quinine."

"Just one sip please."

"No. Get your clothes on, we have to go now, you need liquids."

"Please sir, one sip."

"Olga, you cannot stop at one drink. If you take a sip, I am walking out and informing the Egyptians on your whereabouts."

"You are a mean and cruel man, I do not want to see your face again, please leave."

"Expect the authorities soon."

Before my hand grabbed the door knob, she was hugging me from the back, saying, "Please Gennady, I need you now more than ever. I promise not to drink anymore, please do not leave."

"Get dressed we are going over to the Embassy cafeteria for lunch."

It took all day and night to get the alcohol out of her system.

By breakfast time, she was almost back to normal. Olga wasn't an alcoholic, however she did have a problem with binge drinking. She said her problems started when she was caught stealing exam papers at the end of her third year of university. I had to carefully massage a lot of information from her, if my hunch was right, she must have some knowledge of the Egyptian language. She could be beneficial in helping me get to

Libya, forgetting about Beirut for now.

By late evening Olga was smitten with me, so much so, I took a chance and asked, "Tell me how you started working with the Intelligence Service."

"A man from Moscow came to see me at the university, when I was in trouble. He recruited me, changed my appearance, and made me train for one year with the Army."

"Were you trained, in weapons, self defense, where was this done?"

"After boot camp, I was assigned to a unit of young girls, specializing in hand to hand tactics, and small arms training. The KGB recruited me,then assigned me to a four week course in interrogation techniques. After that course, they made me fly to Paris to join a film company, specializing in blue movies."

"Do you speak French?"

"It was an easy language to pick up. You see, once you master Latin, all languages are easier to learn. The French film crew took me to Morocco to make a film, one that took over a year to complete. That movie was called, "Blonds having fun in the sun" this is why I must leave this type of work, they are using me because of my looks, not my intelligence. Can you help me Gennady you are my only way out?"

"Did you pick up the Moroccan language?"

“Yes. Lots of Arabic words and phrases are similar, even from countries far away, such as Oman and Turkmenistan.”

“Were you trained to handle a pistol?”

“Yes, I told you a few minutes ago. These are strange questions.”

“Olga, I am leaving on a two or three week trip tomorrow, trekking across Egypt with a Nomad Clan. You have to go with me to stay away from the Egyptian authorities.”

“Please Gennady, thank you.”

“First you have to get some supplies from the Embassy. Two pistols, cartridges, one bullet proof vest and quinine tablets. Be back here within two hours.”

“Thank you, I will be back sooner.”

Watching her from the window cross the plaza to the Embassy, I followed, to make sure she wasn't going to change her mind and start talking about the proposal, to the KGB Chief.

Olga headed for the supply store, instead of going up stairs, and being satisfied she was doing exactly as she was told, I headed back to her room.

When she arrived back, with everything, I said, “You have to get your hair back to its original color.”

“Why Gennady, I prefer being blond.”

“Where we are going, blondes do not fit in. Go to a

hair dresser and change it. Then purchase two burqas and pick up four black 18 inch zippers and thread to match the outfits.

When she left it gave me the chance to go to the Russian Embassy to see if they happened to have a small amount of C4 plastic explosives in their ordinance stores.

Unfortunately the stores doors were now locked, fortunately the lock was old and rusty making it simple to jimmy the mechanism, which took all of twenty seconds. Looking for explosives in green wax paper pouches, with Czech or Russian instructions.

No C4 was found, but a box of K-rations was and taken, along with two canteens on a wide canvas belt with a first aide pouch.

Getting the stuff to the room was arduous, looking suspicious if someone discovered me leaving the compound with a couple boxes of gear.

Olga arrived a few seconds later just as the gear was set on the table. Staring at her wasn't good, she looked like another person. Her attitude was one of anger, a demeanor matching the new look was not a happy one. She went to the bathroom, slamming its door hard enough to send a message that men are all bad, demanding things, women shouldn't have to put up with.

Twenty minutes later she emerged with neatly combed black hair, trying to produce a smile.

Hearing a car pull up, I looked out front to see my Coptic Taxi driver arrive. I almost forgot about having to inspect the Gypsy horse and cart.

Before leaving, I said, "You look beautiful. While I am gone, stitch the zippers to each side of the burqas, from the arm pit to the elbow. Cover each zipper with a one inch flap of material taken out of the hem. I will see you in two hours."

"Is it because I am a woman that is why I sew?"

"I do not have time or the inclination to explain every order. You have two choices, follow orders or leave, what is it going to be?"

"Sure, I stay."

At the Cathedral, an old man with his rig was parked in front. His horse was a poor old example of a cart horse, looking like he should have been put out to pasture, years ago.

Feeling sorry for the nag, I asked the Bishop, "Your imminence, please convey to the old man, my concern, his horse may not make the trip."

The old man was not hearing it, his reply through the Bishop, was, "My horse is my friend. We are both going to make this trip together; he deserves to be on this trip he has earned it."

"Alright, tell the man, I would like to purchase an extra horse, to be tied to the rear of our wagon. Let him know I will also pay for the additional oats for the second horse. A horse for riding and one for pulling the wagon."

The old man was given 500 Egyptian Pounds, and after arrangements were agreed, the taxi took me back to the barracks, where he loaded his car with all of my gear to be taken to the Cathedral.

When the driver was gone and Olga had finished sewing the two burqas, it was essential to have supper and get as much sleep as possible, in our own rooms. The next morning at 0500, the taxi was heard arriving and parking next to the entrance downstairs. I got dressed into a typical Arab gown, and then went to get Olga. She was already dressed in her burqa, with two pistols strapped across her chest.

She wasn't shy in hiking up her outfit to show me the weapons, asking, "You approve?"

"Yes, I approve, we had better get going the taxi is waiting."

An old Cockney song entered my mind, "Get me to the church on time" While being driven to St. Marks I couldn't help wondering if the old man was going to show, and if he managed to buy a backup horse.

Not only was he there, the covered wagon was

loaded with all of our gear, with cooking utensils and dry goods. Our extra horse was another sway back old timer, oh well, nothing could be done now. Drat, we or I forgot to purchase blankets and air mattresses for sleeping under the Gypsy wagon. We were told by the old man, to hurry if we intended to meet the caravan when they passed the outskirts of Cairo.

Olga looked alarmed at the prospects of traveling in a wagon, one with no facilities, no running water and on top of that, two men who would watch her every move.

It seemed to take all day to head off the caravan sitting on a hard buck board wasn't the best way to travel. If weeks were needed to infiltrate the targeted Muslim City from riding on top of that thing with no springs or shocks, we may have to consider taking a chance and flying out to Libya's Capitol City.

Olga was as gypsy looking as the others. My appearance was going to be a problem, with fair hair and skin that is unless something could be done.

The Clan Chief looked me over that evening while we had supper around a large fire. I was truly amazed how my new partner, Olga could understand what these people were talking about, and stopping to tell me what the conversation was all about.

We slept together under the wagon, with the old man sleeping up in the cart. Before bedding down for the night, we were both shown how much to feed the two horses, with enough water to keep them hydrated so the old man now had two stable men.

It wasn't long before she asked, “Gennady, are we now officially working together?”

“Yes. My feeling is you are hinting on what your wages are?”

“Tell me.”

“First you must know what you will be doing, then the amount of pay suitable to your position will need to be negotiated.”

“Am I going undercover, saying that, having two pistols strapped to me while in bed is uncomfortable at night, and for that matter, I do not like this woolly tarp covering me either.”

Oh brother I thought, does she want to talk about her duties or take all of her clothes off, making me say, “Get used to it, go to sleep, we have to talk later on your job.”

The next morning I woke up with Olga snuggled so close to me, pistols were not felt, surprising how cold the night was. Moving away from her, it was difficult to get off the ground, by rolling over and out from underneath the wagon. Olga, still sleepy didn't know how to roll over and over. She had to be pulled by her ankles until she was free to stand up, keeping the wagon between us so the travelers could not see she was wearing only underwear. Both of us sore from lying all night on the hard ground, laughter overtook us.

She asked, “Do you know how many more nights we have to sleep on the ground?”

“I may be able to let you know after our trip today, averaging times and distance should be a good gauge on how long this will take. With a little luck we may be on our way soon as there is enough light right now. Hopefully the group time will keep moving forward, not sitting by a camp fire talking about old times.”

We were on our way after the horses were fed and watered. It was a slow progress, even though there was no stopping for food, and watering the animals, that was also a good time for us to go to the loo. My estimation, after stopping for the night, we traveled about 40 miles in fourteen hours, give or take a mile.

That evening while getting ready to sleep, Olga asked, “Well, Gennady, when are we going to be in Tripoli?”

“In three to four weeks, if the lead cart takes a small short cut, when we get to the Benghazi turnoff, at least on a map it looked liked we should save time.”

“Three weeks, I'll be a wreck by then.”

“Go to sleep me old wreck.”

Olga elbowed me in the back, and said, “It's not

funny."

For the next three plus weeks, Olga interpreted my conversations to the group when we sat around oases or a camp fire. Our leader and his family often fed us, or else we would have had to survive on old k-rations. His son a stocky sixteen year old was inquisitive about where we came from and more importantly what countries we have seen outside the Arabian Peninsula. He was starving for knowledge, not inquiring for any ideological reasons, just a curious teenager.

On three separate occasions, thinking about our progress being temporarily interrupted by inquisitive Egyptian and Syrian army bands. Olga and I having time to bed down in the old mans covers to hide was more luck than happenstance. It was good the military vehicles kicked up a lot of dust and sand to give us time to prepare for the worst. Knowing how precarious the situation was and is, I have to be prepared now and in the future to engage the soldiers if it came to fighting or fleeing. There's a strong feeling in my physic, this plan will have to be used sometime early next year.

When we were approximately one day from Tripoli, Olga said as we bedded down for the night, "Gennady, did you notice the old man and his horse haven't had anything to eat for three days."

"No. He probably had something while driving the

cart."

"When was the last time you saw him get off the wagon to go to the bathroom or care for his rig? His horse didn't eat his oats this evening; I believe they are going to die soon."

"That's crazy. Go to sleep."

"I tell you, they have an affinity with each other. I know it sounds crazy, they are both in this together."

Smiling while I dozed off at her intuition, knowing humans go through this from time to time, but an animal feeling that close spiritually to his or her master!

Unbelievable, the next morning we found the old man's horse dead, with the old man next to him, also dead. That was the first time he left the wagon for days. I am now a believer, something a lot of people wouldn't want to hear.

The willingness of horse and master ready to depart this world on the same day or night, was really beyond comprehension. Not wanting to sound or seem harsh, I had a dangerous job to do soon, getting past this sad moment was a priority.

Olga started sobbing, causing the others to come out to see what was happening.

We couldn't afford the time to help with burying the the two. Time was running out to gather information to relay back to Washington.

Olga was asked to convey our feelings to the clan, "Tell the people we would like to pay for the old man's funeral. We have to go soon. Is there a livery stable where we could leave the horse in the city, and have the leader's son pick the horse up and use it to get the wagon back to where ever they were going next?"

"No Gennady that will seem so heartless. These people need you and me to help them through this period."

"It is either that, or we can return to Egypt with them. That would mean another four week trek, that is if the funeral and wake took place immediately."

That did the trick, she carefully explained our situation, with the leader saying, "You two had brought much happiness to my friend on his last caravan before departing to the after world, thank you."

After she translated I asked, "Ask him if it is possible to meet the caravan in Amman on his way back home."

The chieftain replied, "Your husband is a wise man, knowing where we are traveling next."

I was told of his remark, and the old man waiting for me to reply got antsy and said, "Tell him, yes we would like for you to join us. We will be in Jordan for a celebration around the middle of July."

Hearing this, I asked her to give the man some

money, the cash I had ready in a pouch stuffed inside her gown. It was five hundred Egyptian pounds, enough to bury the old man and for his celebration of life party. He reluctantly took the cash and looked at me, nodded and turned around, to address his people while Olga and I packed our gear.

Just as we were ready to leave, the Chief handed Olga a hastily written map, directing us to where we could board the horse, luckily, close to the center of Tripoli.

Several hours later we were outside the Presidential Palace. A strange sight it was several large marquees with roll upflaps, covering about two acres. We showed the paper with directions to the livery stable to a taxi driver. He started to tell us and pointed, then decided we probably couldn't find the place anyway. He told Olga we needed to follow him, and for her to ride in the cab, while I rode the horse. Our taxi being paid, leaving Olga to deal with boarding the cart horse.

After paying a weeks boarding for our horse, the stable owner was asked to call us another cab.

When the taxi arrived, Olga was told, "Tell the driver to take us to the main airport hotel. Then ask him if there was a celebration soon. What was with all the tents scattered around the Palace grounds."

By the time our driver told her everything we

needed to know, he pulled in front of a large American style hotel. A porter coming out to get our luggage was a little startled when I handed him one dirty sack.

On the way in to see the receptionist, I again whispered instructions for Olga to ask the clerk, “After we check in and take a bath, our clothes needed to be washed and dried.”

The concierge met us before we got to the counter, saying in Arabic, where Olga translated, “Madam, sir, you are likely at the wrong hotel. A less expensive place to board is in the city.”

Once we brushed past him, I cautiously handed Olga the money to pay for two nights in this expensive hotel, thinking we should be safe here for a few days.

After paying the top rate, we were escorted to our room, where the porter waited in the corridor, for our clothes.

My two Russian Uniforms were also handed out through a slightly open door.

Olga gave the man a tip that would have at least equaled what he made in one day's wages, telling him we need everyting very soon.

After our baths, I settled down in a chair at a desk, with Olga lying on the bed, enjoying a soft mattress. Eventually she made a pot of coffee tasting much better than what we had endured over the last month. This brought us both back to the modern world. My tan scrubbed off in the bath, made me think about using another alias.

Olga teasingly asked, “Do you want to know what the Taxi man said or do you want to play first.”

“Tell me what he said.”

“You're a spoil sport Gennady, alright then, he said our President is not having a party, he lives and sleeps in those tents, he is afraid of being in the palace if the Americans bombed it.”

“I suspected as much, this is what we came for.”

Olga ran into the bathroom when someone knocked on our door.

I had to pull her out to speak to whoever it was, telling her, “Wrap a towel around you.”

“Wait, if they want to see our passports, we lost them in the dessert.”

Paranoia was taking over, as it was with her, wanting to escape to the bathroom. A huge relief, it was the maid bringing our clothes to us.

We got dressed, Olga in her burqa, me in a Russian uniform. Our aim was to find out airline schedules, and be back within two hours to pick up the rest of our laundry. We had our weapons under our clothes, with the money tied around my waist in the remnants of the feed sack.

A departures board for flights to all over Europe was seen a few steps from the main entrance. It was strange to see so many flights to Frankfurt and Zurich. That meant European countries did not care that an embargo was initiated by America. Abysmal behavior from so called NATO Allies doing business with Qaddafi, or at least his oil ministry.

Aeroflot had a flight leaving at one am. getting to Moscow at six, must be stopping on the way, but where.

A female agent was at the Aeroflot counter looking at what looked like a passenger manifest. She looked Russian, however it was hard to tell with her scarf covering much of her face and all of her hair.

As we got closer, it was clear she was not an Arab, fake eye lashes and a layer of makeup making her cheeks look flushed.

She stared at us in a way she did not believe a Russian General would be with a lady in a burqa.

A yard from getting to the counter, she asked, "May I help you sir."

"Yes you may my wife has lost her papers is this a problem if we wanted to fly to Moscow tonight?"

"Sorry Sir, we are full in the main cabin. A first class ticket would be too expensive for a soldier."

"Even for a General?"

"Sorry sir, you look like a young soldier, I would

have never taken you for a General. In special cases we do allow family members to accompany their partners if they sign for them, you would qualify as a special case."

Leaving the counter, Olga was told, "We have to find some luggage, and a purse for you."

Successfully purchasing two suitcases, purse and a change of clothing, we had a meal at a French Airport Restaurant, with two bottles of Perrier water, no wine or vodka.

Having to go back to our hotel to pack our gear, we got an hours sleep waiting for the rest of our clothes.

The clothes arrived and we were getting ready to leave, when Olga started to take the burqa off.

I had her stop and think about what she was doing, because the Aeroflot Agent we bought the tickets from may also be working the gate, as they often do with other carriers.

A taxi took us to the departure terminal, where we made our way to the gate house and saw the same ticket agent who sold us the tickets.

Once we were airborne, a big relief came over me, if it wasn't for this Russian plane, everything would have been comforting. A couple of hours later we were told to buckle up, the next stop was Prague. I thought for a minute and then it hit me, immigration would be a lot easier in Prague, with Olga as my wife.

I said to Olga, “Are you able to act as if you are sick, reason is we need to get off as soon as we land.”

“Yes. You help me stand up, before anyone gets off, I will moan as if I am pregnant, I look like I am anyway, in this awful gown.”

We were allowed to deplane, as long as we stayed in the arrivals gate. To make sure we did not leave, an airport security guard was called, positioned between us and the walk way leading to customs and immigration.

Olga carrying on acting, was bent over almost double, as if she was about to deliver.

The gate agent seeing this, called out one of the plane's crew, who came over and said, “You will not be allowed to continue, tomorrow evening may be possible if your wife is seen by a doctor. General, we need to see a note by this Physician, spelling out it is okay for your wife to continue her travels.”

“Thank you Miss, however we need to phone my brother to say we have been delayed, is there a way you could make that call for us.”

“No sir, you have to do it. Use my phone while I go tell the Captain you are not permitted to travel.”

When she left, I called Topol, a Gypsy Taxi driver and friend here in Prague. The taxi driver I have known for fourteen years, in lots of my assignments, has proven to be a valuable asset.

Topol said, “English, stay out front, he will be there in thirty minutes.”

We were led through immigration, and Olga in a wheel chair made this a formality.

Standing on the curb, Topol pulled up, opened the back door for us to get in, saying, “English it is better you also sit in back, someone may be watching.”

“English, if they catch you playing a Russian General, you will be shot, you are lucky, no.”

“Sumava Forest.”

Topol shook his head in an unbelieving way, with Olga staring through her burqa slit, expressing a little wonderment.

Three hours later we were dropped off at the path leading to the West German border. After giving Topol all of my left over Egyptians pounds, he seemed pleased, leaving immediately for home.

To say it was essential to stop and hide to watch from the tree line for vehicles coming from both directions on a road used mainly for military traffic, was underestimating the danger we were in.

Warned of our tenuous situation with instructions, “Listen carefully Olga. If two foreigners were seen here in a Soviet Territory this close to a NATO border, they would be treated as provocateurs or spies. Especially if they had suitcases. Now once we start walking there is to be no talking or whispering no matter what. If you have to sneeze cover your face and muffle the sound. If you hear or see anything, tap me on the appropriate shoulder from the direction you saw or heard the disturbance, then point. Any questions before we start?"

Chapter 23

Olga's Extended OJT

"I have to use the bathroom."

Oh brother, well at least she needed to go before we set off.

"Go behind that clump of trees to our left. Use dead grass to wipe, no paper or cloth."

It was essential to drop back to the paved road to see if anyone was coming. No real feeling of impending danger, just being cautious.

Olga was now ready, after saying, "The grass was wet and cold, how awful."

"Remember, once we start walking, do not say a word."

With her head cover pulled off, Olga's eyes were showing a look of danger for the first time since we first met. As she was led towards the border awkwardly carrying a suitcase, she had me quietly stop and take it from her. She tried to ask something, prompting me to stop and put a finger across her lips, to keep quiet.

Unfortunately it was close to being a full moon, meaning frost was going to start forming.

Olga wearing shoes that let in the cold, had me throw caution to the wind to find a place where she was out of the breeze while we dry her feet.

An hour later we were nearing the border when she tapped me on my left shoulder. I froze, knowing anything to our left out side of a deer or fox was not a good scenario.

Blood rushing through my veins and thinking, whatever it was came from our right, it could have been passing border guards. To our left meant it was something stationary, perhaps soldiers have set up camp for the night. This was not the time to throw caution to the wind as we moved forward. I have entered these woods more than a dozen times.

Stopping to listen and see or hear if any soldiers were in the area, my senses started picking up the smell of a cigarette. Darn it, this is not good, I need to get Olga's feet taken care of again, darn, darn, darn. My mind was now on Olga who wouldn't be able to outrun a Soviet soldier.

My attention was soon towards Olga, after a tap on

my left shoulder. She was pointing slightly behind us, and to the left. Stopping and studying the area, nodding my head for her to move to our right.

She was led to a stand of three trees. Carefully laying the cases on the ground, and taking a pair of heavy wool socks out of my case, her shoes were pulled off and the socks were put on while a jacket was taken out of the same case, and wrapped around her feet and legs.

I bent over close to her left ear and said, “I will be back soon. Stay here if I am not back in two hours, you need to walk to the border without the cases. Cross over and keep walking until you come to a paved road.”

She nodded, having me leave to investigate what was close to the path we needed to use. Out of her sight, I stopped for a few seconds to attach a silencer on one of the pistols.

When I was back on the path, it was essential to stop for a few seconds, crouching, moving forward slowly while crouched down.

Two minutes later and fifteen feet off the path towards the area where Olga pointed, faint voices were heard, a female and a man.

Starting to move again, a frozen twig snapped under my boot, causing me to crouch further down and wait.

The female voice hearing the noisc, started to sound

distressed.

This was a good sign, but caution was needed. Still too far away to understand what was being said, I had to be careful not to step on another limb. Moving again, until I was close enough to hear a conversation spoken in Czechoslovakian, it made me once again study the situation.

Fifteen minutes later I was on the camp, less than ten feet away, shielding myself behind a leafless tree. A young man was trying to light a fire, while a young lady was bringing twigs to him to start the fire.

I walked up on them with my weapon pointed at the man's head, causing them both to drop down to a kneeling position.

Speaking in Russian, I asked, "What are you doing?"

The girl started to sob, probably not understanding the language, I then asked in English, "Do not be afraid of this uniform, please tell me why you are here on a cold night."

She rudely replied, "Imbecile, you know what we are doing. With you here, we are doomed."

"My friend and I are also going over the border; you will not be shot or arrested."

"You are wearing a Russian uniform, this is a trick."

"Why would I need to trick you, I have a pistol leveled at your boyfriend's head."

"He is my brother."

"Get your stuff, just enough to carry, leave your camping gear and those cases."

"We cannot do that, this is all we have to wear and set up house."

"Do as I say, you have one minute to leave."

This is not a good situation, I can't leave them after seeing my face and uniform, but crossing over could be a problem if troops or work crews are on either side of the border.

The young lady stridently told her brother to hurry up, and being a little older than her brother, reminding me of my older sister, bossing me around while growing up.

No wonder the young man kept quiet, his silence was causing angst for the predicament he now finds himself in.

Getting back to Olga, the Czech girl inspected Olga's feet, shook her head, muttering in her own language. Handing over a pair of old walking boots.

We took off for the border, which was about twenty

minutes away.

Holding everyone back with out stretched arms, I waited for a few minutes, looking up and down the fence.

Nothing seen, I whispered, “Cross quickly through the clearing and under the iron bar. Let’s go now.”

It took another hour to get to a paved road, where a small milk float stopped to see if we needed a lift. An hour later we were dropped off at the Passau Hotel, the same inn I had used before, as a safe house and retreat.

Olga was so cold she couldn't speak, which was a small blessing.

Alke, an old friend, let us in, letting out a low scream, saying, “Oh Ludwig, how wonderful.”

“Alke, this is Olga, she needs a doctor and hot bath, quickly.”

While Olga and Alke were upstairs, I called Buck at ASA Headquarters, Bad Aibling, telling him hastily, “Listen, do not say anything just write down these co ordinances. Call Thibby, tell him the target is at 13 degrees-53minutes-7.2708-Norths. Do not worry about waking him up. After you hand over the information, destroy your notes, then come to Passau and pick me up, along with three other people. You know where to pick us up. See you in a couple of hours.”

Before the phone hit the latch Buck was trying to

say something. Elke walking in was the reason for hanging up, he could not risk her hearing this conversation.

My sweet Fraulein, Alke put her lips next to my ear, whispered, “Ludwig, are you and her, lovers? What about the other girl you have here.”

“No, none of them are, I need to get some sleep.”

“Yes Ludwig, please give me five minutes to run your bath. You do know if that girl was kept out in the cold another hour, she would have had some damage to her foot.”

“Alke, please wake me in two hours.”

“First Ludwig, make yourself and her in there a coffee, you know where the kitchen is, see you up stairs.”

The Fraulein knew Olga's name, saying her in the other room was suppose to be a warning. This inn is a convient bolt hole when coming across the border, so, I had better make amends. Words are not going to be enough to suffice. If Elke was told there is no one I can’t imagine the look I would get.

Anyway, the bath she drew was such a relief, my toes were starting to turn blue, wet socks and cold leather shoes, exacerbated a frost bite condition.

Alke came into my room ninety minutes later and waking me by lying on the bed and starting to kiss me. I jumped up as if I was in the middle of a bad dream, almost throwing her off the small bed.

After apologizing, she said it was good, she should have remembered how it was dangerous touching me when sleeping. Hearing someone drive into the grounds, she left to investigate.

I went to wake up Olga, and tell her to get dressed in her new clothes, we had to leave.

Buck was down stairs when Olga and I walked into the lounge. He did a double take when he saw the beautiful girls of Alke and Olga.

The two defectors were up stairs sleeping and on their own.

Kissing Alke goodbye rubbed Olga up the wrong way, getting into the back seat of the jeep, purposely looking in the opposite direction from me wanting me to see she was upset.

Driving away, Buck said, "Will, where have you been for the last two months. General Thibodeau is going out of his mind, as he put it, he said, since the first day of setting eyes on you sir, he needed to drink a little more while waiting for you to get back to him."

"Buck, you know better than to talk, this is not the time, drive."

From the back seat Olga asked in her native tongue, Russian, "You speak Russian, German, and now

English. Who are you? How many names do you go by General Vagon? Are you Russian, English? I've got it; you are an American, aren't you?"

"Olga, you are going to find out when we get to our next stop, can you please wait until then."

"Yes, I can wait, whoever you are, I know you have many girlfriends."

She again looked out the window, where I couldn't be seen out of the corner of her eyes. This behavior again was like a high school girl who had been upset by a two timing boy.

Pulling into the Army Base, Buck was instructed, "Drop me off at the office and take Olga to the Officers Guest Barracks. You are to wait for her to freshen up. Then, take her to the mess hall after an hour, I will be there to sign her in.

General Thibodeau was called while going through all the reports and notes left on my desk. By the time we were connected, I had filed most of the paperwork into the trash can.

When he finally answered he opening words were, "Where in the hell have you been for the last four months, and is Beirut taken care of."

"I did not have time to visit Beirut, sir, and it has been two months."

"Don't you dare play semantics with me General

Wright, where have you been, more importantly what have you been up to. The President is waiting to get that Beirut and Lockerbie thing behind him."

"General, getting into Libya was much harder than anticipated. You have the numbers where Qaddafi is, do you not?"

"Yes I got those. They are quite a number of yards away from his palace."

That is correct sir, approximately 100 yards from the front door. He uses the house during the day for restroom breaks and meals. I have made plans to visit the boys in Beirut during the summer."

"Well done, goodbye."

Back in my original office, I changed into a U.S. Army uniform with two stars on each shoulder. Lieutenant Buck and Olga were waiting beside the mess hall in the Jeep for me to show up, getting out after pointing for them to go to the front door.

At the door, I told Olga, "Do not discuss what we have been doing for the past two months. You will be told everything tonight, is that agreeable?"

"Yes."

After we ate, Buck drove ahead to turn the tape machine on, while Olga and I walked going over what I did not want Buck to know, like our trip in July.

Now in the conference room, the first instructions

were, “Olga, speak English, so we can get on with this briefing without having to play games by stopping to interpret your answers.

“There is no way you knew I could speak English.”

“I knew from the beginning of our relationship. Now please ask your questions.”

“What is to become of me now you are safely back in the West?”

“There is a job for you, as a double agent, American wages.”

“That would be good, as long as it is not for spying on my Country.”

“Agreed. You are now officially on the payroll. Your first assignment will be discussed tomorrow in Frankfurt. Is there anything else you need to discuss?”

“Tell me your real name and position?”

“General William Wright, U.S. Army.”

“No, it can't be. You do not look like a hardened criminal who has committed many murders. I do not believe it.”

“Yes you do, no time for being coy.”

“One more question I promise it to be the last one, unless your answer needs further discussion. How did you know I could speak your language?”

“I read your file.”

“What else was in my file?”

"You and I both know what is in it."

"Is that why you do not fancy me?"

"Briefing is over we head to Frankfurt tomorrow, where we are going shopping for your new wardrobe, one where you will blend into Western society. Get a good night's sleep you are going to need it."

Buck drove her over to get ready for bed, which gave me time to call Fran in South Florida. We were still talking when Fran heard the front door slam, and Buck's heavy feet could be heard.

The first sentence out of his mouth was, "General, what was so damaging in her file?"

"How would you like it, if I discussed your weaknesses with her?"

As I was leaving he asked, "What weaknesses, sir."

Laughing and without turning around, I said, "To many to discuss, good night Buck."

The next morning after breakfast, a sedan and MP driver was sent overnight to take us to Frankfurt. Olga and I were in the back seat discussing what the shops were like in Frankfurt.

She asked point blank, "Are you married Billy?"

I saw the driver look at me in his rear view mirror, showing a little glint at hearing her question, making me say, "Keep your eyes on the road sergeant."

"Yes sir, sorry sir."

The driver dropped us off at my residence, taking our luggage inside, saluted and left. We immediately walked out the door and went shopping, which wasn't far to walk to a large department store. Several hours of trying on mini skirts, dresses to weatherproof London Fog's we headed back to the house using a taxi to carry all of Olga's outfits.

That evening I fixed supper, while she tossed salad and laid the table.

She asked, “Shall we have a glass of wine.”

“Yes, Olga, what a good idea, sorry I forgot. Look in the larder, and pick the one you would like to try.”

This is going to be her first big hurdle to overcome. Could she handle having two glasses, without craving a whole bottle?

Over dinner we discussed her first assignment, and her new Identity. Tomorrow morning will be her first briefing as a possible ASA Agent.

After clearing up and the dishes washed Olga went to bed, while I stayed up to read reports from Frankfurt's Headquarters.

A half bottle of wine was left on the table, for the purpose of using it as bait. Bottles were numbered in the larder, starting at #1 and ending at twenty, the last bottle, on the bottom shelf. If she takes the bait, it will be her undoing.

During the night Olga was heard moving around in the kitchen and lounge I couldn't help thinking, she may be seeking a glass of wine. It was useless I had to go see if my fears were right. Creeping down to the landing, she was seen wetting her new shoes, trying to stretch them wider. I thought, do women the world over, purchase smaller shoes than the proper size.

I went back to bed, feeling relieved the half bottle of wine was as we left it, setting the alarm clock to wake up first.

The next morning it was imperative to check if any alcohol was taken from the wine rack in the larder.

With no bottles taken, I Tasted the half empty bottle, the one left over from dinner. It was actually all wine, and not filled with water, I was satisfied she passed her first test.

Olga arrived in the kitchen in her pajamas, when she kissed me on the lips and asked, "Drinking already, or checking out if the bottle on the table was actually wine?"

Knowing my face was starting to turn red, I had to reply quickly. That was impossible, thinking, is she really gifted to be able to know how people behave in the dark, or is it, she knew because of covering her past indiscretions.

"Sorry Olga. I had to know before we entered into a

working relationship, one that could not be reversed, if you had proved to be trustworthy. A situation like that could also be a threat to this agency. I hope you understand all of my people are often tested on their performances and associations."

"Look Billy, are my assignments to include working as a prostitute, or are you going to have me trained for other jobs?"

"We do not use that type of black mail too many innocent people could be hurt. That is the difference between your old employer and us. Besides, we are all under the microscope form a superior."

"Are we both under scrutiny from each other and you with added attention from your many superiors? I am saying, pleasing me and yourself is all I have to do. One last thing General Wright I know my existence will depend on me not having you compromised or the agency, by doing something silly."

Darn, that was truthful, and informative. She has a way of saying the right thing, even during a prickly confrontation.

"Olga, pack enough clothes for three nights, we are going on a trip.

"Tell me where we are going?"

"No, today you will wear something dressy, but versatile. We leave after breakfast, lunch may be delayed. Don't forget your passport."

It took us all day to reach the French Port of Calais, after a delay in renting a roomy Mercedes sedan and several bathroom stops. We finally got something to eat in the terminal Cafe, a basic place to eat, as it was a typical European Transport eatery.

Even though we were in France, we were able to load up on a full English breakfast of fries, grilled tomatoes, fried bread, bake beans, sausages and bacon. This food was going to stay with us for awhile.

An idea was forming while going through the buffet line which required Olga to use her acting skills, asking her quietly, "See the table over there with several truckers grab a seat at the end of their table, then pretend to dry your eyes. Go ahead, I will bring your food over."

Olga was pretending to cry, drying her eyes, made me pause before sitting down, I said in a posh English accent, "Oh my darling, the police may find your passport, it isn't worth you being upset with that dastardly fellow pinching your bag. I am sure the French authorities are going to let us leave in a week or two"

The truckers stopped eating and sipping tea, staring towards Olga, when she said, while crying, "I am not hungry. Mummy is going into hospital tomorrow, do you think the French officials will let me board the boat home."

Olga ran into the loo, causing the men to stand up as she left. She acted out her part magnificently.

I shook my head, putting my knife and fork down, to go after her. The largest and gruffest man grabbed my hand as I got up, and said, "Don't ya worry mate, we ere at dis table will see ya git ome. Ain't dat wite buoys, now wot one of you blokes gonna see dese two youngsters git ome."

Answering him before anyone could volunteer, I said, "Thank you men, I do believe the authorities will see that we are able to board, thank you anyway."

Another man spoke up, "Dose Frogs couden give a toss mate, you lets us 'andle dis, mongst ourselves. Go git that gierl, tell er we fixing dis ting."

I left the table and knocked on the bathroom door for Olga to come out.

When she came out I held her and whispered, "We are about to be smuggled into England, keep your fingers crossed, the customs dogs do not find us. Pick up all of the pepper off the table."

A Scottish man driving a large moving truck, said, "You two berns stay here until I flash me high beams, then you scuttle towards the rear of me rig. Give us your cases, I'll put em in the front of me lorry. Lady stick that vinegar bottle up ya jumper, you mate bring that mustard jar. Wif ya."

I couldn't believe it he wanted us to lift a few condiments off the table, not counting the pepper being taken by us.

We quickly ate our food while watching for the man's signal. Fifteen minutes later we were flashed, making us walk nonchalantly but quickly towards the line of cars and trucks.

When the back door was open, the driver climbed inside, to help us in after I spread pepper on the back bumper, prompting him to ask, "Wots dat for."

"Stops the dogs."

"Breelent mate."

There were four five foot stacks of wool blankets, tied against both sides of the empty truck.

The driver started to move them, saying as he pulled the stacks over, "Rwoit me lady, lay on the blanket, let us cover ya up. You sir, on the other wall, do da same. Now no chattering, till we git to de udder shore, Brit Customs are always walking round da ship, looken for some bother."

Both of us lay still without talking. A rough Chanel crossing kept busy trying not to get sea sick. It was impossible to get some sleep on the four hour trip, thankfully we were tied in, against the wall.

We had to lay flat, moving to our stomachs could have exposed our feet, or worse, dislodge the stack of blankets.

Not knowing the actual time we spent after leaving France, it seemed a lot longer than four hours.

When we reached Britain and feeling the truck starting to slowly roll off the ship, a bump was felt when it finally got off the vessel. Still moving at a snails pace, we stopped.

Hearing an official asking if there was any tobacco or alcohol, our driver replied, “No way Mate, dona drink or smoke.”

The official was faintly heard, laughing and saying, “You must be the only Scotsman not to drink, on your way mate.”

As we drove away, the driver was heard to shout after he was probably our of ear shot, “Up yours, ya wanker. Effing FEB.”

I had to laugh with Olga saying, “Shush.”

It was another two hours before the truck stopped, just as I was thinking, our driver must have forgotten about us being back here. When one of the doors was opened, sunlight penetrated through layers of blankets, blinding us for a few seconds.

After the man untied us, he helped Olga climb down, and saying, “you're on your own mate I don’t help blokes by given em me hand."

We both thanked him, and asked how could we repay him for his assistance.

We didn't notice at first, we were parked down the street from a railway station, until he pointed and said, "That station will git ya any where ya likes to go."

Leaving the Good Samaritan without tipping him for fear of becoming suspicious, we boarded a train for London.

Hailing a taxi from Victoria Station we were in my flat by noon. Olga was impressed with the view of Hyde Park, so much so, she wanted to go for a walk. I decided to have a bath and get some sleep.

Waking up and finding Olga asleep in bed, made me jump, thinking, what if she had been a villain. My reaction didn't wake her, thank goodness, it was necessary to grab my clothes and dress out in the living room.

While getting dressed a car was heard parking down stairs, then I noticed the curtains were open. Drat, Olga must have done it. Now expecting Kenny to drop in, I went to the door to see if anyone could be seen.

Kenny walked in as soon as the door was opened, saying, "Afnoon Guv, aving a late kip are we?"

Olga walked out in her silky pajama shorts, with my robe covering the rest of her, making Kenny say. "I see why your late gitten up, Guv."

"No Kenny, it isn't like that."

"Like wot. Guv."

Olga now giggling and smiling, said, "Hello Kenny, nice to meet you."

"Ello mam, wots your name."

"Sorry, Kenny meet Olga, a new agent."

"She gitten broke in, Guv, sort of learning the ropes."

"That's enough, Kenny. We have a platonic working relationship."

"I"m sure you are, Guv. Before forgetting, the man wants a quiet word wit ya."

"He doesn't know I am in town."

"E does Guv, you see your drapes were seen apart like, earlier and been reported to im."

"Alright Kenny. Olga, come with us, a photo graph of you is needed. We will go to a train station and use one of their photograph kiosks. After that Kenny will tell you where the best places are for shopping."

"Can't elp tere Guv, err in doors does da shoppen."

"Okay, tell you what Olga, we will drop you off in Kensington, where there are several amazing stores. Take this two hundred pounds and buy yourself something a college student would wear. We will show you where you are to be in thrcc hours, then Kenny will drop us off at his local."

We let Olga out and pulled along the curb of the Embassy twenty minutes later. Thinking General Simpson was not informed of the details on the last mission would be wanting to chew me out. Quite sure he should have been brought up to snuff by the CIA Director yesterday.

General Simpson started this impromptu briefing with, "You need to call in from time to time, so we know where you are. I got the lowdown from General Thibodeau, he told me you are not good for his stress level, disappearing like you did."

Okay he was informed, however he must have forgotten what was said in the last briefing. Confused by his attitude, I had to answer in a way that would deflect a finger being pointed in my direction for a possible lack of professionalism. Either way I probably will have to defend myself, even if a charge of insubordination is their proverbial back burner.

"Sir, have you and General Thibodeau forgotten I was asked to take up to six months to complete my last mission."

Yes Wright I do remember, we are covering our bases, that's all do not take it personally."

What a crock, I answered him politely, "It couldn't be helped, sir. When is the information going to be acted on?"

"Imminent, there is protocol to go through first. What about the Beirut connection?"

"In three months, sir, I will be in Lebanon."

"I do not understand, why wait so long, surely you can get the job done way before that."

"Sir, I have to get into Lebanon in a way where it is possible to get close to Beirut and not leave a trail. Then the test is getting inside PLO Headquarters, with out being stopped."

"What is your plan to get the job done? As you know, we may never hear the results from that mission."

"You mean the hypothetical covert action, you want it off the record, sir."

"That is enough of your back talk Wright you will be brought up on charges if you go too far."

He uses more hyperbolic twaddle than a high school principle, however I need to scale down my indignation, with a polite contrite reply.

"Sorry sir, I do understand how you and the General need to be protected. Tell me sir why you need to know everything."

"It has to be done this way Wright. Listen to me. Do you still have a safe house close to Mildenhall or is it Lakenheath?"

"Yes sir."

“We want you to monitor air traffic out of those two bases, tomorrow night. Do not mention this to anyone.”

“General Simpson I need two forged passports ASAP. The photograph was taken from a kiosk, one that has to be doctored. A British Passport with the name of Edwina Heath, a Russian with the name of Polina Rada. They need to be ready in two days, max.”

“Who is she?”

“She doesn't exist she is helping on a non existing assignment.”

“Don't parse words with me young man, I do not take kindly to being part of a conspiracy.”

“Did I hear you right, General?”

“Get out of here I will see you in three days.”

“Sir, what about the funding of a Middle East covert action.”

“The funds will be ready before you leave Frankfurt. By the way on your way up north, be on the look out for protesters, foreign agents and British intelligence, monitoring a last minute anti American demonstration. Those people will be masquerading as anti nuclear protesters.

I couldn't wait to get out of that office; as it turned out some good came into another mission which required for me to act alone. Kenny and I arrived outside Harrods an hour early for meeting Olga.

Iimages of fringe lunatics running through the streets bashing shop windows and cars was disturbing. After hearing from Simpson and his fear of a group of anarchist wanting to storm an American SAC Base, a plan entered my mind. One that would require costumes for blending into the group.

Once inside the department store, Kenny was asked, "Help me pick out something a punk rocker would wear. We have to start in the wig department. Reason being, it would be hard to blend in with a GI haircut. Most of the male protesters would have long dirty hair, clothes to match their locks, with a purpose to disrupt."

"Oy Guv, you want to look like a bunch of tossers, I wouldn't do that, mate. Those blokes ave ben known to carry rotten eggs. Ya gonna doss out like them, or sleep in yur flat? Wot about goin apple and pears, where ya gonna go like, ta ave a jimmy riddle?"

Listening to a Cockney talk, took a lot of concentration. They have a language like no other. Jimmy riddle, is taking a piddle, apple and pears, going upstairs, to the loo, and on it goes, with dropping H's along with vowels.

Olga walked up just after we paid for the hippy gear, interrupting a thinking session on the Cockney lingo. She looked on curiously, but kept silent, probably waiting for an explanation when we were alone.

In the London flat, Kenny was put in charge of making the tea, while Olga and I got packed. We hurriedly finished our tea and headed off to the Cambridge apartment in the Cockney's taxi.

We were dropped off as our driver needed to get back to London to take his wife out to dinner. Walking into the flat, David Chesterfield came out of the spare bedroom looking startled.

"David this is a pleasant surprise, what are you doing, slumming in my flat?"

"Sorry old boy I had no idea you were on the move. We thought you were holed up in Libya, waiting for the fire works."

"Stop that old boy stuff. I have no idea what you are talking about. Meet Olga Prada."

"Come come dear boy, we were privy to what you two were doing all the while, what! However not how you were going to obtain the coordinates was let me say, baffling. Excuse me you two, I am so rude, very nice to finally meet you Miss Prada."

Olga was taken back by that statement and asked, "What do you mean, David. I didn't know anyone in Britain knew me, or for that matter had heard of me. It is good to meet you too."

"Olga, Will, how did you two get together?"

Olga was upset, and in a determined manner asks David, "Answer me please, how do you know about me?"

"Sorry, Prada, that information is a private matter, not to be discussed outside the confinds of my office."

It was necessary for me to respond before Olga said something I did not want MI5 or MI6 to know. That is how we traveled to Libya from Egypt, especially her being one of my agents.

"Now you see Olga that David here is a part of the British Secret Service. We go back a long way, one could say he got into this line of work with my help."

Chesterfield said, "Will how did you meet this KGB operator."

Olga indignantly said, "David, you can ask me, I do not like you talking as if I was a piece of property belonging to General Wright."

That was a big mistake. Chesterfield will digest her remark of belonging to General Wright. He will try and pry for more, saying something provocative or worse, like a misogynistic crude question. MI5 Agents are trained to coerce intelligence by using psychological means of playing on one's weaknesses. Olga feeling inferior to men because of her past difficulties will take the bait if this isn't stopped.

"Oh, my friend Will has been thinking again, not a

good sign Madam, he is wondering was his investment in you Miss Prada worth the price."

"Enough of this you two we are probably here in Cambridge for the same reason, David you go first, why are you in Cambridge?"

"No you don't Will, you are not going to side track my discussing with this pretty little piece, sorry old boy."

"Olga, do not listen to him, he is baiting you with snide remarks. This British Agent has picked up on how defensive you are. David does not look at you as a female you are nothing more than a tool for disclosing any information you may have."

"You are incorrigible Wright. Alright you rascal, we would like to know where you entered Libya."

We can both bait each other now to see if he can be snared. He has already divulged some intel on my last mission.

"Look Chesterfield, no one outside of Washington knows what was going on."

"My dear fellow, do you not think it is strange, a few weeks after you arrive in Frankfurt, Tripoli becomes a target."

"No one knew outside of DC and wait a minute. You feign, Simpson's office is bugged. That is so below the belt, its criminal, you're a villain of the worst sort, pretending to be an old friend and having your hand up my boss's jumper."

"I have no idea what you are rambling on about old friend. Now let's get back to the problem at hand."

He took the bait the CIA office has a mole leaking intel to the Brits. Now to lead him down another path.

"Alright Olga, David, we know MI6 has picked up chatter on an anti Nuke organization in Germany, who are already in the UK, and headed this way. We have to,

I was interrupted by a loud "Hold it Wright; you do not know what is going on. This is not a security probe from Germany its started as a Greenham Common protest."

"No Chesterfield, we need to concentrate on the two RAF stations. We both know what is going on, that is why you are here in Suffolk. How does your company want to handle individuals who are determined to gain entrance into an SAC Base? You may think the CIA some how put out these alerts, and if that is the case, you should tell me."

"You are playing mind games again, Will, for the other matter. What would you do if I tell you elements of Bader Meinhoff may be headed to the the two Bases close to Bury. We picked up two of the groups organizers coming into Dover. They are being interrogated on an RAF Station close to the port where they arrived."

"Look David, if the protest happens and more of the gang are here, we need to get in the middle of them, and listen to what they say."

"The way we look that will never work. Hang about you must have one of your infamous plans in that disturbed mind of yours or you would not have mentioned the need to infiltrate the protesters. Are you working on something?"

"I do have a plan, and the props we need. David, we need to be as unshaven as possible, and a little grungy to make us look like we came out of a camp site. My goal is to seek out Germans, to befriend. Olga has to snuggle up with Middle Eastern protesters, David you need to coordinate surveillance with your agents to have the police arrest Olga, get her out of harms way, if the protest turns violent. I hope to befriend whoever the leader or leaders are. Protecting Olga is a priority, she is scheduled to go home in a few days."

That last statement is to sidetrack his surveillance team, hoping they move to the airport away from Cambridge.

"Wright, you forgot one small item, your names."

"Olga and I have to leave our documents here. Her alias English or Scottish, maybe one from history, like Lucy instead of Lady Chatterley. Her address can be taken from a railway station, say Victoria Gardens."

"She has an accent, Scottish is good."

"Agreed, thanks for pointing that out. How many plain clothes police are going to be in the mix?"

"That's the conundrum we have. Will, listen, I know you, a weapon must not be on your person, my men are trained to look for bulges made from pockets and shoulder holsters. That is one item you would be kept in gaol for, and not released immediately, even after your identity is discovered. Promise me you will leave your weapons at home, anyway you are adept at protecting yourself with knowing hand to hand combat."

"You must know there are going to be shanks, knives and chemicals on the most radical elements. Is it possible to have some type of clear luminous paint delivered here tomorrow morning? A small amount of the substance needs to be masked inside cigarettes. Once an individual is tagged, who may be holding a weapon your men can cull them away from the pack. We also need a VW camper van."

"Good thinking, I will make a call as soon as we are finished here. Now, where is this gear we are going to wear?"

"Wait a minute David. Which base are the B-52 bombers leaving from and are they loaded with nukes?"

"Always looking for leverage no more games

Wright, you know the answer."

"Alright David, lets get on with our aliases.

After the costumes were handed out, we went into various rooms to try on our new attire. Something was missing with David, being a tall man, needing a focal point, to distract from his smug looking facial expressions, telling new acquaintances he was from the dreaded establishment. A garish medallion against his chest where his flowery shirt exposed his not so hairy chest.

Olga said, "You two look the part, I would never guess you were police or secret service agents. There is still something missing."

I immediately went into the bathroom and jerked the bath chain off the tub. Then proceeded to where a string of horse brasses were draped on the hall stand.

The two of them watched as I tied a brass medallion to the end of the chain and placed it around Davids neck. It was so ludicrous the medallion was all one could focus on.

David commented, "It's hideous, and brilliant, bravo, Will, this may actually work. Now what about your focal point."

Chapter 26

Delayed In Suffolk

"There are two large empty birds nest, in the tree by the front door. I will go as Julius Caesar, a wreath upon my head to go with a toga."

Olga asked, "What should I go as?"

"Your outfit is that of a Lincolnshire farm girl, tattered dress, matted hair, with an enticing demeanor."

David asked, "I am wondering, why we need a camper?"

"Chances are, the weather isn't going to cooperate, which could be a positive for coaxing an organizer into a dry place. The police must leave a path towards the vehicle so we may hopefully turn a foreign protester into an informant."

"Not all mischievous disruptive demonstrators are foreigners that is going to be a problem, segregating them."

"You're right. Let's work out why people would travel here with having to explain their reasons to customs officials for entering Great Britain. What is in it for the protesters who is paying the tab?"

Olga added an alarming scenario from a Russian prospective, "Lord David, General Wright, what you are about to hear is chilling. One Stalinist era program for world domination was reintroduced two decades ago, with help from the East German STASI leader, Herr Wolf, a staunch Communist. Comintern is a curriculum taught in a few institutions."

"What does that have to do with our situation here?"

"General, these uprisings are used for subversives to protest America hoping to have others join in for swelling the amount of people showing up."

"Alright Olga, we have to visit that problem later. Our main concern now is keeping an SAC Base safe."

Chesterfield patiently waited before saying, "Olga, Wright is correct we must be briefed on Comintern as soon as this circumstance is over. Are you free to discuss this, say the middle of next week?"

"Sorry Lord David, General Wright is my employer contacts must go through his office."

"Of course."

This was not a revelation I wanted MI5 to hear first hand. If they suspected Olga as a possible agent was manageable, knowing it for sure is disconcerting.

David quickly changed the subject, hoping I would take the bait after he said, "One thought you conveyed many years ago does cause me angst, when you said more than once, one must be prepared for something going wrong. The service has an open file of a few of those wrongs, the murders you are suspected of committing. Your name is in those files, several times."

"Yes I remember one, wasn't that in a domestic disagreement?"

"No. Forensics turned up angles where one KGB Agent was cut by someone who used their left hand, say a third entity, not part of the Apostle Group, since they are all right handed."

"That lets me off the hook David; you know I am also right handed."

"Will, please no more games. I am not the only one who knows about your training. I'm telling you to not have any weapons on your person. I still remember East Berlin and other instances where you had to use your left hand. All I am saying is those files will be reopened, if they have a chance to confront you, face to face."

"Thank you for the heads up, I will not have any guns on me at the protest. You two need to listen carefully on what may happen."

" If it is possible for me to get close to some Meinhoff people, I will need you to cause a disturbance. When I raise my left hand into the air, showing a rude gesture, Olga needs to get in front of the person on my right. David you need to get behind him when Olga is in place and shove him to the ground, on top of Olga. If the gesture is from my right hand, do the opposite. Is that clear?"

"Yes. What is your plan?"

I*gnoring David's last question, because his allegiance to the British Secret Service, had proven more than once our friendship was second to his career or family name, being tarnished. This makes me cautious, in telling him every detail of this or any mission.*

Olga wasn't going to let David's revelation about our past go.

She asked point blank, "Will, are you or were you a hired assassin for the Americans?"

D*avid was shocked at Olga's bluntness. Equally concerned she was kept out of the loop with past CIA missions. Now he knows how secretive I can be or how I like to operate in secrecy. This most certainly is going to be added to a file inside his headquarters.*

Past incursions, in the U.K. was a concern ,not for the villains who had to be dealt with. The Brits do not like foreigners bringing in weapons for any reason.

This time David butted in, saying, "Well, answer the lad my secretive friend."

"What can I say? It seems I am guilty in your mind."

A commotion outside interrupted this confrontation, thankfully a VW mini bus painted with psychedelic rainbows all over it, was delivered to the Cambridge flat. Who ever dropped it off blew the horn several times and disappeared into the night.

We all managed to get to sleep before midnight, with me on the couch and the other two in the two bedrooms. About an hour later, military planes flying low woke us up, causing me to open the curtains to see if they were visible. One did not have to see them to hear what they were, which seemed to be a dozen heavy laden bombers, followed by two DC-10 tankers. They were going to pay the Libyan Dictator a visit at least that was my calculation.

David came out in his robe and asked, "Is it stormy?"

"No, it is military planes. Bombers are on their way to the Middle East, I would safely assume."

"Are you using your dubious skills?"

"Listen David, we have to be the first group to set up a control point, on the perimeter of the airbase where the planes left from. We have to plan on some of the protesters showing up before the planes return later today. Let's try to get some sleep and leave at day break."

"Good night, Will."

A few hours later and being the first one up, it was necessary to load the bus with blankets, sheets, sleeping bags and two revolvers, where David wouldn't see them, more importantly, not finding the two weapons with silencers and several sleeping powder packs stashed next to a bottle of whiskey.

Everyone was up and had breakfast before daylight. It was good we were going to be on the road earlier than planned, with David volunteering to be our driver, so I could go over what we were to do. He was the one to clear our path with local Bobbies and to find out which base was used to launch the bombers.

When David stopped, Olga and I hurried to a corner grocery store down the street, to get provisions for three days. We were back in the bus just before David arrived, with a parking permit from the local council.

David said, “We're in luck, the police station we are parked in front of is the jurisdiction fort for the area we need to park the bus. They have had a memo from Scotland Yard with a description of our vehicle and its license number. Wherever we park the bus will be watched to make sure it stays safe, by these police.”

When we arrived outside the large gates leading into the base, a US Air Force Police Officer watched us back our bus up close to the fence.

When the Air Force AP drove his Jeep towards us David said, “Alright General, your turn.”

When I got out of the bus, making sure no one was around I approached the fence. The Officer was not pleased to see me get out of a vehicle so close to an SAC Command Base.

The Officer said, “You cannot park that thing there. Move it or lose it.”

His rank as a Captain, gave me a sort of relief, knowing he probably had at least ten years in the Air Force. It should be easier to deal with this lifer instead of an Officer, fresh out of OCS.

When he got closer I said, “Good morning Captain. Can I have a word with you?”

“Move your vehicle sir.”

“Captain, that is not going to happen. We need to come to an understanding.

He interrupted my spiel, saying, “Stay right there sir, I will be back soon.”

Back in the bus David asked, “What do we do now Will?”

“My guess he is going to call the local police station, where they hopefully will send a Bobby to explain where we can park. I really do not like so many people being involved.”

A police panda car pulled in front of us, just before the Air Force Police Jeep pulled through the gates. The American Captain was asked to come into our bus, with the two Bobbies standing outside the door.

My explanation was, “Captain, the three of us are

working covertly on a situation that is going to happen very soon in front of your base. I really do not want you to know who we are, for fear of a leak. Will you work with us, I am sure the Police Chief has told you we were cleared to park here."

"I will allow you to park ten feet from the fence. Your vehicle has to be clamped, or else you have to move."

"Thank you Captain."

Our bus was moved and clamped after the Captain said he was satisfied we were far enough from the fence, not to be a threat to be able to compromise his base. He then inspected the bus for ladders and implements to scale the barrier. He was meticulous in his inspection, thankfully he didn't find the two pistols.

Before leaving he asked, "Sir, what do you think is going to happen this coming week?"

"Captain you remember to keep your head, others will be losing theirs, when the excrement hits the fan. All hell is going to break out today, or tomorrow at the latest."

"Who are you sir."

"Never you mind Captain, you just hunker down, be ready to take command of the perimeter. The Brits will have the outside buttoned up."

The Captain is probaly wondering what in the hell

is going on. He doesn't know what is being cooked up from the Greenham Common anti American camp site crazies, to the shores of Dover and Calais, where foreign antagonist will meet and conspire to spread their anarchy agenda in this country through gullible stupid air heads who are thinking they are going to stop American nuclear proliferation, not the Russians.

We had to get ready to make our camp, making sure we looked genuine anti establishment new age wasters. David started a fire pit with dead tree limbs, while Olga found a place to obtain water, where she filled Jerry cans for washing up. As this was going on, a truck loaded with portable toilets started arriving, and dropping off the loos at 100 foot intervals.

With a small bribe, we had a toilet placed between us and the fence, to be used only by us.

David came over to thank the men, when he asked one of them, “Here, mate, how many people are they expecting to show up?”

“We were told to have enough loos for fifty thousand, whats going on here mate?”

David didn't answer, he walked over to me, with a look of consternation, causing him to say, “Will, we may be in over our heads, lets reconsider this plan of yours. I will tell you, 50,000 anarchists are not where we need to be, especially with us between them and their target. Olga, Will, I have to level with you two, my firm has information,elements of foreign protesters have access to explosives. We take these reports as serious as possible threats. To get those gates open will have to be done with using such devises."

"I disagree, all we have to do, is watch for a handful of protesters. Our vantage points will be on top of the bus and in front of the gates. We have to pin point the likely targets ASAP."

"Will, didn't you hear me, we are going to be in for more than a little bother. I am saying, we could be killed if the explosives are only ten feet away."

"That is why we have to target the Meinhoff Gang."

"Look Will if anyone suspects us of being plants. Not to mention, if we are among a group of domestic terrorists and not able to stop the violence, our careers will be over by our demise, for a cause we know is idiotic."

"Okay David, you and Olga remember this scenario. In most Meinhoff bombings, the devises were not armed until the objective was reached. One person, could be a woman, would hold the device while another person armed the device. Old German Army back packs were used in the past to transport explosives. Thinking about it, this may be our way of identifying our targets, a real bonus. Target people who are in the age group of twenty to twenty eight years old that may save us time."

Olga nervously asked, "What happens if one of us is taken out?"

David's answer was not going to help, when he said, "If anyone of us is compromised, this would essentially end our task, perhaps we should stand down, or just monitor the events, I assure you, my superiors would deem a pullback, an intelligent maneuver."

"No, we are not abandoning this assignment if any of us are damaged."

David, shaking his head in an unbelieving manner asked, "You mean if Olga is hurt, you would leave her where she falls?"

"Alright you two, we need to have a back up plan, if one or two of us are discovered. Instead of defending your selves, quash one of the cigarettes on one of your shoulders someone will pull you out. Do not tell anyone about the other two who may be closing in on their target. Let's get out there, look relaxed and excited to be in the demonstration. Wave your fist throw a few F Bombs give the police peace signs."

Thinking as we changed into our costumes because of people starting to congregate. I decided to wear a toga, shaped from a bed sheet, to hide my real costume, which may have to be used later on. It may be necessary to change if I had to evade the authorities or over zealous anarchist.

Joining David and Olga out by the fire pit, David asked, "Why are you wearing that getup, instead of your original one?"

"This one can be discarded while on the run. The other one is under the toga, a way of fooling anyone wanting to arrest or accost me. I am called Ludwig Von Wilhelm my passport under that name is dangling around my neck, in a small cloth bag."

"Alright Will, where do we meet if we have to go to hospital or arrested?"

"At the flat. Now remember the set up. We must find Germans in the groups walking by, with asking likely looking candidates in German and what part of Germany they live in. Take these loose cigarettes; put them out of sight in case anyone bums a smoke. Anyone who doesn't make it back to the flat, we have to call hospitals and police stations to find out where the missing members are."

After agreeing to the plan, we waited by sitting for hours roasting sausages, pretending to drink beer, and smoking. We estimated 10,000 protesters were now here, with several buses emptying its passengers of young and old women, who looked quite rough, as if they came from a camp ground.

Actually some old ladies did come from the Anti American peace camp of the infamous Greenham Common.

I was now atop the VW bus watching B-52's starting to land causing protesters to rattle high chain link fences.

Suddenly three young men and one female hurried through the crowd, acting like they wanted to get rid of something as fast as possible. They were pushing protesters out of the way as they headed towards the gates.

Two tall men had back packs, thinking one was for personal effects, and the other one holding explosives.

A shiver went through me, what if they armed the device and slung it over the gates, where guard dogs and AP'S were standing in line.

Sliding down to the ground, I said, "Okay you two, the game has started. Follow me closely and remember the plan."

We quickly caught up to the group of four, without looking back, I knew my team was about to go into action.

The two without backpacks were brushed against, while ink cigarettes were mashed on their shoulders.

The young lady turned around to face me, lost her

balance, while moving forward.

I managed to catch her and say in German, “Fraulien keep moving, we are close to the gates.”

“Danka, yes we are going to be heroes, tomorrow. Are you part of our squad?”

Olga moved in front of the two men when they slowed down to see if their female friend was still with them. I now know who has the trigger, she does, or else they would have let her fall behind. Clipping her right heel, she stumbled again, allowing me to grab her and reach inside her back right pocket, where a four by three inch cold metallic implement was felt.

Pulling it out and finding it was the trigger, I slipped under the toga and into my back pocket. During this time, I grabbed her arm to help getting her balance, she thanked me once again.

David bumped me into the lady, making her fall against the man to her right. She was now very suspicious with a mean scowl telegraphing her feelings. The other German toppled on top of Olga, the targeted lady was now on top of a conspirator. This resembled a tangled mess, which benefited me in picking back packs and not causing any suspicion.

Slipping my hand under the German girl, I spoke in her language, apologizing again while I picked the man's back pack. Luck would have it there were no wires or tubes, only documents and clothes. After taking a wallet and a leather pouch, and stuffing them inside my inner costume, I got up and to help the woman.

Thinking the third man had the bomb, and hoping to get to him he must have sensed my intentions, causing him to move against the flow, back towards me.

Soon we were close enough for him to try shoving me. Retaliating by using a Judo move, flipping him and removing his back pack at the same time. A loud double snap was heard, similar to dead branches being snapped. Thinking, both of his arms were surely broken.

My wanna be attacker was momentarily left laying in a heap on the ground, with his friend the young lady looking on in disbelief and assessing the possibility of stepping in.

Instead of joining the fray, she started swearing in German and English, causing Olga and I to forget about the other man, who took off. That was David's job to make sure the man did not cause harm or flee. The MI5 Agent distracted momentarily, looking dazed and confused, also forgetting his assignment.

After slipping out of the toga, ripping it to provide straps for tying up the two people on the ground, I whispered to David, “Meet me in the bus when these villains are picked up. Throw some water on your face and snap out of it.”

Before leaving the area, I stopped at the bus to change and get one of the pistols. Walking away from the throng of protesters, I came across a queue of taxis, where I asked the next in line if my German friend was able to hail one of the taxis. He told me the foreigner asked to be driven to Bury Train Station.

"Could you get me to the same station before my friend gets there?"

He said, "No worries mate. The other motor went towards the motorway, which has a ten mile tailback. That taxi is noted for taking clients the long way round, most likely for a larger fare. I'll have you at the station before your friend gets there. Haven't seen this many people since the coronation, why are you people here, can't be for joining the extremist, you just don't look like one of them."

He was right, we got there first. Taking a chance, I decided to buy a paper and wait next to where a London Train was scheduled to arrive in forty minutes.

Thinking, it may be best if I bought a ticket for me and the German, if he was running late, and couldn't buy a ticket and miss his chance to flee this area. The last thing I needed was to have him arrested, for dodging a fare, and me lose him to the Rail Way Police.

The train was approaching, with no sign of the taxi.

An announcement was made over the stations

intercom saying, “The train to London will be ready to board after a clean up in the rear car. Mind the gap when you board.”

Ten minutes went by with another announcement for everyone to board, that meant me, as no other passengers were on the platform.

A cleaner and her trolley moved out of the rear, and hurried to the front where a first class coach was, causing the train to wait for her to get off. The German target approached when the call came that we would be leaving in two minutes. Casually folding the news paper, it was imperative to have the man board first, so I could be in the same carriage.

When the train started rolling we were the only ones in first class, causing the conductor to walk towards us to see our tickets.

He stopped at the German, asking for his ticket.

The man pretending not to understand, infuriated the conductor, causing him to say, “When we get to Cambridge, a policeman will be waiting for you.”

This was my chance to befriend an enemy of the West, by saying in an English accent, “Sir permit me to assist you. Conductor, I am holding this man's ticket.”

When the ticket collector walked to the next car, I said, “This ticket was for a friend who was at the American demonstration. She was supposed to meet me here at the station at least it can now be useful before it expires."

He said in perfect English, "Thank you, I would like to reimburse you."

"That is awfully sporting of you old boy. That will be 50 pounds, thank you."

"You British are unpredictable, may I buy you a drink, and reimburse you."

"That would be very nice, thank you, red wine please."

He was soon back with a small bottle of wine and a can of beer for himself.

After he gulped down a quarter of its contents, he commented how the beer wasn't as good as a German Pilsner.

My new found friend excused himself, and went to the loo. After he disappeared into the bathroom, two packs of sleeping powder were emptied into his beer. Making sure no residue was on the can, or floating on top of the liquid, it was necessary to blow into the can until residue was sticking to the sides.

When the man returned, he took a large drink, expressing his sentiments again, on how the beer wasn't up to German standards. We didn't talk or look at each other, the reason being, I did not want him to eventually remember me if the powder didn't work.

After finishing my wine, I left to go get us another drink. When I got back, he was asleep, with his head on the table.

Twenty minutes later we were pulling into Cambridge, he was still out cold. Taking a chance, and shaking him while saying it was time to get off the train. The German was almost out cold and needing help from the conductor to stand. Both of us managed to walk him out to the taxi rink, where he was loaded into the back of a large black taxi.

We were taken to my flat, which was only five minutes from the station, causing the taxi driver to be annoyed at having to travel a half mile at the most.

Once we arrived and paying the driver to help me get the German upstairs and through the door, into the living room, his demeanor changed from one of disdain to a man who showed gratitude, after a generous tip.

The driver was told, "Please do not tell anyone of this, my friend is a professor at the university."

My hostage now had his own personal cipher, "The Professor."

He was prepared for a swift unorthodox grilling or more precisely a hostile interrogation session, one would not want to go through. The information had to be obtained before David and Olga showed up, with a possibility of disapproving my tactics. Most important was to keep MI5 from claiming this prize, before vital intelligence was extracted for ASA.

A type of tactic one receives from Ranger School cadre for getting quick information had to be used.

Before coming out of his stupor he had to be readied for this act of retrieval, by stripping him.

Next action was to make a crude gurney, by busting up a solid wooden chair its front legs and seat taken off, leaving back legs and the back brace. After that procedure, six leather belts hooked up to make three straps was placed under the frame.

The German was quickly rolled over face down on the make shift gurney. Then tied by the belts, one each across his chest, mid section and ankles.

He was pulled and dragged into the bathroom and loaded into the bath, head first. When the stopper was inserted and cold water hitting the back of his head, he started to come to.

Next item needed as the water filled the tub, was a tape recorder, taken from my bedroom.

With the recorder ready, another item was needed, his identity.

Finding the man's passport, he was identified as Gunther Bader, which made me wonder, if he is one of the senior gang members.

The Professor waking up, his head bobbing as the

tub was an inch away from being full.

He shouted out "Was ist Los"(What is going on) where am I.

I couldn't be seen, with his head bent down, he was dunked before he uttered another word.

Asking him in German, "Bader, how many of you are involved with the conspiracy of bombing the American Base."

"Frig you, water bordering is illegal."

Gunther was raised and lowered seven times he squirmed violently until his head was fully submerged again. After 90 seconds he was raised up, where he tried to shout, he was dunked again and again."

Raising Bader for the fifth time, he was spewing water and bile for several minutes, causing the water to become dirty. Finally being able to mutter a few words, he knew his life was teetering on him being a good informant. He was now ready to spill more than water.

After turning on the tape machine, he was asked,

"How many people are here with your group?"

"Six, two never showed. Please let me up, please."

"Keep talking, from the beginning, when this scheme was initiated. Tell me how, when and where you six traveled. I am going to the bathroom and then make a cup of tea, when you stop talking, you will be drowned. Oh, by the way, all of your friends' documents and explosives are in my possession."

Leaving the loo door open, he was heard spilling the beans, and while in the kitchen he kept the oratory going. What he was saying was very detailed, mixed with emotions of a man who thought he was in a place where reason would not suffice. All total, Gunther Bader talked for thirty minutes.

Going into the bathroom when he quit talking, because of getting hoarse, he started pleading to be taken out of the freezing water. He was shivering from the cold air hitting his back. After hoisting him up, the water was let out, his chest was unstrapped, his wrist and legs were retied.

Pulling him out of the tub, I laid the hostage on his stomach. Taking my pistol out and attaching a silencer, his bounds were cut off. He jerked around to try and grab me, seeing the gun pointing at his forehead, and hearing the hammer cock, the man became as meek as a heel hound.

Throwing two blankets at him to use for covering up and to get warm, I said, "When you are warm and feeling better, put your clothes back on. If you make a move to run, grab, throw something, you will be shot instantly. Do you understand?"

When his clothes were back on, he was tied up and left on the bathroom floor.

David and Olga were heard opening the front door, calling out, “Wright, are you in there.”

Gunther groaned and said, “No one is as inhumane as a CIA Agent, you will be dead one day, by my men.”

Ignoring him, I said, “In here David.”

When he and Olga saw the mess, a wet hostage, the busted chair, they gasped, asking in unison, “Will you didn't.

“David, in the sink, you will find a recorder with everything you need to stop the Bader, Meinhoff Gang. I suggest you call the MI5 boys before they leave the area.”

“Right you are.”

Keeping Gunther at gunpoint, David returned to say, “They will be here within the hour. Get rid of the shooter before they come in.”

“We need to keep quiet until this man is gone.”

Once out of the bathroom, we could quietly talk, with David saying, “Where are the explosives?”

“On the bed.”

Four MI5 or MI6 men came up and when David let them in, they all came into the bathroom, with the oldest Agent asking David, “Sir, tell me, you didn't?”

David replied, “By the time Miss Prada and I arrived, the man was sitting on the floor wrapped in blankets. We did not see anything.”

"Who is that man?"

"Believe me Major, it is better you do not know. Take the man to Stoney Cross."

When they were out of the building, David said, "Once a judge finds out he was tortured, he will be set free. You better give the tape to your people. You and Prada should be out of Britain tomorrow morning, early as possible."

"Are you staying the night?"

"This place is a mess you have a lot of clearing up to do. I am staying on my estate tonight."

"I don't blame you. Give General Simpson a call when the German's are escorted to the ferry. Send CIA Headquarters in Washington, and Simpson photographs of the anarchist."

He nodded and then left Olga and I to clean up the flat, and take off for the flat in London. On the train we went over what was going to happen over the next two months, before we meet up again in Frankfurt.

Once in London we made a copy of the Meinhoff tapes, making notes on the members and their addresses.

Telling Olga, "Memorize their information in case we run into these people again. Are you ready to go out and get something to eat?"

"Tell you what Will go get a good red, I will make us a meal of spaghetti with red sauce. Oh yes, a stick of

French bread please."

Chapter 27

A Gathering Storm

The next morning, Olga was left sleeping, time to recuperate from her first ASA assignment and the long arduous weekend, draining her energy.

It was essential for me to go to the American Embassy to see General Simpson and leave her to sleep and rest. This meeting was not scheduled, meaning he may or may not be able to see me without prior notice.

Miss Peabody was already in the office, amazing, first time she was probably in the office before 0800. As soon as she saw me, she quietly got out from behind her desk, while watching the closed door to Simpson's office. Miss Peabody's mini dress was difficult to ignore. Her tight faux leather skirt looked like it must have been molded on her.

She kissed me on the left cheek, whispering, "He is in a fowl mood, speaking to General Thibodeau, how do you say sometime Billy, the poop is throwed in a fan."

“It's thrown.”

Replying in Cockney slang, “Wot is, oh Billy you are a tease, ain't ya.”

Wait, it is three a.m. in Washington. What is going on, no wonder the Generals could be a little touchy this morning.

General Simpson came out of his office to see his secretary kiss me on the other cheek, making him say, “General Wright, put her down and get in my office.”

Standing in front of the General's desk, while he stopped at Peabody's desk, waiting for me to leave, he was heard saying, “Please type these when you get back from your break. Leave now, lock the door behind you and give us an hour alone.”

Now thinking this ass chewing session was going to take an hour. This must be important, he didn't seem hypersensitive out in the waiting area.

I was being stared at like one would focus on a mischievous high school kid when Simpson took his seat. He evidently was trying to make me feel uncomfortable a smile crept onto my face. That particular reaction infuriated him. He didn't know it was my way of defusing his annoying posturing.

Simpson eased out of his office to make sure Miss Peabody had left the area.

Still standing at attention, he finally said, “You

have done it this time Wright, Thibby is being summoned to the White House this morning, to answer for your actions. Do you have any idea why you are smack in the middle of a cat 5 hurricane?"

*In a storm? This must be serious, no, remembering the two Generals are close to retiring; they are in a CYA mode. (Covering one's a** posterior)However knowing their motives, still made me stop and think, what was it I did this time?Nothing came to mind, that would cause me to be excoriated or verbally undressed, by a CIA Director, much less having the White House involved..*

Simpson was furious when he said, "Answer me, dam blame you."

That remark was as close to swearing this man ever would say. He must be troubled about his future.

Now back from deep in thought, and seeing him on the edge of throwing me out of his office, I said, "Sir, sorry for the delay. You said arrested. Isn't that a little extreme?"

He was so annoyed, he said, "Let me cut to the chase. Where, no, what did you do with a young Russian girl called Olga Prada?"

"Sir, is this all about a young Russian girl?"

"No it isn't, not all of it. Listen, no more interruptions. She was seen with you three months ago, and then she disappeared. Did you know she is an under age innocent high school student. Her family wants the body. You are to be incarcerated today, not tomorrow. Do you understand, this is something the White House cannot get out from under, the Russians have you in their cross hairs. We may have to turn you over to the Russian authorities."

"She is in my Hyde Park flat, probably sleeping."

"What? How can that be?"

"She is not a student, and innocent isn't how I would describe her. She was a seasoned KGB call girl, used to procure politicians and foreign leaders. There has to be a reason this story was cooked up."

"Oh, so you think a conspiracy is being prosecuted towards you. Darn it, why is this so called prostitute with you, and not her family back in Russia."

"She may become a double agent, if need be, sent back to Moscow, for the sole purpose of spying on the KGB."

"Wait a minute, where is Miss Peabody, the phone is ringing."

"Excuse me sir, I'll answer it."

"Where is my secretary?"

Sir, you told her to get out of the office, Wait a minute, sir. Wait a minute, "Simpson's office."

It was Washington, the operator asked me to wait

for the Director.

"General Simpson, it's for you sir."

When he answered he said, "Leave, close the door behind you."

Doing as I was told, I closed the door and pushed it back, so it was cracked open by a quarter of an inch.

Hearing him tell Thibodeau word for word, what he heard from me, he then waited and listened to a long diatribe coming over the phone, finally saying, "Yes Thibby, we will be there, see you in Florida, goodbye General."

Simpson shouted, "Wright get in here, right now, I know you've been listening, you can't fool me."

"Sir, I am hurt you would think I would eavesdrop on a CIA General."

"Hurt my eye, you are in no doubt the most impertinent person, our agency ever had the misfortune to have darken our doors. We have to be on the Phosphate Docks in two days. A C-130 is being sent for us. Be at Mildenhall in forty eight hours."

"General, I have a few chores to finish. Expect me in Florida on Friday, if you don't mind."

"Your behavior will not be tolerated any longer, you be there Thursday afternoon, understand? You have to find your own transportation, and we will not reimburse a first class ticket, we are firm about that, understand?"

"Yes sir, may I go now."

"Go find Peabody, send her back up here."

I knew where to find her she had to be in the bathroom down the hall by now.

Walking into the loo, she was putting lipstick on, and seeing me, she said, "Billy, are you crazy, you are not allowed in the ladies."

"I want a kiss from your painted lips, before leaving."

"You are a dangerous young man, Billy, one kiss that is all you get."

"Umm, Billy. How is the old man's demeanor?"

"He is now worked up, asking for his secretary to get back. Oh my, your lipstick is smudged, want me to fix it."

"Billy, you have to leave, before we get into trouble, please. Wait, walk with me, the passports you requested are in my desk."

We walked towards the office, and almost at the door, she turned around, kissed me on the cheek, pushed me against the wall, whispering, "Stay here love."

Back in two seconds, she said, "Here they are, see you Billy."

"Okay. See you again soon. Oh yes, keep an eye on him, let me know what he's doing, see ya."

Back at the flat, Olga was up sitting on the couch, drinking a cup of tea, watching the rain. She was probably thinking, what is on his agenda for today, as the rain was hitting the windows.

"Any tea in the pot?"

"Yes, just made it. What are we going to do today

"It's up to you Olga. We have a couple of months before we have to meet up with the Nomads. Would you like to attend a fire arms training team in the States, work undercover in a Middle Eastern Country, or go home."

"What are you going to do?"

"I have to be at a meeting in three days, in the States. After the meeting, I will be visiting friends and family, that may take up to three weeks. Let me know within a few hours where you would like to go."

"What part of the Middle East?"

"Azerbaijan."

"What about the small arms training, where is that held?"

"In the States, with a special forces team."

"All boys?"

"Yes."

"No, not if I am the only girl. Middle East is fine."

"Why not home?"

"Does it matter, anyway, it is too risky, someone

will see me and start asking questions. It is best I stay away from Russia for a few years."

"Pack your bags, I will escort you there. The place you are going to is beautiful, however it is hard to find, wait a minute, the change over in personal is happening soon. I have to call someone before we make that decision."

Pierre had to be called, unfortunately, his wife answered the phone, meaning, the needed info was not going to be given.

Mrs Farouk said, "He is at the doctor's. It seems he has had some kind of Asian flu for several weeks. Pierre is getting a prescription today to knock out his virus."

"Thank you, have Pierre ring me as soon as possible, I am at the London property, thanks again."

Pierre called within the hour, sounding hoarse, and apologetic, when he said, "Sorry Will, I had to leave my post because of getting some kind of virus. I am much better now, planning to return to Astara in two days. Is that good?"

"How are you traveling?"

"Through Moscow, flying to Baku, you know the rest."

"I need you to take a new agent with you, is that alright?"

"Is Paul leaving your agency?"

"No. This is a new agent I will need elsewhere. Make her reservations on the same flights you are traveling on. Go first class, so you two will be expedited through Russian Immigration."

"Will, you do the arrangements. You know why. I will cancel my ticket when you call me and say it is taken care of."

Pierre's wife would go spare, if she knew he had to go on an extended posting with a young lady. This may turn out better, by purchasing the tickets through W. W. Holdings and Olga being appreciative I had actually put up the money.

It took less than an hour to have airline tickets bought and Pierre notified, he was leaving in three days.

So this is how it plays out. From Boca Grande a phone call will be made, to make sure Olga was on her way. It would be hard to stay in Florida after the briefing, if my new agent was not in a place where she could be watched by another experienced agent. She has to be on probation for at least a year, without her knowing, before I had the confidence she was going to work out.

Getting to Florida one day ahead of Simpson and Thibodeau was necessary to get over time differences and jet lag. On top of that, preparing mentally for the two power brokers was essential.

Knowing the time the two Generals were arriving the next afternoon, had me hang around the Inn for a last minute phone call, if Simpson had a delay in his MATS Flight. Those hops are notorious for delays that could be a few hours to days.

When the two walked into the inn after lunch, they scheduled a briefing in the late afternoon, on the outside deck, overlooking the Gulf of Mexico, conveniently at happy hour for General Thibodeau.

Chapter 28

Calm Before The Storm

While the Generals were unpacking and up in their rooms, it was necessary for me to get lost until 1700.

Coming off the beach at a quarter to five, Thibodeau called out as I was approaching the outside deck, "You're late General Wright."

"I thought the meeting was at five, happy hour."

"That program starts at 1630 here on the island. Have a seat we have to get to the bone."

What kind of statement was, get to the bone. He sounds like he has had an early cocktail or two. *Simpson was grinning while drinking a glass of dark ice tea, as if the excrement was about to hit the fan.*

"Yes sir General, can we forego the alcohol that is until our briefing is over. We need clarity discussing my next what ever it is we are going to debate, since it is my life that will be on the line."

"There is no debate, you impertinent ass and, for one thing, your life isn't important when our national security is at stake. I'll have you busted down to a buck private. Do you understand me, Private Wright?"

Simpson beat me to the punch with a statement of concern, "Now General you know you shouldn't let anyone get your blood pressure up."

Thibodeau started laughing and saying at the same time, "Yea, I know, but, that insolent SOB needs to be told how it is. Thank you Jerald."

Tell us Wright, where is the teenage Russian girl?"

"General, she is not a teenager, or a student. General Simpson, I am sure you were informed of the girl's status, and what she was when I discovered her working as a KGB Agent. I was told yesterday that she was on her way to Moscow in the last twenty four hours."

"We are still getting flak from the Russians, concerning her disappearance. I will let the Vice President know she landed in Moscow yesterday."

"Generals, before we go any farther, I need to brief

you on what actually happened with the four protesters we encountered outside the RAF Base."

Simpson spoke up with, "Wright, your mission was successful, according to our sources. We also heard from your friend in MI5, he was the one we always rely on for needed misinformation and snippet on what is going on inside the United Kingdom."

"Well General you two may be getting a different story from the Germans."

"What do you mean?"

"A rumor will be circulated that the head of Bader Meinhoff was tortured or coerced into giving damaging information by a CIA Team, by water boarding one of the gang."

"Don't worry about that, Bader is on his way to a CIA holding cell in North Africa. Next subject, tell us about your schedule of administering retribution on the Beirut Bombers. The President's time in office is running out."

"Sorry General a plan is not ready yet. There will be something for you in less than three months. A means of getting into Lebanon with needed gear. It is being setup by friendly foreign CIA Allies. Funds in the sum of $100,000 dollars will be needed in seven weeks the cash needs to be delivered to Frankurt ASA Headquarters before then."

“Now see hear Wright, we never received receipts from the last hundred grand you were given.”

“Sir, it is hard to demand acknowledgments from foreign informers and their politicians. I have it sir, let me write a receipt for you now.”

“Yea right, just forget it we will smooth it over with GAO. The first time you are not successful after receiving lots of cash for that mission, will be your undoing. You understand?”

“Yes sir.”

Simpson hesitated before he said, “Tell us about a shadow agency being set up in Europe, Moscow, Soviet Satellite Countries and the Middle East, by a CIA Agent.”

“Sir that sounds like something the British would do.”

Thibodeau had smoke coming out his ears, making him show an agitation and saying, “Who in the hell do you think told us about you setting up a team of black OPS Agents. Let’s cut to the chase. Are you responsible for a company called WW Holdings stuffing cash into an off shore account, writing checks, from a Merchant Bank, out of Guernsey to pay bills in Moscow and Jordan, not to mention a bogus account from the Cayman's for expenses paid in Azerbaijan.”

“General, let me clear the air on that bogus rumor,

by saying and proving the British are involved in the Caucases, stretching down to the country in question."

"Where is this proof?"

"Sir, my word is the proof."

"Your word isn't worth a damn, Wright; we know you are up to something. Let me say, if it is found out that one of our agents is doing this, a charge of sedition will be levied on that person, or persons. Do you understand the gravity of that charge?"

"It is beyond my comprehensive, sirs, to even contemplate anyone getting away with putting together a ghost team."

Thibodeau quit ranting and calmly said, "You are so full of it that is all, this briefing is closed. Wright lets get a drink, Simpson is going to order a pot of tea, ugh. Have them put the cocktails in plastic cups we need to walk the beach."

On the way to the beach, Thibodeau said, "Off the record Wright, I know you have different opinions on where and what we should concentrate on, like putting assets into the Middle East. My thinking is you are probably spot on. Now that is between you and me not Simpson or anyone else. You had better be alert with so many agencies believing you are up to something that's it. We will not discuss this again."

"Alright sir."

“Wright, what is Comintern about?”

“It was a Stalinist era program, sir?”

“Alright we will leave it for now. Tomorrow morning, we are having an abbreviated briefing, Simpson and I are going fishing you can go do your own thing. We will get back to you before you leave for Lebanon.”

My time in Florida was well spent, getting ready for a covert mission in the middle of an ant hill of extremist. Even though the time was spent dating Fran, fishing, not with the Generals, and working on the Wright family farm. All the time my mind was churning over possible scenarios in making Beirut a success.

After seven weeks of relaxing in a warm spring Florida, I flew to London, where a letter from Olga was waiting on the floor beneath the mail drop in the Hyde Park flat. She had heard that the Nomad Caravan may be passing close to Astara. The post mark was from Birmingham, England, which meant Pierre was back, which is disturbing.

Pierre's wife answered my call, saying, “My husband is very upset he had to come home. Pierre did say the young agent taking over was up to the job. He has a doctor's appointment, a consultation in three days. We think it is a viral infection. Where can he reach you?”

"In my London flat."

The phone rang a couple of hours later, waking me from an attempt to beat jet lag. He started off with an apology, sounded genuine, which helped me in judging his commitment to the cause, even though he cut out early from his posting.

Hesitating to speak his mind, he finally said, "You probably have read the note by now. It was strange to say wait for a way to your target area, the caravan is passing Astara before your original jumping on point. Does that make sense?"

Yes it does. How is the new agent working out, any concerns I need to know about."

"Maybe one small problem General Wright, that is, there is an air of invincibility, which caused us some bother when we traveled to Tehran on the back of your motor scooter, one weekend. We were almost noticed when the agent stopped to watch a group of young men playing football."

"Was the interest physical, or one of studying the attitudes of Muslim men while relaxing?"

"It seemed it was both."

"How many trips did you make to the Iranian Capital, and what did you discover."

"We went three weekends, Friday evening to early Sunday morning in your old students digs. It seems that most of the populous were depressed, except for the young men who played football, which made us think, they were part of the extremist guards. Your new agent's actions were not out of the ordinary on our first two excursions.

"Okay, thank you Pierre. Maybe I should fly out in a few days, to surprise the agent. One last thing, was the safe house operational?"

"Yes. We stayed on Friday and Saturday nights, watching activity that was feverish around the large Mosque near the city center."

"Did you use all four floors for observation points?"

"We would spend the nights on different floors, viewing the area out of several windows, making sure the building was not watched."

"Thank you call me when you are through your illness."

Two items to think about. One, Pierre never said she, her or Olga" when talking about the young lady. Second item, Olga must be needing physical contact, now that is a problem. His wife doesn't need to know who the agent is, especially when it is a woman.

Who could help in the area she needs, or is there a way she could take care of her itch and captivate a young extremist leader at the same time.

Time was precious in getting to Azerbaijan, prompting me to take off for Moscow this evening. Two days later I walked into the Astara Inn to find the owner and Olga in a game of dominoes. At least she wasn't drinking, that was a big relief.

Olga ran up and embraced me with a strong hug and kiss. We walked outside and and sat on a picnic table.

After all of the nice chit chat, we got down to the nitty gritty, when I said, “Olga, I need you to take me to Tehran this weekend.”

“Sure Will, what is the reason?”

“You need to show me what you think is needed to get close to the young men who have turned into extremist. It may be necessary to infiltrate their collection of friends. What do you think about gaining access to extremists?”

“General, I would like to try it. It sounds dangerous and exciting. I know I am able to turn many head's, especially young men. It would be best if you leave me there on my own for a couple of weeks. Is that good?”

“Yes, that is good, but dangerous. We leave tomorrow morning, if you are sure about going covert on your own.”

“Thank you sir. This is my first solo covert action. The one to Libya was yours this one belongs to me, I am so excited to show you I can do it. One question, should I have a revolver for getting out of a dangerous situation?"

"That would not be wise, especially if a young man gets fresh, wanting to touch you in a place he shouldn't venture. If a pistol was felt you would not survive very long."

"Pierre and I took enough food and water to last for three days. He said many times, it is too dangerous to shop. General, that makes good sense, how does one shop for food in Tehran, especially a woman on her own."

"It is safe around the university, no where else. I suggest you take provisions that would see you through for the amount of time you are going to stay."

"Yes sir. Lentils, cereals and dried beef are easy to transport, water is a problem."

"Take quinine tablets to purify tap water. Wait ask the inn keeper how do Gypsies keep water potable."

Chapter 29

Comintern

We have a few hours for you to brief me why and

when this Comintern Program started,"

"General Wright, this project is mandatory for all top echelon Party Leaders and field agents. It was mandatory for all of them to go through speciallity workshops on counter espionage, using psychological means to tear down Western Societies. This started as soon as Nikita Khrushchev became Chairman of the Communist Party, sanctioned by Georgy Malenkov, who was a devoted Stalinist. We were all taught how Malenkov was a true leader of the Soviet Supreme. He was soon deposed by Khrushchev, thinking he was a threat to staging a coup."

"Alright Olga, that was yesterday, the Soviets have spent all of their capitol nothing to worry about, or is there?"

"This all ties in with Greenham Common, recent protest and more importantly the media, like the BBC, all of the American news outlets and now West German broadcasters."

"How was the Western media swayed?"

"By indoctrinating elites in academia to believe, low IQ citizens are a problem and if they go against established left wing teachings, the poor and minorities would suffer. Our instructors gave everyone a book to read called Uncle Tom's Cabin. This was the basis for us causing upheaval in the United States between the white working class and minorities. We were amazed it worked as quickly as it did, because of a spin off program to finance and train white university students in the North East United States and California. So you see how this is still working with the anti Nuke crowd as it did with the anti Vietnam demonstrators. If you notice, when a Democratic President is elected, everything calms down. That says it all you do not need to be very smart to understand which party are left wing."

"Yes Olga, I see where the Russian leaders would benefit in getting away with their agenda of world dominance. So you are saying that if Johnson was President this anti nuke stuff would never have started."

"No. He was an anomaly. The Politburo did back the fat man in 68, through Labor Unions in America. He barely lost, even with unions assisting in stuffing ballot boxes in all fifty states."

Chapter 30

Sirocco Brewing

"Thank you Olga for a discouraging briefing. Two items, first, no one has to know of this program. Second, we have to curtail this intrusion by ourselves no one would believe it was possible to indoctrinate so many Americans. We need to get back to the issue of Tehran."

Olga wanting to get on with her own agenda, interrupted by saying, "Please General Wright, give me four weeks to infiltrate the group. You and I can meet at the safe house, say, on the fourth Sunday, reason is Friday Prayers is such an important time of their week, they seem to celebrate and feast afterwards with family members and friends. Saturday's are for feasting. This way I should be able to infiltrate one of the groups by the second or third Friday."

"Alright, in that case you move into the female student's dorm down the street from the safe house. Do not compromise our building for any reason. You will be given enough money to live on and bribe anyone that needs to be bought, like the dorm patron for gaining access to a room outside curfews."

"Your right, living on my own in your place would certainly send up an unnecessary red flag, especially when masquerading as a student. It is hard to think of another reason for being in Tehran. Secondly it may be possible to investigate if a weekend course is available, to get away from any dangerous association."

"That reminds me, myself and another agent, years ago witnessed students being preached to on weekends while congregating on the steps of the school. If you nonchalantly walked by and stop for a moment with a curious look, they may invite you to join their group. That ploy worked for another female agent in the same place back then."

"Universities in Russia also indoctrinate the young, with the professors molding their minds into a state sponsored propaganda curriculum. On top of that problem their own personal beliefs are pushed into what they believe the students should hear. That's it sir, brain washing starts during informative years."

"It is the same in England. Let me finish. These Tehran students are being brainwashed into joining an extremist Jihad. If you are able to befriend that particular group, follow the examples of other females, for instance, they do not offer opinions or speak out against lies."

That evening we went over and over Olga's escape plan, if she was suspected of not being a Muslim. It will be easier for her to get away with not knowing anything about the Koran, being a female.

The next morning we took off on our scooter to Tehran.

Not only getting to the Iranian Capitol City and inside the safe house without any hassle was a huge relief but finding the safe house clean which meant it was left alone by the police.

Olga and I took our time making sure the house was still safe. Olga was allowed to go shopping in the local grocery store for provisions, her first test. She was given instructions where the shop could be found, and not showing any jitters she grabbed a shopping bag, taking off down the stairs.

Two hours had gone by without her returning, paranoia sinking in, prompted me to climb to the top floor and gaze out of the bedroom window.

Watching for a short time, Olga was spotted coming down the street, at least the covered up person was the same shape and height, seemed fairly docile, until two men were seen following her, about one hundred yards behind.

They stopped fifty yards from the building, with one of them taking out a radio.

Hurrying down stairs, I stood under the stairs until she closed the door. Quietly stepping out, startling Olga, she almost dropped the groceries.

I quietly said, "Come with me quickly. Leave the bags on the floor, I want to show you two men, who seemed to be following you."

Explaining to Olga when she was led up to the top floor, "When we reach the window, look out and see if you recognize these guys."

Olga looked out from the dark side of the room,

peering at the two stalkers, with one of them talking into a radio. I gave her a pair of binoculars, which took her several seconds to focus on the two men.

She finally said, “Yes, the one talking into what seems to be a radio, served me at the corner store. The other man came in as I was leaving. I think they are secret police, thugs wouldn't communicate like he is doing.”

“That was what I was thinking. Go down and put the groceries away. Leave your gown on. If I knock on the floor, that means they are coming towards us. If they see the scooter, they will assume a man is in here.”

“Sir, we must bring the scooter inside. Hurry; help me hide it in the first floor toilet. Then you can go back upstairs to monitor them, while I fix sandwiches.”

She was showing leadership, by taking command and assuming I would do as I was told, it was essential to stop and put on a dirty white Muslim gown on the way down to the bottom floor. We got the machine into the house in less than three minutes. Back upstairs the two were still there, leaning against a wall fronting the alleyway. Their radio was put away, which meant they were staking this building out.

I went down to where Olga was preparing the food, walking in, I said, “We should leave, I do not like this situation. They may be waiting for backup. Let’s go

Olga."

"You go Gennady, I am determined to get this assignment done. Stuff a sandwich in your shirt."

Carefully pulling the scooter down stairs, Olga was outside watching for eavesdroppers, and seeing it was clear she called out to say it was safe if I hurried.

It was essential to have the block of buildings shield us, especially when it was time to drive away in a direction avoiding being spotted by the two stalkers, thinking how confident the new agent seemed to be.

On the way to Azerbaijan all I could think about was how I wished, Olga was asked about hooking up with the Nomad Caravan in the Astara area, and not in Jordan, It was puzzling. Oh well, we can discuss this after I go back for her in four weeks.

That night, the Hotel's owner went over how well Paul and Pierre connected with all types of Azerbaijani's regardless of some language difficulties. He asked if Pierre was an Arab or another Middle Eastern.

The inn keeper was told very little, only that it was a mystery where he came from. After his inquiry, I was handed a bevy of information on Iranians coming over the border to get a beer. One item worthwhile remembering was vodka, bought by the case, taken back to Iran by the soldiers.

One week of listening to the man was definitely a

case of info overload. On one hike to the Iranian border, I had an uneasy feeling Olga was in danger prompting a plan to go and make sure she was okay.

The inn keeper watching from the rubbish bins, the bike taken out of his garden shed went back inside, shaking his head in disbelief. Without knowing, the hotel owner had placed two bottles of vodka in my backpack. They were seen when I pushed in a shirt.

Before leaving at 0400 the next morning two pistols in shoulder holsters were strapped on under the gown. These last eight days seemed like weeks, because of not knowing if my agent was in trouble.

I arrived at the Tehran safe house, as the sun was coming up, too early for police or students to be on the streets.

Pushing the scooter inside, and hiding it under the first floor stairs it was time to find a place where Olga could be seen coming out of the dorm.

She was seen a few minutes after 0800 coming towards this building. No one was following her, which allowed me to hurry downstairs and greet her.

She was pleased that I was already here, saying, "Gennady, I am so happy you have come early. These people are never going to change. They spew their hate for anyone who is not part of their religion. One man I have dated wants to get together tonight, with two other men. The two men are regarded as heroes for being part of the group holding American hostages some years past. That is strange, I thought he wanted a date, but not anymore after thinking about him wanting two others to join us, using me to impress his friends. Do you think I am being a little too cautious?"

"You have to go with your intuition. When was this invitation offered?"

"Last Friday evening, after Prayers."

"Where is this meeting taking place?"

"In the dorm. Most of the residents go home, for a week's holiday. I am terrified they want me to provide the entertainment in the way of offering me to one of the men who was the leader of that Embassy takeover."

"Go ahead and keep the date. I will be in a room close by, in case they do anything to you that is dangerous or demeaning, we both will deal with them."

"Thank you, I am relieved you are here. When a few of these men get together they act different to when I have been alone with my new friend. All of this talk is about me when did you have a premonition I was going to be in danger?"

"An uneasy feeling started started three days ago."

"That is when the man asked me to go out with him and his friends. You must have a gift of sensing danger. Whatever it is, thank God you have arrived early."

We discussed our plan and how soon I should sneak into the dorm, and then Olga left for university giving me the day to rest and store up sleep for a late night.

Just before five pm, the ground floor door opened, waking me. Knowing it was Olga, I had to hurry, strapping on two pistols, the old dirty Arab gown was then slipped over my head. Both vodka bottles had large quantities of barbiturates mixed in, to knock out the three men. We needed the villlians to be put to sleep, or at least incapacitated. Now I was ready to start the first phase.

When Olga led me to the dorm, up the flight of stairs to the third floor, and showing me inside the room next to hers, I thought how dismal this place was, with a smell of damp or mold.

Sizing up the place while being taken to a large communal room with a galley size kitchen, where residents could mingle and brew their tea or whatever resident students needed. The idea to place one bottle of vodka on a window sill in the kitchen area, partly covered by its dingy lace curtain, where it could barely be seen. This would make the men assume it could be anyone's property, not necessarily Olga's. It was very important for her to be seen as a naive young student.

Her plan was to meet the men in the communal area, where we set up a table far from the entrance, where eavesdropping on them would be possible. The hinges were fixed where the door could not be closed, and according to Muslim teachings, an unmarried woman is supposed to be visable to others when in the presence of males. We both hoped that room was the only place they would want to visit, meaning her dorm room was going to be off limits, again keeping within the perimeters of their beliefs.

Of course, when alcohol is consumed, perspectives change.

Setting up an area in the next room, where a small pencil size hole had to be punched through, where it was possible to observe her dorm room if it was visited. The hole had to be where it was not noticed, that meant it was necessary to make the puncture close to a base board, angled upwards. Not happy with just one peep hole, another was bored through up high where it was angled down towards the area between the bed and her door.

We had just entered her room when someone was knocking on the dorm's front door. I hurried into the next room, leaving the door ajar, for the purpose of hearing or seeing who was wanting in.

Olga answered the door, asking the three men to go into the kitchen area on the second floor.

Two men were slender, the third man was heavy fat

and much older, who was seen back when this area was investigated. If my memory is right, he is a lecturer, a religious Professor, the same one who organized the American Embassy take over in the late 70's.

After thirty minutes I quietly walked barefooted downstairs to see what was going on. One of the younger men had the vodka bottle in his hand asking Olga a question, having her say something and motioning no.

It seemed they did not approve of alcohol being in the building. He poured some vodka into a large glass, took a big drink and passed it around. When the glass was offered to Olga, she refused by, shaking her head and saying something in Arabic or Urdu.

I went back upstairs, took the other bottle of vodka out of the bag, and sat it outside another room. This was going to be a long dragged out association, one where at least one of the three will probably become amorous.

Two hours later, I was heading back downstairs when voices were heard getting louder. The three men and Olga were coming out into the hallway, ducking back inside after they were seen coming up the stairs.

Now in position, peering though a peep hole, and seeing the fat man with his arm around Olga's waist, showed he was having difficulty in keeping his balance.

Holding on to her she lost her footing and landed on

the bed with the big man tumbling on top of her.

She must have kneed him in the crotch, as he rolled over groaning, falling onto the floor off the narrow bed.

One of the men trailing behind found the vodka bottle that was across the hall, after tipping it up into his mouth, he then passed it to his other friend.

They immediately stopped laughing, when the fat man said something, making them rush in and hold Olga by her arms from opposite sides of the bed. He tried to stand up and pull up his gown, falling onto the bed, showing his old worn out underwear.

Pulling one of the revolvers out a holster, I quietly walked into the room unnoticed. The big man was shot in the back of his head. The other two were shot in a way, where it had to be staged, looking like a suicide and double murder.

Olga's whispered, "You were a bit late coming to help."

I took a few strands of her hair into my right hand and said, "This is going to hurt, do not scream."

Jerking her hair out, the strands were then placed into the fat man's left hand. Cleaning the weapon of fingerprints, it was placed into the hand of one of the younger men.

We hurried down to remove the scooter, when Olga turned to go back up, and said, "I need to get some things."

Grabbing her and saying, "No, this has to look like another person could be involved, you being missing will add to the suspense."

"I need to get a few feminine items."

"No, we need to make it look as if you were taken. This would have an investigator going around in never ending circles. Let's go before someone comes looking for the big man."

Two a.m. we were parked outside the Astara Hotel, three hours after leaving Tehran. The innkeeper came out to see who had arrived, ordering us to go to our rooms. He must have been annoyed at having to let us in I hope that was the reason for his rudeness.

Later that morning, we were eating breakfast when Olga thanked me, and was sorry she sounded cross when she was rescued.

After we ate, it was necessary to be briefed on what was found out in Tehran. The briefing had to be done outside, away from anyone listening in.

Sitting on an outside picnic table, Olga's summation of the Tehran Affair, in her own words were, "General Gennady, do you mind if I call you by your Russian alias. Those people are living as if it was 2,000 years ago. Wanting to add them to your list of allies is a waste of time they would be of no interest to any of our causes."

"Thank you. Answer one question. Why should we meet up with the Nomads in this area?"

She hesitated, making me elaborate.

Let me put it this way, when the caravan has passed the closest safe point, while traveling here, in other words, the caravan will be going away from our intended targets from where you think we should join them."

"I thought this area was the safest point for a thousand miles. You have a base here, where else would you meet up with them?"

"Amman, Jordan. That is one Middle Eastern city that is friendly to the West, no one suspects the Jordanians of being our friends."

"You're right; the Russians are in the dark on an association between them and Washington. But why in that area, it is out of the way."

"That is the only Arab country we can use as a staging area. Agent Prada, we need to leave as soon as possible if we are going to intersect with the caravan."

"Today? I have to find suitable clothing, this Arab gown is rather dirty, and get some personal items."

"You can shop at the airport and in Jordan, we leave in one hour."

We were lucky to hire a man to take us to Baku

Airport where shops were scarce. We boarded a flight to Cairo, where shopping for Olga found everything she needed in the international departures. Waiting for our connecting flight to Amman while Olga shopped, it was important to call Thibodeau, leaving a coded message on his home phone, Turieb in sight (Spelling Beirut backwards).

Finally arriving in the Jordanian city one hour past midnight, we checked in at the expensive American Airport Hotel, where luxury was a welcomed reprieve from the Astara Inn.

The next morning, while Olga slept, Lieutenant Els was called, to see if we could meet me today.

She looked at her schedule before saying, "Only one period is available, noon, meet me in the cafeteria, please be on time."

Her answer seemed curt, no sir or General, a take it or leave it scenario. It was as if her course work was more important than her duties as my agent. That could mean comfortability has set in, for a Westerner in an Islamist State, it is saying something. Dannie can be brash at times with a quick reply when her feathers are ruffled, especially when the source of a question needed answering was about her. No, that would be aloof, I think something is bothering her.

Back in the room, Olga was waking, mumbling,

"Where have you been? Couldn't sleep?"

"So sorry, however I slept good. Had to call a fellow agent to meet me for lunch."

"Can I come? Or do you not want me there."

"Sure, you can join us, since you are going to be one of my agents. Maybe we can find out together what is happening here in this city. We need a friendly place where agents could go, or if need be, extracted to, this will be a good time to get this familiarization session started. With a little luck, Amman is going to become a sanctuary, in the Middle East."

Meeting Lieutenant Els again was going to be an experience with Olga probably taking offense to Dannie's attractiveness and assertiveness.

Walking into the cafeteria, Els started waving when she saw us, prompting Olga to ask, with whispering, "Is that who you are meeting?"

Ignoring her question, the two ladies were introduced to each other when we got to the table, with Els asking, "Is Olga a friend General or a twenty four hour escort?"

"That is uncalled for lieutenant our situation here does not need any animosity. Hold your fire you are both needed in this endeavor, one that has to be stealthy for now. Let's order some food and then I need to get some information from you Lieutenant for Olga to know why you are here."

Els was reticent at first, assessing the situation and saying, "General Wright I do not know this lady, this is causing me to be a little cautious. Does she know why I am here or what I have done while in Jordan? This could be a set up this lady seems to have turned your head. Is she privy to my position?"

Olga interrupted with, "I have a name I am not the cat's mother. I have a name beetch."

Oh oh, here we go I better step in forcefully by saying, "Pull your claws in ladies. No one outside of your crew here in Amman Els knows about us, you have my backing. I appreciate your concerns. Tell me about the other four associates."

"Everyone is virtually fluent in the local language, Arabic, however that is not the case when it comes to writing it. Darlene had corresponded to her lecturer in short notes, when she was asked to respond to certain current events. Saying that, I wouldn't say she was confident enough to contact Middle Eastern leaders by writing. We all need another six months course work, on top of an actual face to face contact with Jordanians, finding out if we could actually produce an Arabic resume."

"Alright Els, see if you can set up a meeting with the other four agents. Miss. Prada and I have to leave soon or when I find out where we can join a group of Nomads who are willing to get us close to our next objective. You can contact us at the International Hotel Airport."

"Alright sir, what room number is yours and Miss. Prada's room number or are you sharing a room to keep expenses down, sir?"

Chapter 31

Impasse In The Desert

Letting that statement fall dead, I replied, "Lieutenant, ask the hotel receptionist for General Vagon's room. One last item, see if you can find the phone number for St. Mark's Cathedral in Cairo."

"That should be no problem sir. Shall we set up a tentative meeting for this evening, inside the hotel lounge, around 1900 hours?"

"Yes, 1900 sharp, and dress for dinner. Els call a taxi and tell the driver to be back for you in two hours ."

"Thank you sir, see you at seven."

Olga was handed two hundred dollars to shop for clothes she would need for tonight and the trip to Beirut.

It was just as important for me to go shopping at a bazaar for items needed to mask Western features.

Luck would have it a merchant selling thawbs or what we would say in the west, a gown. The merchant's customers were the poor, who would purchase and wear a color that would not easily show dirt or stains.

Wealthy Arabs were often seen in white pristine robes, where garb would be changed if a spot appeared after a meal. The merchant was quite pushy, determined to sell two robes, one for chores and one for mixing into more formal activities. It was necessary to blend into several Arab communities, and having the correct head gear matching each Thawb, was important. That was what I originally went to the market for to cover my features and an American hair style. Feeling comfortable that these items were going to do the job, it was time to get back to the hotel and see if they actually would do the job.

It was quite late when Olga arrived back with so many packages her taxi driver had to help carry her goods up to the room.

Her driver seeing me in the white gown and head gear, said something distinguishable, sahib was the only thing I understood.

She looked pleased with herself as soon as the man left she closed the door, asking, "Do you know what he said to you?"

"Not really."

"He apologized for coming into a hotel room with a female he did not know."

"He must have thought I looked genuine, why were you not fooled?"

"Polished military shoes, sir."

"Very good."

"Olga shocked me when she slipped out of her shoes and gown.

Pulling another similar gown over her, she asked, "Well?"

"It looks good you could be taken for a Jordanian."

"Men! Please leave while I dress."

Taking the elevator down to the main floor, I thought to myself what did I say this time.

The Jordanian five were in the lounge ordering cocktails when I heard Els say, "Put these on Vagon's and Prada's room."

That was brash, reminds me of my earlier days when I was under the thumbs of all of my Commanding Officers. She blushed, when I heard what she said.

Darlene was the first to speak, saying, "General, we waited patiently for you here's to our astute and generous leader."

"Cheers, thank you Darlene, it is good to be with

you all again. Now tell me, was it worth the expense to have you study and train in this country?"

Every one of them had reservations at first, living in an Islamist State, as Westerners. They were unanimous in saying it was well worth the cost, where dividends will certainly be paid back in many ways. However, as Els said before, a further six months is needed to hone their skills, in this city.

Els stridently asked, "Where is that new friend of yours, Miss. Prada?"

My agents all had an inquiring look; I needed to respond to this awkward question.

An unwarranted explanation was needed, having me say it anyway, "She is getting dressed. All of you listen, Olga Prada is not a girlfriend and we have never as much had a kiss. Olga is going to be part of our organization, stationed in Russia, the exact area she will be needed in, has not yet been determined. She was a Russian agent, procuring clients for blackmailing, in other words, she was used as a call girl. We will not bring this subject up again, is that clear?"

It was understood and agreed. Just as we finished making that pact, Olga walked in very gracefully, having the agents aghast at her flowing gait, especially the guys. Els was very courteous in introducing the new agent to her associates.

Watching everyone, reading their faces, it seemed she was acceptable, showing smiles instead of grimaces, was a relief. Olga likewise, showed her appreciation for being included in the group. No one was in a hurry to order dinner; they'd rather talk to their newest ally to get to know what she had to say in an Eastern European accent. Speaking with a sexy broken English accent was an attention gatherer.

Lieutenant Els traded places with Darlene for the purpose of relaying information that was previously asked for.

After sitting down, Els whispered, "I have the phone number you wanted. First, let me tell you, I took the liberty to call the Cathedral, to see if the Bishop was available. A man called Paul eventually came to the phone, and when I said your name was General Vagon, he laughed, and said, is that his name. That comment took me by surprise, how does he know you that well?"

"Long story Els. Go on, what else did he say?"

"The group is in Alexandria at present, you will be able to join them tomorrow evening at the latest. The man wanted to know if you needed anything."

"Thank you. Call him tomorrow and ask if a motorcycle could be purchased."

"Sir that is somewhat vague. What if he needs to know a make or vintage?"

"You're right. Just tell him to buy it from the same garage as before, he will know where. Ask him to let me know the scheduled stops and dates the caravan hope to keep."

"Can you tell me what mission you are going on?"

"No. That is for your own safety.

When our food was being served, it was a perfect time to study everyone to see if anyone looked like they really did not want to be here any longer. Thankfully our new agent was receiving more attention with her stories on the mission into Tripoli. Even the two American women were enthralled with her story telling.

Towards the end of the meal, the conversation turned to a more personal one, everyone asking Olga, what it was like working for the KGB.

Needing to leave and have the six of them come together, for the purpose of creating a close cohesive association was asking a lot, so soon. At least they may get to know each other without their boss listening in on their conversations, which may hold them back from being themselves.

I leaned over close to Darlene and said, "I have to go to make a couple of phone calls, and if I do not return, that means Washington is keeping me occupied. The tab is taken care of have them order anything they want. You all stay safc."

On my way out, I had a quiet conversation with the concierge, giving the following instructions, “Sir, my guest will need a taxi to get home, when they are finished for the evening. Whatever they order put it on my tab, please.”

He was given a sizable tip, which he appreciated, by replying in broken English, “Is fine, they are my guest now thank you. A moment sir, the desk is saying you have a call, you like to have it transferred to your room?”

“Yes please.”

Hurrying up to the room, my phone was buzzing as I stepped inside.

It was Paul from Cairo, causing me to say, “General Vagon here, this is not a secure phone.”

“Understood. Nomads moving towards your position.”

Code for Amman.

The group needed to be brought up to date with this new information, discussing it tonight is out of the question, when alcohol is being consumed down stairs.

Spending a few minutes, asking them to be back for an early breakfast, caused them to get up and leave with Els asking Olga, “Go to your own room and let the General have some rest.”

What Els said was a little catty, best way to handle

that remark was to let it alone. Back upstairs, it wasn't long before sleep overtook me, day dreaming about how we were going to travel to the PLO hotbed in Beirut.

The next morning over breakfast we all decided our best course of action was to have a way to escape in a hurry. That meant having a motor cycle available, one that could be driven in the desert. Collectively we determined the caravan could hide the bike until it dropped us off on the edge of Beirut. With the nomads arriving here in seven to eight days, we had plenty of time to prepare.

After our breakfast we split up into pairs, except for Els and Olga who joined me in canvassing the city center for a bike, while the other two groups looked elsewhere. We agreed not to purchase anything, until everyone could view all prospective motor cycles.

We agreed to meet back at the hotel at three pm. to discuss our findings.

During our search, Olga peeled off to enter a junk yard and garage, asking on the condition and price of a suitable looking bike. Els and myself standing outside the small office, asked, “Will, why doesn't Olga get started early in her Russian assignment, leaving me to go with you to Beirut.”

“No, Dannie that would not work.”

“Why not? Do you like her company, more than

mine?"

"Quite the opposite. I know when I am with Olga, she will not be compromised. With you, there is a slight possibility we may go beyond a professional relationship."

"General, you really think I would jump into bed with you. Trust me sir, you are mistaken, if you think I am that loose."

"Thank you Lieutenant. It is not you I mistrust. Now, no more talk about Miss Prada."

Olga came out at the right time, saying, "The machine needs work before it would be ready to drive."

We had no luck in finding what we wanted, having to report our findings at the afternoon meeting.

The other two teams found several prospects, which had to be viewed the next morning. One of our group grew upon a farm, had worked on tractors and small motors and said he knew a little about how a bike should run.

The next afternoon we all decided on a motor cycle, one that was made in Britain, equipped with saddlebags, large front light, wide tires and a passenger back rest. It could be the right motor cycle, as it was used by British forces during the war.

After buying the machine we all headed to a desert area. Driving into a soft sandy place the bike turned sharply to the left, throwing Olga off, causing her to dislocate her right shoulder when she hit the ground.

At the Amman Hospital, Olga came out of the emergency room with a sling. She was told to rest the arm and shoulder for at least two months.

Lieutenant Els said in a sarcastic manner, “Do not worry Olga, the General and I will continue on.”

Prada struggled to smile while saying sarcastically, “Thank you Lieutenant Els, you must be alert at all times, those Arab men will be watching to see if a woman is acting like she should. I'm sure you can act feminine with some training.”

With that prickly confrontation over with, it was necessary to see if Els could actually handle a revolver and driving through sand in the same afternoon.

My new sidekick and I left the hospital for my hotel room, where two revolvers were put into saddle bags. We immediately drove out into the desert, to give Els her instructions. With Olga being injured, we learned the first lesson of caution when driving through sand.

Far into the desert, safe from being spied upon, we had to be cautious of soft sand, remembering what had happened to Olga, could be our fate.

We had to slow down gingerly before stopping, allowing Dannie to slide off the back. With the grace of a dancer, she may be extra vigilant to show she doesn't always have the movements of a tom boy. Not waiting for me to find a hard spot to push the kick stand down, she was actually helping and using a little common sense.

Once the bike was stable, the two pistols were pulled out. It was time for target practice by drawing an outline of a man in the sand, with an X where a heart should be.

"Okay Lieutenant, all you need is two rounds to kill a person, one each in the heart, and forehead, in the hip area, if you need to keep him alive."

She fired three shots in rapid succession, all of them finding their intended targets.

Els asked, "Why would you want to graze the hips?"

"Just in case we have to terrify a suspect with you pointing your weapon at a man's private parts and grazing his hips, he may want to talk before you have time to fire another shot. Where did you learn to shoot a pistol like that?"

"Sir, one mustn't assume a female is less than adequate to handle themselves. Do you think we will be in a situation where we have to use torture?"

"It is always a possibility, when quick information is needed to save lives or the assignment. With that being said, tough physical persuasion has to be a last resort. An old cliché, it is easier to receive favors with sugar than vinegar.

"General, not privy to the information of your last mission, I need to know our objective on this mission, or is it too soon for me to know?"

"The timing is perfect. Rest on the bike's seat and listen carefully. In a couple of days we are joining a caravan of Arabs, who are willing to take us to the outskirts of Beirut.

Chapter 32

Playing With Fire

"Wait a minute sir, why would Arabs help us, we are foreigners, and in their country?"

"They aren't like other Middle East people, they are nomads. Dannie, after hearing what we are going to go through on this trip, may give you second thoughts about going. Both of us have to live and sleep in a covered wagon for approximately ten days. That means no bathroom facilities, we will have to use a bucket, burying our waste when we stop for the night. Traveling in close quarters is easy until we have to sleep together in a four foot wide cart. Since we are of the opposite sex, may be our undoing."

Well sir, you traveled with Miss Prada for three months in close quarters, were you never tempted to try your luck?"

"Never."

"Good, we should be alright for a ten day trip."

"One more issue. When we get close to the PLO enclave, a motor cycle will be used. This is all the information you need to know for now."

"Sir, what if something happens to you, how can I continue on with the mission, if you do not level with me?"

"Alright Lieutenant, you asked for it. We have to root out the vermin who was responsible for the Beirut Marine Building bombing. Rat bait will be used in the form of three types of poison, money, women and the last option has to be fear."

"Wait a minute sir. You haven't discussed the reason you need someone to tag along."

Give me time Lieutenant; everything is going to be spelled out by the time we get to our destination. Believe me, we are going to have a bunch of time on our hands to discuss everything and teaching you how to covertly enter a hostile environment. Listen, what ever happens towards the end of our assignment, you must keep your composure. If you or we are taken, no one is coming to get us. Anyquestions?"

"Yes sir. I take it, we have no written orders, is that correct?"

"We are on our own. You still want to continue with this action."

"I believe it is necessary for me to go with you, if I want a future in your agency."

"Good. You and I are going to experiment with skin dye, mascara, tea staining, anything that will hide our whiteness. When we get back to the city, you have to shop for Arabic underwear, sanitary items, soap, and tooth paste. I have all I need for this trip. Lastly, we have to stay in my hotel room trying different skin tones. Oh yes, one last thing, pick up a lot of skin cleaner. Before we go shopping, gather as much information on how to get into a Swiss Bank account having lost the codes. It may be possible to get into the account from the phone number of the account holder."

"Is there someone I can talk to for that information, the one where our allowance checks are cashed?"

"Fantastic, we may not need the info, just in case we do, we will be prepared."

We spent the next two days eating and living in the room, room service providing drinks and meals. After thirty hours of experimenting wearing many types of make up, we found that a strong tea dye made from loose leaf Indian tea, was successful in making us look a little darker, except for our eyes, which was altered with head dress, scarfs and Egyptian made sun glasses. Our last day was used to make phone calls to several Swiss Banks, using fake accounts to try and gain access.

The next evening after honing our telephone skills all day, we left on the motor bike to join the Nomads. Before we left, Els was required to strap a pistol under her gown. This was one insurance policy that may prove to be useful if I was eliminated and she could use it to end it all one way or another. She knew, being taken alive was not an option.

We eventually found the caravan by seeing a camp fire a mile away. It was good they were expecting us and having our wagon ready for us to live in. After waiting for our bike to cool down to load, Els was introduced to the clan, and started a conversation with the chieftain. It was quite impressive the way she handled herself.

That night before we settled down to sleep, Els asked, “General, are you sleeping under the wagon?”

“No. We are both sleeping in this wagon.”

“I am sorry sir my bed will be under the wagon.”

“Okay Els, be careful of the cobra's, they like a warm body to snuggle up to on a cold night.”

She didn't need to hear anything else we ended the

day with a small briefing, and then finally settled down to sleep, with Els wedging the seat from the buckboard between us, to keep our bodies from touching.

Luck was on my side, waking up first in the morning, correcting an embarrassing situation. The seat used to keep Miss Els and I separated, unfortunately, had worked its way down, ending up at our feet, and partially out of the covers, our bodies touching from our bottoms to the shoulders. Even though we were back to back, it could have caused some angst for a short time, if she woken up first.

Gently sliding away from her and out of the wagon, to put the coffee pot on the fire's hot coals, my agent ventured out within thirty minutes.

Lieutenant Els was ordered to study the terrain bordering Israel if we or she needed a place to run towards a friendly country.

During the following week, Els was asked to speak in an English and French accent, answering to the name of Suha Rahman.

Finally on the penultimate evening before arriving at our destination, Lieutenant Els asked, “Tell me what you suggest for getting out of here if you are killed?”

“The route studied when we began this trip. You have to work your way towards Israel, traveling only at night. What else is troubling you? I have noticed how uncomfortable you were at times, usually when we were getting ready to go to sleep.”

“Okay General. Why are we doing this if there are no written orders?”

“The President had ordered this mission a year ago. He doesn't want this pinned to his administration, if it goes sour. This will be hard for you to understand why it was sanctioned with no trails.”

“What? There is nothing of value we have to get?”

“No. lets get some sleep.”

“Wait a dam minute General. That means we are on a mission of revenge, I do not think we should carry this out. Wait a minute, you're out to eradicate someone, is that it?”

“No, its four someones, you want out?”

“How do I get out, we are surrounded by Arabs.”

“That's the conundrum Lieutenant. You had your chance to back out, the game is about to begin.”

On the evening of the eleventh night we were

dropped off on the edge of Beirut in the dark, with instructions from the chief, to the direction we needed to travel.

Carefully driving around potholes and bombing debris, we were on the perimeter of our targeted compound within an hour of leaving the safe confines of the caravan.

Having to wait inside a derelict building until it was deemed safe to infiltrate the PLO fence, two women stopped to see what we were doing.

Els asked them in Urdu, “Is it possible to provide a good time to the soldiers for some cash?”

They both quietly giggled, telling Els, and whispering to me the translation, “Yes, very little money, they do not earn much.”

I whispered back, “Ask them, if the soldiers were willing to leave their post for a little fun. Also ask if they were coming back tonight, if not, what time would they be here tomorrow, so you could join them in earning some money.”

After they left Els relayed, “They are going to be here late tomorrow evening. A welcoming home party is planned for returning Jihad trainees.”

“That is good news Lieutenant, we need to observe the arrivals from this area, and camouflage our position tonight with mounds of rubble.”

All night Els and I built a covered igloo type hide. The next day we went over her strategy in case she was assaulted. We both decided she had to leave her pistol, exchanging it for a small sharpened piece of metal.

Our plan was to have her start a commotion as far away from the main building, for me to gain entry. We both thought, starting a fire would be the best way to grab their attention. If that wasn't possible because of being watched, she should get involved in a fight, with two or more men wanting her attention.

When I was inside the main house, she had to slip away and help out, that is, if she wasn't already in the targeted building.

It was important to get as much sleep as possible, with one of us keeping guard. It was up to me to stay awake and on guard the rest of the night, knowing she needed to look her best if she was to attract more than one of the rebels.

Later that afternoon we talked again about strategy, Els had to find out where the arms and fuel were stored, and start the fire in the area.

There was a chance she could take a pee break close to the stores, where a fire hopefully could be ignited with the help of gasoline. The last resort was to have her scream out she was being raped in Arabic, hoping one of the other women would come to her rescue.

A convoy of three small pickup trucks drove up to a pair of rough chain link gates. Good news for us, the gates were not pad locked, however it took two guards to drag them open, wide enough for the convoy to enter the compound.

A small overweight man, with a hounds tooth head dress, came out of the building, along with a man dressed in a Russian uniform. After hounds tooth kissed each soldier, they all vanished inside the building.

My side kick counted the number of soldiers, then saying, "It is going to take more than two ladies to satisfy a dozen sex starved men."

I laughed and said, "With you, there are three women, so let's see, that is four dudes each, unless you are greedy."

"That is not funny General."

She finally saw the funny side of that last remark, and said, "Why don't you dress into a burka and be the forth prostitute?"

"You're a genius Dannie. When you get inside, tell the other two women your younger sister is showing up an hour later. I see you have packed an extra outfit, it may be a little big in the rear for me."

She hit me on the arm while I was laughing, and said, "I do not have a large bottom. You may think that was humorous, I do not. I may get even with you when you get into the compound."

That remark could be taken a number of ways; anyway she got out her dirty burka for me to try on. Being a little tight, Els popped out a few hems around the waist area, and the bottom to make it longer in length. She made it adequate looking, giving me the confidence to actually believe this may work. This would definitely be the easiest way to get inside without shooting my way in. The two women showed at the time, with Els waiting a hundred yards from our hide towards the fenced in area. When Els left with them, I decided that it would be smart to use charcoal to darken the skin around the eyes and nose. A Russian General's uniform was hidden under the gown, to be used for a quick escape. The burka was also helpful in hiding a pair of spit polished Russian boots.

Chapter 33

Escaping A Ring Of Fire

Dressed with gloves to hide pale hands and the gown over my Russian boots, I was totally hidden from being recognized as a Westerner, Russian or a man.

Walking up to the gate and through it, where the guards were preoccupied with the other three women and unaware of me walking in.

Els walked over, hugged me and whispered, “Your date is the oversize Russian. He doesn't speak Urdu or Arabian, is this your first time?”

Without replying to her humorous jibe, I whispered, “Meet me in the house.”

The Russian must have shared his vodka, by the way the men were acting. With the PLO fighters not used to hard liquor, they were not too far away from being half way incapacitated.

Making my way through a dozen jihad-est on the way to the main building, followed by one jovial Russian Colonel, hot on my heels, who wanted my attention, causing us both to fall onto the floor, as soon as the front door was opened. The leader of this group, the one with the fancy head dress was on his way out, just as we fell at his feet. He laughed and said something indistinguishable, as he stepped over the

Russian.

The Colonel following close behind made me dart straight upstairs, giving me time to plan a diversion, where the inebriated man could be quietly taken out. A room to escape into, preferably a bathroom where it was impossible for two people to squeeze through its door, giving me a chance to turn around, hoping to subdue the randy old soldier.

A door at the end of the hall looked the most likely however it was actually a linen closet.

When the door was pulled open, the Russian bear wrapped his arms around my waist, asking, "Please madam do not run away again. You are muscular as a man what is this, who are you?"

My fist thrown in a backward motion, was mashed into the man's groin, making him he hit the floor in agony.

Turning and dropping to my knees and holding a revolver, I said in Russian, "Colonel, listen very carefully and you may live if the information I get is what I came here for. Answer quickly, where is Rahman and his wife?"

He groaned asking, "Why do you care? Who are you?"

"I am General Vagon of the KGB. Where are the PLO leader and his wife?"

"Please help me to my room. We can talk there."

Once in his room, he was willing to speak freely, answering, "The Wife is in Paris spending billions of Yankee dollars. The PLO leader is meeting an Egyptian on a yacht. I knew you would come for me one day. How did our Politburo know these people were paying me to say nothing on shipping low grade oil last winter instead of good military fuel for our jets?"

How many years have you been on the take?"

"Ten Years."

"Who were the ones responsible for planning the attack on the U.S.Marines and the ones planting the devices?"

"The four outside, three cadres and their leader were responsible. What will you have me do?"

"Go into the washroom, and splash lots of water on your face, you have to be alert for this to work. Go outside in fifteen minutes, hold a weapon in your hand, ready to use. Stay close to the building, if you see anyone running your way, shoot to kill, Understand?"

Els walked in and said, "The soldiers are busy with the two girls. What do you want me to do?"

"Go downstairs to the office empty all the files into those pillow cases over on the bed. Take everything; I will be down in a few minutes."

As I was taking off the gown, I suddenly became a

Russian General in front of the Colonel who had just returned from a bathroom down the hall.

He was still drunk,obeying an order, "Colonel, go down to the entrance, close the door behind you and stand at parade rest with your pistol ready to fire. Do not let anyone in, I have to call Moscow. Understand?"

Els was almost ready to leave when I stopped her and asked, "Did you see any letters from a bank in Switzerland?"

"They are in one folder marked confidential, Banque of Zurich."

"Good. Call the number and tell the operator you are Suha Rahman and you need all the funds in your account transferred to WW Holdings, Jersey, UK. Here is the account number. You have five minutes."

"What if they ask a personal question to prove I am Suha?"

"Her mother is French, she is French, so answer in Urdu. Wing it."

In the five minutes, two safes were opened and emptied with everything in them and placed in a trash bag. Fires were lit, starting at a second floor bedroom, kitchen gas stove turned up all the way and a fire started in the office as soon as Els hung up the phone and took it off the hook for it to seem it was being used, in case the bank called back before the fire damaged the wiring.

The next move was made a lot easier with everyone busy and occupied out by the guard shack. Els carried the contraband as we moved towards the targets, getting no reaction from the PLO rebels.

Walking through the group assassinating as many as was possible with shots to the back of heads and foreheads as we progressed towards the gates. Extremist were dropping at the sound of bullets finding their targets.

Els, was almost in shock with a man laying dead where she had to walk. She was manhandled and thrown into the back of a white Toyota pickup truck, conveniently parked near the gate.

By the time the truck started, the Colonel was seen standing on the top step with his weapon drawn, causing two gate guards to shoot him, just before they became hood elements when I busted through the two gates.

Taking the silencers off the pistols and sticking them in my jacket, I threw my weapons out of the truck's window. Since they were both Russian revolvers, my plan was to have Russians accused of these murders.

An hour later I passed the cutoff to Tyre, with the vehicle running on fumes. It was lucky our speed was enough to let us coast close to the Israeli Border, where a squad of Israeli Soldiers noticed us approaching shouting for us to stop. Els was now in a situation where she was needing medical attention, shock was carrying her onward, she had no idea what was going on.

Responding to the soldiers and asking them to call General Ito, they helped us through the barricade. Their practice of separating unknown intruders was standard procedure, causing me to tell them the lady needed medical help before she succumbed to a permanent state of shock.

Dannie was taken to Haifa, I was blindfolded, loaded into an Israeli Army vehicle. From a radio conversation in Yiddish, I worked out I was on my way to Mossad Headquarters.

We were traveling about fifty miles an hour, by my calculation, and should be inside a fortified Israeli Army Base within ninety minutes. Placed face down on the back seat, the driver and guard didn't say anything the whole way there after their original radio transmission.

The timing was right; we got there in an hour and a bit. One reason a conversation never started up, wasn't because of rudeness, it was typical protocol, leaving the professionals to grill a suspect.

Once inside a holding area, the blindfold was taken off. That was after an Israeli Colonel walked into the room. Knowing this would happen, it was essential to show as little shock as possible, to light coming into my eyes.

He stood in front of me, about three feet away, while a fit looking commando was over looking my right shoulder, making sure nothing was going to happen.

My interrogator started with, “General Vagon is that who you are?”

“No Colonel. I am General William Wright. ASA CIA Agent.”

He smirked and said, “How can you prove you are the infamous BTK?”

Just as he got out the BTK, I chopped my minders leg at the side of his left knee causing him to fall, with me on top of him in a split second, having his pistol in my right hand.

The Colonel helped the guard to his feet, indignantly asked, “What was that for, give the man's weapon back to him.”

The minder was told to leave, soon after I gave him his weapon, I had to say, “Colonel we do not have time to read resumes or call credible references.”

Before the Colonel could ask another question, General Ito walked in and said, “Wright, you are becoming a nuisance. Tell me, what is coming down the road towards my country. By the way, your bags are being investigated.”

“Sir, your country will not be in the cross hairs, at

least from my mission."

"I take it you have no orders to what you call your mission."

"Correct sir."

"Tell me what were you doing in Lebanon?"

"Sorry sir, that is far above my pay grade. Saying that, I am sure you were quietly alerted to me showing up."

He coughed twice, clearing his throat, meaning he needed a few seconds to come up with a reply. Staring towards him and waiting to hear what he could come up with, he was going to take the other road, because of me side tracking the question, that's their M.O.

"The number of PLO killed was about a half dozen? Am I wrong General Wright?"

Hearing that statement meant Els had been interrogated, probably while she was sedated. Now hoping she wasn't given any help in the form of a shot of sodium pentathlon. That would be unethical to say the least. I mustn't say anything.

General Ito tired of waiting responded with, "Are you going to answer?"

"Sorry sir, I was counting."

He laughed out loud, while saying, "You are way to good for this old Israeli General. Tell me how you had covered your tracks, or more importantly diverted attention to my country."

"Russian evidence was planted to throw off Lebanese investigators."

"What do you suggest we do with your trail leading to my back door?"

"Sir, I would assume you move the pickup to Israeli Territory, and all foot prints raked over."

"Your associate is saying some incriminating things about you."

"General, she is out of her mind. You can't trust a crazy person."

He let out a quiet laugh and asked, "Do you think our Prime Minister will be called in front of the U.N. again, because of you."

"Sir, you must know, I am not here."

"Yes General Wright, we have a dilemma, you are not here and your sacks of documents never fell into our hands. Are we are going to be blamed for executing a PLO Squad and their leader?"

"You are going to get blamed if a dead fish floats to the shore in Beirut."

"So true."

"General Ito lets trade my agent for the documents. Put Lieutenant Els on a Red Cross plane to London. I will use an alias to board an El Al flight to a neutral country, lets say Buenos Aires."

"Yes that should do the trick. We will allow you to travel to London under an assumed name, so you can meet up with your agent, say after you spend a week on a certain Kibbutz, with a beautiful Israeli female officer."

"Thank you sir, would that be Miss.Devorah Tobias?"

"Wright, we do not like your incursions into our little country, please let this be the last time we see you, for many years."

Strange, he didn't ask who Els was working for. She must have told the Israeli's everything. Now what is to become of my dream agency?

That evening I was allowed to see Els in the hospital, where she was groggy but aware enough to understand one special order, which was to have a blood sample taken on the Red Cross plane.

The next morning waiting for Pete I was hauled in front of Ito, knowing this was for one reason, money.

Served thick hot coffee with bread sticks in a drab interrogation room, the General walked in with a huge grin on his face.

He started with a strange question, "Well General Wright, we have a situation with a half billion dollars missing from Rahman's bank account, do we not?"

"No sir."

With a hearty laugh he asked, "How was the money transferred that quickly? Forget that last stupid question. Thank you for the left over treasure, we now know where all PLO funds are coming from. I believe your ride is here. Do us all a favor, do not come back to Israel after this trip is over."

Rabbi Pete Tobias picked me up, saying his sister will be arriving later this evening.

The biggest surprise, Els was delivered to the Kibbutz the following day with a nurse and a Doctor of Psychiatry. This was something else, what a kind gesture. I wondered what was going on and where is the charity flight.

The nurse took a needle of blood from Els and placed it in a sterilized tube, which was stored in the communal fridge, with a note, the sample is to accompany us to England.

We all talked Dannie through the ordeal of witnessing so much killing, with her apologizing for being weak and deciding to get out of the spy game. It was a shame to loose a budding agent who was going to run the Middle Eastern Operations. I was thinking, she could be an asset by leaving field work to others and staying in an office.

A few days later Els had a set back, long periods of weeping. She was sedated, and the next morning we were taken to Tel Aviv and put on an El Al flight at the last minute under Israeli Aliases and flown to London, the file of blood was packed in iced, placed in the cockpit.

While sitting in the last two seats at the rear of the aircraft, Dannie rested her head on my left shoulder, then pulling her legs up under her body. With her window shade pulled down she drifted off to sleep after the plane was in the air.

I was restricted from having anything to drink or eat, after she draped her left arm across my waist.

Whispering to a flight attendant that we should be left alone, having her take a curtain out of the storage bin, segregating us off from the rest of the passengers in our cabin.

Just before arriving at Heathrow, the attendant told us we had to get ready to land. I woke Lieutenant Els up to get her to put her feet on the floor, as we were on our approach.

Dannie woke up and kissed me on the side of my face, saying, "Thank you Will for taking care of me. I hope we can now be close friends."

I was now in the middle of a huge problem. One, she is too valuable of an asset to lose. Two, I was not willing to forgo the money spent on getting her ready to take over the Middle East OPS Center. She had to be handled with kid gloves, not making her condition any worse by letting her seduce me into caring for her for an unforeseeable future.

Kenny was alerted we were flying into Heathrow by General Simpson, for the purpose of delivering us to the London flat. When we arrived, I gave the blood sample to Kenny, instructing him to take it to the West Ruislip RAF Station to have it analyzed.

When we were up in the Hyde Park Flat, it was chilly, causing me to turn up the heat and draw a bath.

She was led to the bedroom, where she said, "Will, please come to bed with me and keep me warm, I need you now more than ever."

Once again my mind was in overdrive while helping her undress. Dannie was taken to the bath tub and told to relax, a cup of tea was being brewed.

In the kitchen, I thought of rejecting her, which would probably exacerbate her fragile condition. An idea came to me that she had to be broken in reverse. Instead of turning someone into a submissive person, she had to be turned into a feisty fighter, now how was the question.

Leaving her and going back into the kitchen, I made another pot of tea. This time with five times the grounds needed for two teas, putting a tea cozy over the pot to keep it hot.

Back up stairs, Els had left the tub without pulling the plug, which meant she was hopefully tucked up in bed and drifting off to sleep. Quite the opposite, she was laying on top of the bed with a sheet over her, asking for me to keep her warm.

Going back down stairs and bringing up a tray with tea and sugar, she said, "No more tea darling, I want you, nothing else."

Without undressing, it was necessary to save an agent, not an enjoyable task of making love to a beautiful young lady.

Taking a chance I climbed on top of Dannie, kissed her hard enough for her to move her face away, where pressure was quickly applied to her solar plexus. This maneuver was taught in Ranger School where the air was pushed out of an opponents lungs.

Her eyes slowly closed as she struggled underneath me, it was apparent she was trying to catch her breath. This went on for a few more minutes, panicking, she tried to squirm away.

The bed sheets under us were now saturated with sweat, causing her to become even more uncomfortable.

Lieutenant Els was now at a point of trying to shout, making me press even harder, until she conjured up enough strength through sheer determination to throw me onto the floor.

Gasping for air, “You filthy pig, I will have you prosecuted for abusing me.”

She got out of bed, grabbed a small bedroom chair, ready to beat me with it as I lay on the floor. She caught herself just as the chair was held high into the air, about to be brought down while in a frenzied state.

Finally catching her breathe, she shouted, “I need to get out of this place. Please leave, now, allow me to get dressed. ”

After pouring her a sugary strong black cold tea, I instructed her, “Drink it down or I will force it down you, then I will leave the room. Drink all of it.”

After she had gulped the tea down, it was sat down hard on the tray I was holding, with her again shouting, “Get the hell out of this room.”

Waiting in the kitchen, Els finally appeared, saying with a menacing smile, “You bastard, you bastard.”

I laughed and said, “Welcome back Lieutenant, want some tea?”

She laughed and said, “I have had enough tea.”

Moving over to her, I embraced her saying at the same time, “You don't know how much I wanted to make love to you, it took a lot of control, not to cave in.”

Calling my bluff, she said, “Okay General lets do it.”

Then she let out a nice laugh, when several seconds went by, not knowing how to respond.

After a few seconds I told her, “You shouldn't tease a General, it could be construed as an insubordinate offense.”

“Arrest me, or is it an agent you need?”

“Lieutenant Els, are you ready to go back to Jordan to finish the university course?”

“You are a SOB that is it. Nothing about, I will miss you when you are gone?”

She was back, even more feisty if that's possible, this was making me struggle to reply to her question.

Els started on another angle, asking, “Tell me about Beirut. Why wasn't I let in on your real objective?”

“Can you deal with a shocking revelation, one that is straight out of the White House? This is information that could get you assassinated.”

“General, do I need to know?”

“No. You have a choice to make it right now. Shall I draw the curtains so we can see the park, or do you want to go out for supper?”

“You're right. Get a jacket on, it’s a long walk to a great restaurant that is if our stroll isn't interrupted.”

Thirty minutes into our walk, Kenny's cab pulled alongside of us, barking out, “Goen sommers Guv, giv ya a liff.

Els weakened, pleading, "Lets ride my feet are killing me."

It wasn't long before we were outside Flanagan's Pub, Kenny parking his taxi and walking behind us.

Kenny looked like he had just lost his best friend, causing me to ask, "What is it?"

"Our old gaffer is ill. E as ben taken to that big Yank Base and shipped ome. Ere's a note from the other General. Ya thingme results ere from the Yank Base."

"Thank you Kenny."

I stuck the letter into my jacket and the results of Els blood test, and ordered a beer with fish and chips.

Els asked, "Aren't you going to read the note?"

"I know what it says. Let's eat."

Kenny shaking his head and saying,"I'll pick you at 0700, you kids 'ave a good time."

After supper we walked back to the flat, where Els was told to pack her suitcase for a morning flight.

After reading the letter, I made reservations for her to travel to Amman, and me to Washington.

Our night together was strange; we slept in the same bed, as if we were still in the wagon.

At the airport the next morning, I kissed Dannie goodbye on the lips, making her smile and saying, "You take care and I need to know I will have someone looking out for me if our group is exposed."

“Okay, you do the same, Dannie. See you in Amman, when you graduate, stay safe.”

We got a ride to the airport with Kenny, where Els was told at her gate, “Be aware who is close to you.”

On the way to the States, I thought of only one scenario that was going to happen, the London CIA Office had to be manned. Hoping this was a temporary setback for Simpson, because of a selfish reason, I wanted to take over.

At Dulles, General Thibodeau was waiting on the curb. He sent his MP in to take my bags.

Once in the sedan, and before the driver took off, Thibodeau said, “Simpson is officially retired. You are taking over the London Office. Now tell me, was your assignment a success?”

“Yes sir.”

Not offering to discuss it in the car infuriated him.

Thibodeau was not a patient man, showing his disdain, barking out, “Well, damn you, what happened.”

“I said it went okay, what else is there to say.”

Thibodeau was so agitated he shouted to his MP chauffeur, “Stop the damn car, he's walking.”

Starting to get out he said, “Keep your seat. Driver move on. You didn't have to kill the PLO Leader and all of his men. No that wasn't good enough for you, two guards ended up as hood ornaments. What were you thinking of. Oh yes, a half billion dollars are missing, any idea why that is?"

The driver looking in his rear view mirror, quickly turned back to watching the roads after he was seen, causing me to slide the privacy window across.

Saying to the General, "We need to talk about this in a formal setting, not in the back of a car."

"Damn you Wright, there will be no formal setting, or for that matter, there is to be no official briefing on something that never happened. Now listen to me, when you are in London, you will be watched and your actions will be evaluated weekly. Do you understand where I am coming from?"

"Yes sir."

I was taken to a barracks guest bedroom and told to get dressed in a suit. I had a meeting in thirty minutes.

An MP escorted me to a conference room where Thibodeau was waiting. Within minutes, my friend Jeff entered the room. We shook hands and after the accolades, Thibodeau muttered something like "Unbelievable" just then the Vice President walked in.

The VEEP, said, "Well done General Wright. You look familiar, have we met?"

"Yes sir, several years back when you awarded me with a medal."

"Umm, that must have been it."

Chapter 34

Conspiracy

Thibodeau being right behind me, whispered, “You had better not screw this up. He never gave you a medal, where do you come up with this stuff.”

Causing the VP to ask,” What was it you were saying, Wright?”

“Sorry sir, I am a little shy in asking, and wanting to know if you miss your CIA days.”

Thibodeau put his fist into my back just before the VEEP said, “Yes, I do miss those days, General. How about you, do you like the agency?”

“Yes sir. I cannot think what I would rather do than serving my country with this great American iconic organization.”

“General, I do not believe you are shy at all, there seems to be a reason you want me to remember you, is that correct?”

“Yes there is sir. I know you like to visit the UK on certain business association matters and since my new posting is in London, I would like you to feel safe and secure in letting me handle your security team.”

“And after I am no longer a VP, what then?”

“You will need much more security as the next President.”

He laughed and said, “Shy, that is going to be your tag, when you are needed to be on our team, good day General.”

“Sir.”

As soon as the VP was out of the room, Thibodeau said, “Wright you came mighty close to stepping over the line. What game were you playing? And while we are at it, how do you know Jeff Jones? Please don't tell me he was planted.”

“I honestly can't remember the time I met him, sir.”

“Maybe not the time, bet my bottom dollar you have some relationship there. All that crap about wanting to serve your country, you sounded like a political pimp.”

At that moment, Jeff stepped into the room to pass on a message from the veep, saying, “The VP wants you to make up his foursome at Greenbrier on Saturday. Tee off time is 0800; a room will be booked for Friday night.”

Thibodeau was shocked, saying, “I do not believe it, unbelievable,” heh heh heh all I want to do is ha ha was heard as he walked out behind Jeff.

The General's car pulled away from the building, leaving me to find transportation to wherever I needed to go.

Shaking my head in disbelief, Clint in charge of base security and an old friend rode up in a golf cart, saying, “What did the veep want with you.”

“It seems he needs a golfing partner. Call me a taxi Clint, I need to get to Washington National.”

“I'll take you.”

“Wait a minute Clint, I need to call Tel Aviv.”

“At this time of night, it's around four in the morning there.”

“Who would have a phone number of a certain General in the Israeli Army?”

“Thibodeau.”

“You have a key to the Director's office?”

“No, I never had one. You want to go to the hotel?”

“Take me the old man's office.”

“Don't tell me you're going to break in?”

After being dropped off in front of the building, a security guard held the door for me, asking, “Working late General?”

Reading his name tag, I replied, “Always Williams.”

The CIA door leading into a foyer was easy to open, by sliding a credit card up into the latch. The old man's secretary's desk was also opened the same way, where her Rolladext was stored.

Getting through to Israeli Army Headquarters, I asked for General Ito's home phone number. Knowing the CIA number was seen on the Operator's screen, I had to confirm it was General Thibodeau who wanted this information.

After being told it was half past four, the General was most likely asleep and would I call him after 0700.

General Ito answered, sounding half asleep he asked, “Who is this?”

“CIA Headquarters General, wake up we have to talk.”

“Wright, I recognize your voice. Are you out of your mind or stark raving mad? Let me speak to your supervisor.”

“My Lieutenant had traces of sodium pentothal in her system.”

“You called me to tell me that, you are really unstable.”

“I’d rather be unstable than untrustworthy. I just wanted you to know, that is all.”

“Wait, do not hang up. Yes, we wanted information. Everyone caught coming into our country through the desert gets the same treatment.”

“That is the last lie I want to hear from you, goodbye General.”

When the phone was on the way down to its hook,

he was heard saying, “Wait, one dam.”

That was that, end of the conversation. Knowing he was on the phone to his headquarters to call me back, I waited.

Within two minutes the phone rang. This time in Thibodeau's office.

Hurrying to answer I feigned my accent to sound like a Cajun, “Yees, what is it Wright?”

“It's not Wright, General Thibodeau that crazy bastard called me from the CIA building. Is he there? Can he hear you?”

“Yees, he is in the Secretary's office, hurry what's up?”

“I think he knows.”

“Leave it with me.”

What was that about, he knows, knows what? Maybe there is something in Thibodeau's file cabinet, No use, it will be coded.

No, probably under a fictitious heading of a name or number. I have to get the information from the Director, by devious means. Hold on, the Rolodex had strange numbers at the bottom of a card.

Bingo got it. 8/08/46, my birthday. In Thibodeau's file was a file heading with those numbers, showing correspondence. Not only with Israeli Intelligence, but with British Secret Service and more importantly with

MI5 and MI6.

A copy of a letter to each agency reading the same.

Lord David Chesterfield, copy in-General Ito:

Please be alerted, General Wright is under investigation of sedition per his Director. Forward all interrupted wires out of Amman, London, Azerbaijan and Moscow.

Was this a precursor for going on the last two unofficial assignments? If it was, the Veep is part of this conspiracy theory in squelching a ghost agency being formed. That's it, they are throwing darts towards a missing dart board. Got to go, Clint's waiting.

Clint dropped me off at my hotel after midnight, where sleep overtook me, and I was awakened at 0800 by the phone and Thibodeau asking me to be in his office within the hour.

Once in the CIA building, two over sized MP's were waiting to escort me up to the Director's office.

Inside Thibodeau's office, his secretary was told, “Mam, leave us. Come back in one hour. Wright come in here. You two MP's wait outside.”

He stared through me, not at me, causing me to ask, “This is rather dramatic, sir, what's up?”

Saliva was coming out when he shouted, “You insolent SOB, I am going to have you taken to the Brig for breaking into my office. Don't you tell me it wasn't you Wright. Every time you visit Washington, CIA files and property are compromised, either at Langley or here in Washington, not to mention the White House Press office being burglarized last year on one of your visits."

"I must object to being accused of those allegations, sir."

"You are way past being annoying, in fact, your presence is starting to make me feel uncomfortable."

"Alright General sir, lets clear the air. I had to get Ito's phone number so he could be called and confronted with a despicable act of treason on the United States. I had to enter your office to get a phone number, where you would not be implicated if this confrontation with an Israeli General went awry."

"What the hell are you talking about?"

"Soon after being granted sanctuary in Israel, which you had warned them I may showup, Lieutenant Els, my agent was tampered with. She was given an injection of truth serum while she was in an Israeli hospital. Do I need to go any further sir?"

"I find that hard to believe, can you prove it?"

"Yes sir. As soon as we arrived in London, Els blood sample was delivered to Ruislip for analyzes. Please call them for the prognosis."

"Anything else you find out?"

"You know the the Israeli's were handsomely

compensated, sir."

"Get out of here. Wait! Where are you going to be for the next few days?"

"Florida, Marco Island."

Compensation was not questioned. He knows about the files and must have been told about the wire transfer. Why didn't he mention the half billion dollars.

The General's driver took me to the Hilton and waited for my bags to be packed, to catch a flight out of DCA.

From the airport Fran was called to see if she would like to go to dinner tonight.

My pickup truck was still at her parents house, parked in the back where no one could see the old beat up vehicle. Flying into Tampa and catching a Florida Airlines plane to Marco Field, Fran was there to meet me in the truck.

We were glad to see each other so much, it took several minutes to kiss and hug before we headed towards Everglades City. That evening we had supper at the Dog n Suds drive in and then went to see what was playing at the drive in movie. It really didn't matter what was on, this was a place we could be alone. That night we drove back to Marco for some beach time

After spending several days at the Marco Inn, Fran and I left for Washington on Friday after her school duties were over. That evening while having dinner in the palatial Greenbriar, the VP and his wife walked in and over to our table.

They were introduced to Fran, with the VP asking, "What is your handicap?"

"Ten, sir."

"Umm, you're not a bandit, are you?"

"No sir. I have my registration in the room."

"Yea right. Wright, you wouldn't be the first to produce a bogus golf registration."

Chapter 35

London CIA Posting

"Bring it with you and at least two hundred dollars. Your wife can spend the day with Barbara."

"Yes sir."

That was a strange statement. Did he not know my wife was on the Pam Am flight, and I was now widowed? Doesn't give me confidence on his security team investigating who he is playing golf with, unless Jones had me passed.

Fran was taken aback and then eventually asked,

"What are you thinking about. How do you know the Vice President and his wife?"

"It's a long story. How would you and your daughter like to spend this summer in London."

"No thank you. The last time I was invited to stay with you there, you went missing for months."

"It will be different this time. Both of you will travel with me to some of the places I have to go."

"No thank you, anyway your place has only two bedrooms and one bathroom."

"Fran, I will be moving into the CIA Director's residence, close to the Embassy."

"You mean you are going to be taking over? Yes we will gladly come, one condition, my daughter can bring a school friend with her."

"Agreed. Your parents can move into the flat if your father can get away from his bank."

The next morning, Fran and I were on the practice range when the Defense Secretary walked over, introducing himself.

He was the third player, and asked, "Have you seen Jones?"

Great, Jeff was the fourth. Jones pulled into the front of the club house, hurrying to unload his clubs, waving for me to get him a cart. I thought, oh brother, he was almost late, what would the VP think. We could see the entourage driving up the hill just as I got to Jeff, then asking Fran to park the man's car, so it would look like he was waiting for his boss. Secretary North was laughing at Jeff struggling to get his spikes on.

Our golf match turned out well, with the VP making a putt to tie the match. No money changed hands that day. Monday morning, Fran was back in Florida and I was in Thibodeau's office at 0900.

The General walked in thirty minutes late causing me to ask, “Semi retired are we sir?”

“Don't you start with your smart ass crap I can still have you in front of a court martial before you know what day it is.”

We both laughed, with him bellowing out a hearty chuckle, and saying, “You need to be in the Embassy by noon tomorrow for a meeting with British Intelligence. I believe you know the man who is in charge of that service. Get him to do us a favor we need access to his files.”

“Chesterfield will never let us see his files. He is as straight laced a Brit as you would ever find, anyway, I burnt that bridge long ago, he doesn't exactly want me around his filing cabinet. What is it you need to know?”

“I need all files on Simpson, because of them wanting to destroy his reputation. His service to our nation will not be impugned by over zealous foreign agents, wanting a CIA scalp to place in their showcase."

Sir, Simpson is never controversial, or confronts anyone."

"Precisely."

What a strange thing to say. I was asked to leave and ordered to call tomorrow, from London.

Fran flew out of National for Florida and I from Dulles.

On the red eye long overnight flight, there was plenty time to think, doze and think again.

There has to be a reason for not hounding me on the money and more important, where is the outrage from Rahman and his wife. They will have to curtail their lavish life style until aid was again shipped from the USA. Is it possible something like that would be placed on the back burner or ignored, no way, Washington never will give up that much cash. Okay, why not call me out or at least investigate the missing funds.

Arriving the next morning at Heathrow, Kenny was waiting in his taxi as I walked out of the arrivals hall, hearing, "Oar ere Guv, welcome ome."

Kenny talked as I dozed off, having him wake me when we arrived at the Embassy. Kenny was still talking when I got out and walking towards the front door.

In the office, Miss Peabody was distraught, until

she saw it was me who was going to take over. It seemed she had some bad news, thinking I hoped it wasn't General Simpson.

She finally said, “This office has been broken into. My files that were left on the General's desk are gone.”

“Miss Peabody make us some tea, and gather yourself.”

“Alright me duck, I mean Billy, I mean sir.”

She settled down as we sipped our tea, asking her, “Do you remember what files were taken?”

“It was a file on you Billy, I mean sir. Mister Simpson and that Chester bloke who was here when Mister had his funny turn, General Simpson, I mean.”

“Calm down. What was it that caused the General some stress?”

“It was when that Chester bloke said you were seen in some Arab place before holding up a bank.”

I thought, now where could that Arab place be? Oh yes, Amman, has to be the area. Those files are useless, unless CIA practices or notes about covert actions were assimilated. I have to ask the obvious question.

“Miss Peabody, were the files on assignments?”

“Oh no deary, they were personal. You know, on your be haven.”

“How do you know those were of a behavioral matter?”

"I typed them Billy, then filed in a section called patterns of ASA agents. You weren't the only one in those papers."

We finished our second cup of tea when David Chesterfield walked in making Peabody go completely back to her Cockney roots, saying, "That's im, that Chester bloke, E's tha one who caused mister to turn fun-nay."

"Miss. Peabody, take the rest of the day off."

When she was gone, I poured David a cup of tea. We started talking in a civil manner, he did not need to know how mad I was knowing one of his men broke into this office, following his orders.

David politely started by saying, "Will, congrats on your new posting. I am sure we will be a formidable force if we are able to share intelligence. Who would ever have thought we would be where we are today, back when you recruited me to be a CIA Agent."

"Yes me Lord, we are going to be a great team. You need to give me a month to get settled in then shall we meet once a fortnight to discuss what has to be done or more important what we are up to."

"Very good idea, say we get together on the last Saturday of each month on the estate, a fortnight is asking schedules to be changed."

Is he acting coy, not mentioning my file. It is

important to remember the dirt he knows I have on MI5.

"No David, that would never work, you like your home to be void of business. We need to meet at the Cambridge flat on the first Monday of the month, as close to 0800 as possible. You still have the key?"

"Yes, I have a key. Good idea. Is there any concerns you have before we start this new association?"

"None. Shall we treat each others office as one of our own? I will give you a key to the Embassy and you give me the combination to your locks in Whitehall. It would be much easier to walk through the door instead of climbing a drain pipe to gain access through a window, do you not agree?"

"What gave it away?"

"The putty is still pliable."

"Oh dear. Your files are in my case. Start anew then."

Those misappropriated files were most likely copied by now or else he would have said, they would have been in my hands by the close of day.

Responding as fast as I could with, "Yes, let's get lunch at the local and toast our new association."

"Jolly good. Tell me one thing before we get lunch, why did it take you so long to get to Amman to see how your associates were progressing."

So that was it, the British big wigs are suspicious of a mysterious rogue agency being formed. David knows all about this venture, why would he need physical evidence instead of taking my word on this subject?

Chesterfield is looking uncomfortable at the delay in my response, telegraphing just maybe, there is more to this conspiratorial feeling on my stealth agency feared by Washington and Whitehall.

"Sorry David, it was essential to answer you without wasteful hyperbole. As you know I was on my way to an Amman meeting with a few prospects. A stop over in Moscow was essential for visiting a friend. Now enlighten me on what this paranoia fervor is all about. Wait a minute, Montague is now reassigned to the desert, for what purpose?"

"Will, lets discuss this over lunch in the Lord's dining room, my driver will take us."

As we left the Embassy. Kenny was signaled to follow us.

In the back of the Jaguar staff car, David was told he had a tail, making him to say, "It seems your driver has decided to follow us, pity, my man is willing to take you to your new residence. I take it the flat is to be sold. I may be in the market."

"No David, it is to be used as a sanctuary for me and my friends, including you and your wife."

"Thank you old boy, we may use it next weekend, if that works for you."

"Yes, it works for me."

Lunch was enjoyable, David and I reminiscing about our exploits in Cambridge, when we worked as helpers punting tourist up and down the river Cam while going to Cambridge University.

This new life in a grown up world was not supposed to be easy, especially in the intelligence community. It is a situation we had to get used to. Polite lunches instead of grabbing something to eat while on the run, avoiding STASI, KGB or Middle Eastern Terrorist, was not David's forte, as it was for my life during and after university.

For the next two months I flitted between London, and Frankfurt where Buck was now the Chief ASA officer in Europe. On the first of May, it was necessary to travel to Amman, to meet the kill squad from Ranger School and to see how close the Amman 5 were to graduating.

Our team took up a good portion of the top floor at the international hotel at the Amman Airport, where we were given a conference room to hold our briefings.

This get together was more of a home coming than a strategy session. A couple of the group needed a few more weeks of one on one help in conversational Urdu language skills while Els needed to hone her English accent.

Instead of going back to London when we broke up, Els and I flew to Luxor via Cairo, for a lesson in proper English dining at the famous “Old Winter Palace Hotel” on the Nile which Agatha Christie called her winter home. We had a few good days, Els mixing with well to do Brits, pretending to be from Lincolnshire, where she was asked multiple times if people in her county really had webbed feet.

We both flew into Cairo, parting after a few hugs, with her going back to Amman and me to London.

On May 21st, Fran arrived in London, with her daughter and parents. Having child minders on call, allowed me to take Fran on a trip to Jordan, to see the graduation of my new agents.

Olga arranged to meet us, along with Pierre, Combs and our kill squad from the States.

Lieutenant Els after graduating was promoted to Captain, and given a choice of taking over the Bavarian ASA Headquarters in Bad Aibling, or staying on in Amman as a coordinator of all Middle East activities.

We then traveled to Langley to see the graduation of Phil, Alison and Lupe.

All of this going to graduations then tea and lunches in London was not exactly stimulating. I wanted to go one more time across the Czech border, running through the forest and stopping to see if anyone could be heard or seen trying to catch this American artful dodger.

In the middle of August, Fran and I were having dinner in our favorite pub when she said, “Will, I am so proud of you staying in London. Now saying that, you were noticeably restless for some time, are you missing your cloak and dagger life?”

“Yea, the rush one gets while moving around in a country of nasty oligarchs who rule by violence is stimulating. However, I have enjoyed our summer together. What's the highlight of your summer?”

“Showing my daughter museums, old buildings and having afternoon tea in different places it will be such a good grounding for her, my little girl, thank you Will.”

At the end of summer, all of the Millbanks left for South Florida, leaving a large void in my daily life, one that only Fran could fill.

The American elections were progressing, with the VP having accepted the Republican nominee. In two months he would probably be elected; inaugurated in the New Year, and hopefully having the CIA granted a new budget. Just maybe, my expenses in Jordan, South America, Europe and the Middle East will be paid back in full. Maybe not if the money from Beirut was traced.

It wasn't long after I was on my own that a call

from Buck, wanting help in closing down a surveillance team which was set up in a highway works van, across the road from our I. G. Farben Complex.

Buck was given specific instructions, "Alright Sergeant, sorry Lieutenant Buck, leave the building and go to the train station now. Call me from the phone exchange across the road, I will be at Simpson's on the Strand in thirty minutes, the number is in the company's daily planner."

Kenny dropped me off at the restaurant, parked his taxi and joined me for lunch. A table was being arranged in the back of the large room while we ordered a beer from the bar.

Chapter 36

Setting The Table

A few minutes after our meals were ordered, the waiter came back to say a call has come in for me, would I please take it in the booth out in the foyer.

Lieutenant Buck accepted instructions on dealing with his onlookers, "Take photographs around the clock, by using a high powered camera with telescopic lens. Develop all of the photographs daily blow them up as much as possible, without blurring the images. Meet me at the Airport Hotel with all of the photographs next weekend, say Friday evening at 1800 hours."

Clearing the top of my desk, while telling Peabody to take a three week holiday was necessary. I did not want information leaked out to where I was going or for that matter to what this next trip was about. However, it was important on her return that messages left on the machine needed taking down in chronological order by time and date.

Arriving at Frankfurt International Airport Hotel, Buck was early, waiting in the lounge and joining me at the front desk, saying, "You're checked in sir."

The clerk was confused with Buck carrying a leather suitcase, telling the concierge, "I am not staying the night. Please have our dinner brought to the room, along with drinks ordered from the bar."

Dam! Buck was organized, I was impressed.

The Lieutenant took off the bed's heavy quilt, folding it up and laying it on a luggage rack. The top sheet was pulled back, where it was folded, resting on the foot of the bed. While he was busy spreading out photographs, I had a quick shower to refresh myself after the plane ride.

Feeling much brighter and dressed, our drinks were delivered as soon as I sat down at a small desk. Buck pulled the sheet over the photographs, in case the waiter pushed the trolley in.

Our drinks and food were left on a cart outside the door.

While we ate, the photographs were looked ove and rearranged with different characters placed in separated stacks.

Buck was asked, “After you studied profiles, were any of them noticed in other areas, like walking around town, in bars, catching a bus or taxi. More important, did other agents notice someone following them?”

“Yes sir General, all of those scenarios happened. We in Frankfurt feel our entire organization has been compromised.”

“Which one of these men followed you here?”

“That one sir, the one with the dirty trench coat.”

“Alright Lieutenant listen, most of them are British, with two local dicks being used to shadow you and your men.”

“You know those guys, sir?”

“Yes. Listen this is important, we need to use these stalkers to further my plans. How are we going to do this? By calling the Russian Embassy and have one of their agents come over and pick up a letter from Washington. When I get back to London, I will send you letters for not only the Russians, but the Egyptians,

French and the Turkish Consulate. They will have five scenarios to worry them, and with four men we may be lucky, since the work patterns here are more or less the same everyday. First they will follow me as they know I am here, then operation sidetrack will be initiated, we have time on our side"

"That should work sir, but where or more important how are you going to get the foreigners to fall into your trap?"

"By going fox hunting, where I am the vermin. If my plan is successful, the MI 5 agent in charge is going to follow me for a quiet walk in the Sumava Forest. Is my car in the complex?"

"Yes sir. Serviced and parked in the garage area.

Are you going to eradicate the man?"

"No. Have the motor bike in Bad Aibling ready for me on Sunday morning."

"It is ready sir."

"Gather your stuff, I will walk you out to the curb, I need to be seen in Frankfurt."

The next morning I got into a taxi for a ride to the ASA Complex.

Right on cue, a German gum shoe followed the taxi to the complex gates. Hurrying up stairs to catch the man entering his hide was essential for seeing who he relayed information to.

Binoculars were positioned near a large window with drapes parted far enough to eaves drop on the eaves droppers. How ironic, observing the surveillance men talking to the one who must have spent the night in the cold watching my hotel.

The bait is is about to be placed in a sports car owned by the fox.

Purposely driving slowly out of the gates, stopping to watch for oncoming traffic, I took off using side mirrors peripherally, and noticing a stalker walking quickly towards a call box. It was also necessary to take my time driving onto the autobahn on the ramp going towards Mannheim.

Another ploy was to stop at my old unit to see if any of the old guys were still there. Ah haw, a black Mercedes sedan was seen about a mile in the rear view mirror. Looks similar to the one we rented for the old ASA dick.

An hour later I pulled into Taylor barracks, asking the MP to call the 68th office if he noticed a large black Mercedes driving slowly by. Parking in the lot next to my old barracks where this old car had spent many cold nights, it was back home, wonder if it knew.

One hour later, I stopped to speak to the guard, on my way out. He informed me, no one was seen eaves dropping on or towards the base.

That meant, the guy was good or the MP wasn't as sharp as he should be. Three hours later it was necessary to stop at a rest area the other side of Munich. This was a chance to see if the Mercedes was actually going to play the game.

Off the motorway and on the exit ramp, the car was accelerating towards the parking area. I hurriedly parked and walked inside, stopping by a window to see any car pulling in. Waiting for ten minutes, two cars came in with families but no gum shoes. He was good, probably parked along side the motorway waiting for me to exit the rest stop and getting back on the autobahn.

Looking into the rear view mirror, a black Mercedes was seen pulling onto the motor way. Okay, the shadow was now back with me, he wasn't as astute as I first thought. Yes, he did a good job hiding, but one would think MI5 would pull a switch by now, they must be short handed on weekends.

An hour later I pulled up to the Bad Aibling gates, with the MP walking up to my car, saying, “Welcome back sir, thought I recognized the car.”

“Thank you Corporal. If you see a suspicious black Mercedes drive by, let it be. Do not call the local police, or try to see what they are up to. I need him or them to be available later on for an old fashion get together. You put in your report everything that was said and call the

Officer of the guard, tell him my instructions."

"Yes sir General Wright. Are you going hunting?"

"Hope so."

The ASA weekend CQ opened the door, and immediately said, "We've been expecting you General. Lieutenant Buck advised us to have your uniforms ready, weapons oiled and serviced, along with two box lunches inside your saddle bags."

"Thank you sergeant. Anything from Washington come in for me?"

"No sir, before I forget, in the other saddle bag is a nylon pup tent if you needed to camp."

"Thanks. You have not seen me, if anyone calls, except for Buck, is that clear?"

"Yes sir."

"I will be in the back office for a few minutes."

My old office was left as it was from the last time I was here. Dressing into a heavy wool Russian uniform, packing two revolvers, I went out of the back door and into the parking lot to get on the waiting motor bike.

Stopping at the front gates, taking my helmet off, the guard said, "General, the Mercedes is parked to the right, about a half mile away. The driver of the car got out and walked back towards the base, I believe he knows who you are now with your head gear off. Was that on purpose?"

"Thank you Corporal, good observation."

I waited for a few minutes to let my shadow get to his car, couldn't let him fall to far behind. Knowing his car could keep up with the bike, I had to gun it, once I was on the motor way, to give him the confidence he was not spotted.

Three hours later I pulled off the main road and onto a forest track on the West German side of a border fence three miles away.

My follower knew now he was very near the Czech border from a bill board seven miles back, warning all American Military traffic to turn off immediately.

Thinking his car should be low on diesel and too close now for him to abandon the chase, it was necessary to coax him closer to the border. He wouldn't know the Czech territory had a buffer, where it stretches a mile on this side and is actually in the Soviet Zone, so far from the fence, one could not see it through the dense trees.

Slowing down, gingerly picking my way northward, he could be heard behind me about a quarter mile away, must be a diesel engine making a noise like that, or else it was burning oil.

Looking back when rounding a slight bend in the path, he was seen exiting his car, following on foot. Nice to see a plan come together.

Well inside the buffer zone, stopping at the last line of trees, observing the border, a Russian Jeep was seen far to my left, slowly approaching from the East German direction. This guy was so consumed at following he came all the way to the edge of the forest after I moved to the border so the guards could see me.

Stopping where bike tires were almost under an iron bar, I used to go under in the past, was too much for the approaching soldiers not to hurry towards me.

When the Jeep was fifty yards away, I turned the bike around, taking off into the trees, with my stalker only ten yards from me.

The Russian vehicle ran up alongside the tree line, letting out one of the biggest and blackish German Shepherds I have ever seen. The dog ran towards the area where the British Agent was hiding. Beautiful, it could not have been scripted better than this.

I quickly made my way back to where the Mercedes was parked, finding the drivers door wide open. Going through papers on the passenger seat and then the glove box, his passport was found.

Stuffing the documents into my jacket, I pulled out the car's back seat, throwing it away and wedged the bike into the vehicle.

Attempting to drive away, one of the soldiers ran up and pointed a rifle at my head.

Knowing the man was a Czech and his weapon would not be loaded, I laughed and said in Russian, "You have the man on the border, no?"

He knew a little Russian, enough to say, "Yes, you a Russian Colonel?"

"I have to go. Private, have that man taken to Moscow, he is the infamous Billy."

The private all of a sudden looked excited.

Thank God that was over. I drove to the closest garage to get some fuel, which happened to be at the entrance to the autobahn.

Arriving at Bad Aibling, the guard let me in after seeing who it was. He shook his head when he noticed the bike in the back.

The next day I had a meeting with Buck and boarded a BEA Flight to London. I stayed in my flat instead of the official residence for two days with the curtains drawn, to sleep and rest up before showing up at the embassy office. All of this was essential for Kenny to think the flat was empty and for me not to be hounded by people who needed my help or one particular cab driver stopping for a cup of tea.

On an early October morning, the MI Director and I were having breakfast inside the Whitehall confines, our first scheduled briefing, when David asked, "Can you talk over a problem this morning and not let your mind wonder, since today is your anniversary with Nicola."

"I can do both. What is on your mind?"

"Our Agent was finally released from a Russian torture house two days ago. He was accused of being BTK. Where do you think they got that idea? Do you have his documents?"

"Now how did you get the Soviets to release one of your agents? I am astounded you think the Russians will collude with Americans on fitting up one of yours."

"Nothing astounds you Wright especially me wanting to know why you do what you do. Leave it at that. We need someone to get into Moscow very soon. A British Agent is under strict surveillance inside his flat, which is down the street from the Kremlin. He has a dossier from Mikhail's KGB Director, one that describes the man as an American mole. Will, is he one of your agents?"

"What's the address?"

"I take that as a yes."

"Dam you Chesterfield, address please."

Chapter 37x

Moscow CIA Mole under Threat

"What agent would you send? I need to know who he or she is, for the purpose of getting word to him, and with luck the agent would be let in and not shot."

"Give me two weeks to provide that information. Is your agent called Montague?"

"You saw the documents Will; we suspect you have his passport. Why can't you let me know right now if that is true and who you are sending, do you not trust me to keep it inside my office?"

"You have a leak in the pipes, sorry old friend."

"Alright Will, promise me, you are not going to be the one to go."

Wanting to get out of here and see if this dossier is legit, it was necessary to look at my watch, and say, "Oh my, Nicola's parents are expecting me in twenty minutes. Before I go, are we good for another meet up four weeks from today?"

"Yes, that should be good. I will call Miss Peabody in three weeks to advise her where we are going to have our scheduled monthly briefing."

He motioned for one of his minders to come over, instructing him, "My driver needs to take this man to Harrow, two panda cars should escort the car, and then return here, after the General is delivered to 24 Harley Crescent."

Saying goodbye to Chesterfield, I was taken to Harrow, making the get together without a minute to spare. Kenny arrived as arranged at the house one hour later, joining us for a cup of tea before we took off for Grosvenor Square where the American Embassy is.

David may assume I am spending a few days in Harrow, relaxing surveillance outside the Embassy, the flat and my official residence. Not to mention spending time looking in Cambridge, where it is known my place there, is used as a bolt hole.

Back in the Embassy by one pm. I called Lieutenant Els in Amman, telling her, "You are needed in the London Embassy this evening. Go immediately to the airport, a ticket will be waiting at the Jordanian Airlines ticket counter, for a non stop flight to London."

When Els walked into my office that evening, Miss. Peabody had left after she was giving instructions to tell Kenny on her way out, a ride was needed to Mildenhall RAF Base tomorrow at noon.

It then took an hour to discuss what duties Dannie had to perform in my absence, however, she was not told what or where I was going to be or go. I would be phoning in from time to time for messages. Keeping my travel plans secret was essential for now.

We left the Embassy to get something to eat, with Kenny providing our transportation to Flanagan's Pub, and then to my flat.

While having tea before we went to bed, Els asked, “One thing bothers me Sir, what do I say to the Washington CIA Director if he calls, asking for you?”

“You are going to have to think about that more often than you would think. When you give anyone an answer, you write it down along with the time and date and what you said.”

“Who is likely to call?”

“There are only two people you have to worry about, General Thibodeau and a Brit called Lord David Chesterfield. If Chesterfield invites you to his estate for a getaway weekend retreat, go, but be cautious, he is a smooth operator.”

“Why should I go, if all he wants is, to use me to get information? Maybe he can be worked, two can play that game.”

“Very good Els, keep him off his game, and make the MI6 Agent assume you will be an easy touch, if he doesn't divulge any intelligence.”

“You have to help me sir, what if he asks when you are returning to England.”

“Els that would be a trick question, hoping you would bite and answer him.”

“Wait a minute sir, is he as conniving as that.”

“What do you think? His conversation will be in

the form of an off the record interrogation. He may say at the offset, Miss. Els, may I call you Dannie? Your name has a hint of Irish or Scottish, isn't it Gaelic meaning, quiet waters."

"Oh sir, that is so nice, I like him already. Quiet waters, I never knew there was a meaning to my name."

"You see, Els, those few choice words threw you off your game. He knows how to get inside another person's mind, with nice words. Now listen, what are you going to say when he asks, when is my friend William returning to London? Think for a minute. Play your own game, play a weak defense to draw him into your lair."

"David, I never knew you two were good friends. Where did you meet General Wright?"

"Very good Els. Now he has the ball, one he needs to keep playing with."

"You think the game would be over at that moment."

"No, he is in an endless game of chess. He is going to ask one more time, When is my friend getting back to London, I would like for you and him to join us on Guy Faulks night, a sort of celebration of a British Rogue."

Els thought for a couple of minutes, and then said, "Oh didn't I tell you, he did not want to be disturbed he went hiking. When is this Guy Faulks celebration going to take place?"

"Excellent, you didn't lie and he now has to think of another angle to get the information. Els, it's almost midnight, we need to get as much sleep as possible, Kenny will be here at 0800."

The next morning Kenny was early, catching Els in her pajamas at the kitchen table with us having our breakfast, making him say, "I see Guv, wait in the motor, shall I?"

"No you don't see pour yourself a cup of tea."

"Right Guv, off to foreign lands today?"

Those comments made Els giggle, amd leave us as she walked towards her bedroom.

"Alright Kenny, where did you get the idea I was going someplace?"

"That lady secretary of yours, the one in the big ouse, you know Guv, er upstairs said you told er wot I ad ta do."

"Okay Kenny, we will be ready soon."

In side the Embassy, Els was introduced to Miss. Peabody as my assistant, Captain Els was to take all of my calls.

After briefing the two ladies was over, Kenny came in to tell me it was time to go. We headed to my place to get my bags and to get a passport with the name of Ludwig Von Wilhelm.

Packing everything I needed, Kenny was told to head for Slough Station, close to the airport, and watch to see if anyone was tailing us.

He was seen looking into his rear view mirror several times and just before we pulled into Slough, he said, “Guv, a white escort seems to be following us.”

He dropped me off and headed back to London, with me quickly going into the gents and waiting to see if I was followed.

A white car pulled up with two men getting out, coming into the station.

After approximately twenty minutes, one of the men entered the bathroom as I was drying my hands. He was dressed in a dark blue pin stripe suit and black highly polished shoes, meaning he should have a neon sign on his back saying MI5.

When he went into a toilet cubicle I left, wedging a porter’s trolley under the outside door handle. A London train was spotted waiting on the opposite side of the tracks, making me jump down and run across the tracks, instead of taking the pedestrian bridge. I was on the train just as the British Agent busted out of the loo, he was seen staring as the train started to move.

Unfortunately the other man, with a full beard, boarded the train, where he was ignored, causing him to set down beside me.

Brazen, wasn't the word, maybe a little over confident in his ability to appear as a commuter.

The tube train stopped at the next station, we both stayed in our seats, causing him to ask, “Are you an American, do not care for those chaps.”

That comment really got to me, I had to act like I did not understand, saying in German, Nix ferstein bitte, he took the bait, espousing his hatred for another race, saying, “Krauts, do not care for them either.”

The need to get away from this oaf overtook everything else. Staring at him in a smug manner, he followed the bait, when I got up and moved towards another car, he also rose.

Our train was slowing down, causing me to hesitate, and walk past an open door leading out to the station, I picked up the pace and just made it through the next door, with him close behind he was pushed back hard enough for him to fall backwards. Needless to say the oaf failed to get off.

I hailed a taxi to Heathrow, knowing the man would get off at the next stop and work his way back.

Able to shake the maladroit on my train, I made it through to the international air side and into the departure gate unscathed.

Arriving in Frankfurt that afternoon, Buck was waiting outside the immigration hall, to escort me to

ASA Headquarters. He now has General Neuhofer's old job, meaning I must remember he is in command here in Frankfurt.

In the staff car he wanted to convey his thanks for a problem we solved, with him saying, “Sir, the nest of eavesdroppers have vacated their hide. It seems they moved on.”

“Remember this Buck, if roaches are swept away, they come back, that is why you may need an exterminator one day.”

“That is quite extreme sir, if you don't mind me saying.”

“Buck, you have always gone by the proverbial book, one day that principle is going to get you killed.”

“Talking about that subject sir, are you still going over the border this week?”

“You want to go with me?”

“No sir. Thanks for asking.”

Together we called Bad Aibling to organize a few men to assist me in getting over the Czech Border and make sure a motor bike was fueled along with two revolvers being fitted with silencers and four magazines filled with cartridges.

General, sir, I would like to once again be part of your team. Give me ten minutes to pack my camping gear.”

“You stay in Frankfurt and have all calls to Bad Aibling go though this office. No one has seen me, and if you feel you cannot lie to Washington, do not answer the phone, understand?”

“But sir.”

“No buts, this mission depends on a total black out of communications. You will understand later. If you feel like this is putting your future in jeopardy, go on a two week leave, starting now.”

“Yes sir. Sounds good, going to the States in the morning, an early Christmas visit. Thank you sir.”

“Alright Buck. Do not mention that I was here. Call Bad Aibling again, tell them I didn't show, have them leave the bike in the parking lot.”

“General, your car will be brought out in a few minutes. We had it stored down stairs, since the last time you used it. Of course I had to run it from time to time to keep it charged up.”

“Thank you Buck, I may be here when you get back from stateside.”

Driving the three hours gave me a chance to go over how to cross the border as it was dark when I got to Bad Aibling, I could get my gear, change into a Russian Uniform and be at the border around 0200. Choosing to be a General or Colonel was the most difficult decision. Colonel with the General's insignia's in a pocket, just in case they were needed. Night infra red goggles, pistols and enough rubles taken from my old desk drawer for payoffs was all I needed for now.

Another three hour ride on a vehicle that kept me alert with a very cold wind brushing inside my helmet. This also helped me to contemplate all types of scenarios that could get me into trouble if a Russian scouting squad was between the border and my way to the main Prague road.

Three hundred yards from an old entry point, barely inside Austria, I watched through the goggles, with no images of soldiers, I decided to crawl under the fence.

Once under the fence, the bike was pulled to me and stood up. Walking the bike towards a thicker part of the forest I heard someone mumbling. Kneeling down in the middle of three trees I looked again into the goggles, picking up images of three men, approximately fifty yards directly in front of me. Their language was Czech, one where I only knew a few words, except for words like Cossack s, Soviet and krauts.

Knowing Czech Soldiers always had Russian minders made me think a Russian Officer was probably sleeping in a vehicle somewhere, most likely close to the only paved road out of here.

Having to walk around the group, it was necessary

to skirt their position by half a football field. Stopping to train my goggles on them every two minutes.

These three Soviet Soldiers was a mere hindrance, slowing my progress down to a point, where I would be at the main road when the sun was going to be coming up.

Back on the path again, I stopped where I thought the road was a hundred yards away, again gazing through the binoculars, a faint image of a vehicle's engine was showing up. Whoever was in the thing must have kept turning the engine on to keep warm, but now the occupant was most likely asleep. This vehicle was now ten yards away, while approaching a door creaked, seeing a large man get out to take a pee, I waited.

The man turned around, facing the Jeep, grabbing something off the front seat, he was then pulling on a sweater, giving me time to walk up and hit him over the head with the butt of a revolver. After pulling him out of the way by his feet, I started the vehicle up, loaded my bike into the rear, taking off slowly so the three other soldiers couldn't hear the engine.

Now driving away on the Prague road, I turned off on a small farm track that led to East Germany, and Leipzig. This route was so familiar because of its use in the past, mainly for coming back this way when having to escape to the West.

Once the Autobahn was above me, the distance to Leipzig was about thirty minutes away. The fuel gauge was almost on empty, prompting me to veer off into a forested area and ditch the jeep. A Gerry can of petrol was taken out of its holder, used to fill the motor bike's tank, in case a chase was initiated by the dreaded Stasi Secret Police.

It was now possible to go around Leipzig and head for the Polish border, where the location of a service station, owned and operated by an independent Gypsy Clan was a place that was used several times in the last two decades. During this long arduous trip, I thought of several plans to deal with the Brit who had the skinny on my mole.

Several hours later I pulled into another Gypsy Village thirty miles from Moscow, needing sleep and food. Also knowing these people from the past, I was well fed and rested, as usual, they were well paid, allowing me to leave and get to my friends house, Petro and Isla in the dark, at 2100 hours.

Petro the KGB Director was so glad to see me, he and Isla wanted to go out and celebrate. After having a meal and a few drinks, we were back in their flat, which incidentally was my safe house many years ago.

Isla went to bed, leaving Petro and me to discuss something that produced a worried look all evening on my friend's brow, causing me to ask, “Are you being investigated?”

“Why say that. You must have some intelligence on that subject.”

“Montague is holding up close by with a dossier on you, stolen from an informant, who had it handed to him last week in a park close to the city center.”

“My wife and I had a feeling we were in a bit of bother. That is mild compared to an environment of despair coming from the Kremlin.”

“Apart from the Brit, I had a premonition that Petro had crept in and out of my mind for over a year. Tell me when the wall is coming down?”

His look was now one of fright, making him stutter. I have known Petro for many years, he never got nervous, much less stuttered. It was as if he was told he was going to die.

He finally said, “It is impossible, you knowing that.”

“It's hard to distinguish between logic and intuition, because of suspecting for a long time the Soviets could not keep supporting nonproducing countries.”

Chapter 38

Cross Country Set Up

"Petro, you and your wife need to think about defecting."

"What do you want us to do?"

"We would like for you to stay in place. Any Soviet Agents who are non Russian, working the Middle East will be needed, only the best, no slackers or over the hill Vodka drinking idea-logs. There is a possibility we can work with the Soviets in curtailing a larger threat festering in Egypt and its neighbors. Second item, I need to have Herr Wolf detained in the gulag he uses as a re-education camp in Leipzig."

"Wolf will not be arrested or detained. He could be moving back to Moscow before the hand over."

"How about your family?"

"We are safe for now. The Russian oligarchs are friendly to my office, even though our leader is acting like a CIA plant; he is revered because of the body of supremely powerful people who are there because of him. Thanks to your President Reagan, we Soviets are within a few years away from being totally broke."

"Do you not think it is because of propping up Eastern Europe?"

"Not entirely, the economics of the Kremlin propping up an Afghanistan war and a Nicaraguan policy of supplying arms to rebels are burning our reserves the fastest. As you have seen first hand, neighboring Soviet territories have quit producing at an unsustainable rate. Our military doesn't have enough fuel to fight a thirty day war here in Europe. I'm curious how you came to this conclusion the wall may be crumbling, years ago."

"You know why. I came to get you two, now that you are willing to carry on, I will head back tomorrow. Do me a favor, I hit a Russian over the head at the Austrian Czech border and stole his vehicle, cover it up for me, please. No, wait, hold that answer. Back date a release of British Spy Montague Marlborough, say, last week. Have him handcuffed inside an Army jeep tomorrow morning, one with ten cans of petrol stored around him to hide him being there. Two jugs of water, one laced with a strong sedative, is that possible?"

"We can do that. One of these days you are going to be shot, without asking questions. I thought you were now sitting in London with those shiny shoes on a desk in your Embassy."

"Me to. Wake me before you go to work, I need to leave as soon as you do. Oh yes, Marlborough will be finished working the Soviet zone, which may be beneficial for us to recruit former Soviet operatives, away from the British."

“Something tells me he has crossed the Rubicon.”

“Yes.”

The next morning getting an early start with my passenger shackled in the back of a jeep was not a good start for my man Montague. He assumed he was on the way to the woods to be shot and burned, until he recognized me, even in a Russian Uniform.

Marlborough in his old English public school accent, sounding like Terry Thomas, the late English actor, said, “I say old boy, you did give me a fright. I thought this was the end, and all of that you know. Take these shackles off of me, that's a good man, what.”

For psychological reasons, speaking in Russian, which he knows very well, is going to help in gathering information from this irritable slug.

“You are going to a special place to be permanently interned, where no one will ever find you.”

Marlborough responding, “Sorry Colonel. You resemble an awful American Agent called Wright.”

“Marlborough, your nemesis BTK, or Billy is dead. My forces killed him on the German Border, trying to cross to our territory.”

“Yes, yes, I see, when was that, I mean what date was he killed?”

“It does not matter, he was eliminated once and for all.”

By not rebuking Wright was a thorn in the side of the Brits, meant it is most likely a shared view inside in Whitehall.

"I say Colonel It's awfully stuffy in here, close even, do you have any liquids, what?"

Giving him the jug of water with sleeping powder did the trick. He fell asleep within ten minutes as he gulped down almost half of the quart jug's contents.

We were waved through the Russian Border check point and were now in Belarus headed towards Poland, where we or I will skirt the area around Warsaw, while driving towards Czechoslovakia.

My passenger slept through all of our refueling stops, border check points and a short power nap was taken by me. He must have consumed most of the sedative in that one long drink, with sleeping for many hours.

When we crossed into Czechoslovakia it was pitch black, using my lights was dangerous but necessary, since going under the autobahn which was well behind us, diminishing our main obstacle of having GDR patrols seeing us from an overpass.

Arriving in the area where I crossed five plus days ago, it was necessary to stop by the path on the edge of the main road, to monitor the situation. The area was clear of soldiers confirmed by looking through infra red binoculars. It was a good time to set up MI5 by planting evidence with taking an article of clothing belonging to Montague, throwing it out the window, so the Soviets will think he was the one who caused the bother a few days ago.

Stopping a quarter of mile later to look through the binoculars and seeing no warm bodies of soldiers stirring through the forest, we proceeded down the narrow path. Side swiping a few trees was better than dragging a passed out body through this thicket. It was now three in the morning when I decided to bust through the iron bar over an old farm track.

By the time we got to the autobahn outside Passau, I emptied the last can of fuel into the jeep, which meant I had to stop and top up before we got to Bad Aibling.

Pulling up to the base gates, the MP guard looked as if he had just seen an advancing Russian war machine, with a Russian Colonel inside. When I told him who I was, along with my American ID, he waved me through and immediately got on the phone.

By the time I got to the Office, the Commanding Officer pulled up, along with two other ASA Agents, all of them armed with semi automatic M16 rifles.

The officer poked his head into the Russian vehicle and then back out quickly, saying, "That took my breath away General, how long have you two been living in that Jeep."

“To long, call an ambulance for my passenger.”

After a medic and doctor looked over Montague, the doc said, “This man has a very weak pulse. We have to take him to Munich right now.”

“Alright Sergeant, he's yours for now. Keep him cuffed, he may be playing possum.”

“No sir, he is almost expired, seems like an overdose, if his pupils are anything to go by. Also he has messed his pants, which is a sign of comatose setting in. Who and what rank are you, sir?”

The Base Commander step up and said, “That man is none other than General William Wright.”

The medic in disbelief climbed into the back of the Army ambulance, shaking his head and muttering, “Yeah right.”

The commander asked, “General what should I say in my report” What is that man's name?”

“Nothing, you haven't seen me or him.”

“That's not how we are supposed to operate around here sir.”

“Do we need to get another man to run this station?”

“Yes sir, I mean no sir. Thank you sir, you were never here.”

“Lets go inside, I need to make a call.”

Once in the office I had the Commander call British

Army Headquarters in Hamburg, telling them where they could pickup Montague.

After getting out of my clothes, I instructed one of the agents to have them cleaned, pressed and hung back up in the back office. He was also told to send the pistols to the ordinance supply officer for cleaning and oiling.

It was time to shower and get some sleep over at the Officers guest barracks, before heading to Frankfurt and then to London.

Ten hours later, arriving at Heathrow in the evening, I was taken to my flat by Kenny who was called beforehand by ASA Headquarters, to be at the airport to pick me up.

When I walked into the flat, Els came out of my bedroom in her pajamas.

Looking pleased, I asked, “Are we sharing?”

She blushed and said, “No. It's that your bed is much more comfortable, that is all. What did you mean by saying sharing, sharing what?”

“My bedroom.”

“You kind of fancy yourself, don't you sir? Your trip must have been a success, by your demonstrative demeanor.”

“It was alright. Any cold claret in the house, I need a drink. Then brief me on what has happened in the last few days in the Embassy."

"Few days? It is almost a week of non stop inquisitions from Washington to Whitehall. You have thrown me in at the deep end, if you don't mind me saying, sir."

"You haven't seen anything yet, wait until tomorrow morning. My physic powers are telling me, Thibodeau will call, telling us he is on his way to London."

"No telepathic sensing of Lord Chesterfield coming over when he knows you are back sir."

He already knows. Chesterfield is going to send two goons over to arrest me for breaking some type of secrets act. We need to get as much sleep as possible, keep the curtains closed, and pretend you haven't seen me."

The next morning Lieutenant Els was awakened at 0500 and told to get dressed, we were going out for an early breakfast. Knowing British intelligence were aware of an American CIA Agent, arriving at Heathrow under the name of Ludwig Von Wilhelm. It may take a few hours for MI-5 researchers to work out it was me.

Knowing how the Brits like to surprise villainous suspects in the wee hours of the morning, to get an advantage in taking the subject to jail. Today is going to be a valuable lesson for my Lieutenant.

Now in the cafe across the street we were served with two cups of hot tea, a short time later we had two full English breakfast shoved in front of us.

While we were eating, three police cars, one dark blue paddy wagon and a dark green sedan came to a screeching halt in front of the apartment building, all vehicle doors flung open dramatically.

David Chesterfield dressed in a full length trench coat was following a contingent of a dozen officers; I got up and said, “Come on Els we have to go.”

Our waitress came over to get the money, saying, “Ain't that your place sir.”

“Yes it is. When a posh sounding git comes over to inquire about me, tell him I was watching the whole thing, having to hurry and finish my breakfast.”

Els and I were in Hyde Park Tube Station within seconds, headed to the closest station to our Embassy, which is Grosvenor Square.

Safely arriving inside the Embassy CIA office without mishap, my Lieutenant asked, “Sir, what is going to happen next?”

“Plenty. Go downstairs, get six of the biggest MP's out of their barracks, and have them stop the British contingent from entering the building, except for Chesterfield. Let him pass through, I need to see him.”

She left while shaking her head, staring at the back

of her head, seeing her hair sweeping from side to side.

Within the hour David was standing in front of my desk, Saying, “Will you have to come with me.”

“Sorry David, you are now standing on American territory.”

“That isn't cricket old boy.”

“You are correct, Control. Back home we call it playing a game of old fashioned hard ball, pal.”

“Now, let’s be civil about this. You are going to have to leave this building one day and then we will have you, so let’s be grown up, shall we.”

“What is this all about? Maybe you are barking up the wrong tree.”

“You know very well what this is all about. Our man in Moscow is now a wanted man he is finished as an intelligence officer. Wait a minute, that was your plan all along, wasn't it? You are a bastard General Wright; you will not get away with this. Oh yes, he could have died, ingesting your poison.”

“Look me Lord, be in the Cambridge flat at noon tomorrow, alone. If you have any backup with you, I will cancel any thoughts of bringing your agency into my plan.”

He left in a huff, causing Els to ask, “You're not leaving the Embassy, are you sir?”

“Don't worry, he will have us followed, but not

detained. I need you to continue on with running this office for a few more days, is that okay?"

"Yes sir, I could get use to living here."

"One day Els, not yet. Meet me at Flanagan's Pub at 1900 hours tomorrow evening."

Kenny was downstairs, and when I got into his taxi he asked, "Let me guess, the place where all the sheep are."

"Yes, only after you shake the filth, who will be following us."   "Leave it wif me, I'll ed em down the North Circular, that street is not fit to be called a main road in this manor."

After twenty minutes we still had a tail. Prompting me to ask Kenny, "Drop me off at Watford Junction, double back to Waterloo pick me at the High Street exit."

"Leave em to me Guv, see ya in alf an our to shake these coppers."

Forty five minutes later, Kenny was waiting when I came out of the station, saying, "Those fellas needs a new motor, I reckon. Laughing and continuing his diatribe, hee hee, that round about through the gardens was their Waterloo, hee hee."

Finally, when we were out of the city, Kenny was told, "Drop me off at the gates to Mildenhall RAF Base and wait."

When we got to the airbase an AP at the gates was instructed to call the Base Commander, and tell him a General needed to see him.

Being asked to get into an AP Jeep that was sent to fetch me, I was taken to the commander's office. After explaining a conference room may be needed tomorrow at noon, to accommodate a three star general arriving in the morning on a C-130 at his base, he interrupted me to say, he had already been alerted that General Thibodeau and the Vice President were landing on board Air Force Two at 0900. A secure room had already been allocated.

Kenny then took me to the Cambridge flat. He left to go back home, and get some kip, as he would say and he would be back at 5am.

Els called to say she had just heard from Thibodeau.

The next morning Kenny was opening the front door just as I put the kettle on, seeing me he said, "Morning Guv, just getting up are we?"

Ignoring him He answered his own question with a little laugh, "Thought so, ya Yanks ain't use ta this early lark ares ya."

His sense of humor is hard to get use to so early in the day, especially when it involves taking down an American verbally, in the process.

I knew it was a mistake to banter so early, when I

sarcastically said, “You want a cup of coffee or is it a cup of weak tea you need?”

He really didn't respond as he said, “Now let me tell ya bout dose Yanks we ad oer ere in the war. We showed those boys whot life was about.”

“Changing the subject, Kenny, we need to get to the station for breakfast. Do you think those New Scotland Yard boys are coming by train, or down the motor way?”

“ I reckon they will motor down, easier ta git back ome when the works over, if ya catch me drift. There's a caf just before the motor way ends, we can watch to see if they arrive. They make a good breakfast there Guv.”

“Good. You go and wait to see if they turn off the motor way. Call and let me know how many and where Chesterfield's car is in the procession.”

“Right Guv, I'll go soon as dis Yank tea is gone.”

When Kenny had gone I left a note for David, as a back up, reading;

Evidently you do not understand, no police, means no. Meet me inside the University Chapel, now or go back to Whitehall.

There was a strong chance a two prong attempt to arrive simultaneously at the Cambridge flat by Lord Chesterfields men is plausible.

So a decision was made to arrive at the station

before the early London train pulled in and have something to eat, setting up a surveillance area inside the small track side cafe.

Just as I imagined, the 8am. train pulled in with two men dressed almost alike, black spit shined shoes, dark wool overcoats, pin striped trousers. When one looked to the right, the other one looked to the left, definitely Bill and Ben the flower pot men.

Finishing my breakfast, making sure no one else was getting off the same train. I was about to get up when a man I recognized as a stalker from the past walked into the station cafe. He ordered a cup of coffee to go and then looked around; by this time I was outside watching him from a station platform. Time to head off towards the University through a small alleyway.

Inside the Church, and joining several students in an early Mass communion, kneeling at the altar, waiting for the Vicar to issue their bread and wine. This tranquil Holy Communion was halted momentarily when the Priest recognized who was kneeling in front of him.

Chapter 39

The Triad

Tipping the wine cup, and bending towards me, he whispered, “See me in my office.”

By the time we met outside the door of his office, it was a quarter to nine, saying, “Come in my son. What brings you back to our beautiful Chapel?”

“I need to meet Lord Chesterfield here, is that going to be a problem?”

“No indeed, it will be nice to see David again. Are you two still thick as thieves? Who would have ever thought you two would wind up running Governments.”

Smiling and saying, “We are still thieving, sort of in the same business, on opposite sides of the spectrum, one might say. We are only small cogs.”

“Oh dear, can I be of service to you, my long lost friend?”

“Yes Vicar, I need a taxi to Mildenhall?”

“I will gladly take you I always wanted to visit the American side of the base. One never knows where lost sheep are until they are found.”

“Thank you Vicar.”

David walked in mad as a wet hen saying,

“What is the meaning of this General Wright?

Sorry Vicar didn't see you at first.”

“Anger is a deadly sin my boy. So we have two fellow students in my presence, one a General, one a Lord, I have never been so taken back in my many years as a Vicar, how wonderful. You two have always been amenable to each other. Please tell me, this has not changed."

Smiling again, knowing David just had his fanny smacked caused him to say, "You can wipe that smirk off your face for starters Billy boy."

The Vicar once again entered the fray, saying, "Now Lord David, be civil, shake hands and be friends again."

"Sorry Vicar. Wright, where do we go from here?"

"We are going to Mildenhall, in the Vicar's car."

"That's fine, I need to make a call first."

"No call."

The Vicar stared for a few seconds, eventually saying, "Shall we go?"

We arrived at the airbase just before noon. An Air Force dark blue police pickup truck with a large sign reading "FOLLOW ME".

This scenario was quite comical, a small car following a large American truck across wide swathes of concrete ramps and runways. When we turned, several giant hangers were seen with large C-130's emptying their payload of two Marine helicopters,and several large black Limousines.

David had to bend forward in the back seat of this mini cooper, with the Vicar listening in to our conversation and excitedly asked, "What is going on?"

"Sorry for the secrecy David, Vicar, my Vice President and our old boss General Thibodeau are here to find out what went wrong or right in Moscow one week ago. Vicar, after you are introduced to the two men, you will have your tour of the base. Give us two hours to conclude our business."

After the introductions, the Vicar was taken away, and the Veep started the briefing inside his plane, and was first to ask, "General Wright, why did you venture behind the Iron Curtain, and what happened to the British Agent who almost died in your care?"

"After meeting with my friend, KGB Director Apostolic, who wanted me to convey to you sir, rumor is, the wall will be dismantled within two years. There is also talk of the Russian Chairman, being a CIA plant."

David's boyish grin turned into a glare, spoke up saying, "That's preposterous, the wall coming down."

The Veep ignored David's out burst, asking, "They want to work with us?"

"Yes sir, I expressed an interest in Russian Agents who were serving in the Caucuses and the Middle East, especially the ones who could speak Arabic or Urdu."

General Thibodeau listening finally said, "Mr. Vice President, I am going to have General Wright arrested for putting together a shadow agency. He will be charged with sedition. I now have the proof with his admission of knowing and working with the KGB Director. I am not part of his scheme and never wanted to be, sir."

The VP asked Thibodeau, "Let Wright continue on how he was to finance a rogue agency. Go on Wright."

"Sir. I am not financing a rogue agency, shadowy yes. My feeling is that I will head the CIA within a few years, a job I want to be prepared for, not inheriting a smoldering fire that is going to explode very soon in the Middle East."

David spoke up before the VP could respond, saying, "You're crackers Will, We the British are not going to be part of this fanaticism."

"Lord Chesterfield, I promise you, the Brits will want to join or be willing to play catch up in the near future."

We all hashed over the problems in the Middle East for the next hour, with everyone now agreeing that problems did exist.

The VP got up and said, "We have to leave now, Wright I want to see you in March."

The Vicar was waiting outside the gates for us when we were dropped off.

In the back seat David said, "Where do you come up with these ideas, its lunacy?"

"It must be a gift of clairvoyance."

"That is so much BS. Answer me this question, why would you sacrifice a great career on an assumption? My bosses believe you have been lucky so far, they do not want to be seen as an associate when your scheme blows up in your face."

"I am not assuming anything, it is based on logic. When Nicola was murdered I made her a vow something good was going to come out of that horrific crime."

David was sure he had the answer to this paranoia, when he said, "You are on a one man vendetta."

"Good try. Let me continue. As far as this so called scheme blowing up, I assure you whatever comes out of this, we will have over a dozen well trained agents in the field, who are going to specialize in Middle Eastern surveillance."

The Vicar purposely interrupted us, by using a low reverent tone, "Yes, I now remember hearing when your lovely Nicola was in that plane. We said a prayer for you and her that Sunday. Did the culprits ever come to justice?"

"Yes Vicar, they all were prosecuted."

David spoke up again saying, "Prosecuted, yes, without a trial."

"Listen David and you too Vicar. No one knows

outside of our two agencies, how many other bombings were stopped with the CIA working with the ASA to thwart many Middle East extremist from carrying out their dastardly hijackings and subsequent bombings."

For the rest of the way to Cambridge, the Vicar preached on the virtues of being contrite or in other words, turning the other cheek.

Several MI6 men and local police were inside the flat, gathering forensic evidence, wondering why David had disappeared. They were told to leave.

The place was a mess with everything in large heavy duty black bags, even my bedding, causing me to say, "Wait a minute before you go, there is some cleaning up to do."

David gleefully said, "You do it. Send us a bill, you know the address. Oh yes, General you need to see me Monday morning in my office. Have a nice time cleaning up this sty old friend."

My once imperceptible team is scheduled to be briefed in England, (Brighton) to be more precise, the day after the presidential swearing in. The new President, a former CIA Director, should be one we can work with, not saying we are going to be allowed an open ended budget or given a cart' blanche' policy, which would be beneficial in carrying out future stealth missions.

However, I am sure we or I will be given some latitude, when missions are successful, behind the Iron Curtain. Traveling to Washington had to be remembered in the month of March.

I arrived back in London on Sunday, Els was sent back to Jordan, while thinking my next two months was going to be attending afternoon tea's and sitting behind a large desk. That was until Lord Chesterfield arrived at my office on that Monday afternoon.

Miss Peabody showed David in, she was told to take the rest of the day off.

When she was gone, he asked, "Are we going to be taped? I know how you want everything on the record. You were supposed to be meeting me in my office this morning what happened?"

"Busy. Should I have the tapes turned on?"

"I do not trust you; can you hear a humming noise? My driver will drive us out into the country. We can talk while we ride."

"Yea right."

"Do you have a case of paranoia?"

"When MI-5 is around, just say caution is needed."

David laughed, just before saying, "Let's go to the Pub, we both could use a drink."

In the pub, David ordering our drinks, showing a concerned look while walking over to the table with two pints of beer and having a look of consternation all over his brow.

When he sat down, stumbling to find the appropriate words it prompted me to ask, “I take it your Bosses have had a change of heart?”

“Damn you Will, do not tell me you can read my thoughts.”

“Like a road map. You and I both know, after Montague was named as the culprit on the Czech Border, your agency was finished operating in that particular Soviet zone. You and your superiors wonder what papers they found in his apartment, he isn't about to say he was careless.”

“Yes, we are worried, not about what was left behind, about how you have manipulated this set up. We think you have an agenda to feather your own perverted future. Do you have a plan to take over all agencies or put them out of business if they do not conform to your way of thinking? I just figured it out; you need us in your web. How are you going to engineer this, is the question?”

“Do you not remember our past conversation, when you were told the Soviets are spent? Western societies are under threat from a new incursion, you won't admit it but we are all in a later phase of a caliphate.”

“That is insane. Saying that we have to be involved,

without being involved, if you know what I mean."

"Unfortunately I do know what you mean. Most of my assignments were of that nature, straight out of Washington and may I say, one recent mission planned out of your office."

"That is past history. When are we going to consummate this new alliance with our partners?"

"I don't like that term. We need to consolidate this Triad, after the new President is sworn in, say early spring in Florida."

"Who do you think will agree to your meeting, certainly not the Russians?"

"Apostolic, General Thibodeau and British Intelligence. Each country's Intelligence Chief is going to be the power brokers in charge of carving out these territories. Each area will overlap and work in unison in targeting houses of hate. That could include individuals and department heads."

"I do not understand, when you say our own territories. What do you mean by that?"

"Yes you do."

"Are you insinuating we have an ethnic problem in Britain, that's preposterous? We seem to have everyone in tow."

"You must be blind, what about Brixton and the Leas in Oxford? Manchester is next."

"Look Will, I know there are disagreements on how to police some areas that are considered no go zones, that's all in the past."

"Before we meet in Florida, send in agents, informers or what ever you like to call your friendly Elders in certain communities, to monitor what we consider preachers of hate and racism. Would you do that in all areas?"

"Yes, I agree, let me say, we will not find any problems with the Imams."

"I hope that is still the case after your compilation of the facts. Reading your findings when the dossier is handed over in Florida, would be instrumental in determining just how apathetic all of those preachers are."

My long time friend, Lord Chesterfield and I would have the odd weekend on his estate, walking his black labs, hunting pheasant, without talking much about our agencies and their agenda's. It seemed we were now growing older together, not exactly being put out to pasture, but enjoying a rest that comes with maturity and an afternoon nap after a large Sunday lunch.

In February, the day after an inauguration, the shadow team and I met in Brighton to discuss their future in a new world of espionage and spying. 14 members, including five trained Rangers who graduated from helicopter school in Alabama, atttended.

The most valuable asset this five man team possessed being long range rifle marksmen, who could be used as snipers in hostile situations. They will be known as our extraction team, based out of Bad Aibling and Amman.

For the following two months they all trained for extractions out of desert locations, roof tops in Amman, and evacuations from a beach in Cyprus. These different locations were logistical nightmares, where choppers were used off carriers who were on maneuvers in the Middle East.

Els orders for promotion to Captain arrived in London, just before heading off to Florida as my Aide-De-Camp. The reason for her promotion was so she could officially take over Command of the ASA Bad Aibling Headquarters. This was decided after the Captain carried out official duties as interim London CIA Director, as an acting Captain.

We got to Boca Grande three days before the actual briefings were going to take place the reason was, General Thibodeau wanted his own briefing, before MI6 and the KGB representatives showed up.

The next afternoon Fran arrived, finding Captain Els and myself on the beach sun bathing.

My girlfriend was not happy to see a bikini clad

blond lying on the same blanket next to her fiance. After an hour of explanations and telling her I understood why she would feel the way she did. Fran calmed down a little, not enough for me to feel a little more comfortable.

General Thibodeau showed up in the middle of one of our discussions, the General, being himself, told me to go outside, he needed my full attention. Fran, I thought felt sorry for me, as she walked away, she said that she now understood everything.

Trying to channel my thoughts on what was about to be said, I asked the General, “What do you think she meant.”

At that precise time Els walked up with a towel draped across one shoulder, and showing all of her curves, causing Fran to stop and turn around, just as Els said, “Thank you sir for bringing me here, lying on the beach with you was so, so nice.”

Thibodeau said, “That is what she was telling you. The way Dannie looks at you is not one a junior officer should give a superior. Wright you may be an astute spy, but when it comes to knowing women, you have a long way to go. You had better go and see her, our meeting can wait.”

Boy Howdy was he was right, Fran walked so quickly to our room, leaving the door open, she was seen throwing her clothes into a suitcase, packing up.

After telling her again, Fran decided to finish packing and said on her way out, "When you get rid of her, come see me. You know where I live."

Speaking out loud as she headed down the hall, I said, "Fran, be reasonable, Els works for me, nothing more. Tomorrow is when everything is happening, you know how important this weekend is for the agency. I need someone to listen while I rehearse my lines, ones that may sell my ideas to prospective partners."

Fran left without saying another word. That is a problem for the proverbial back burner. Being here when Petro and David arrive is far and away more important than my love life.

Back on the deck, Thibodeau asked, "Well?"

"It's complicated."

"She left then?"

"Sir, I need to be here when our guests arrive. We need to hash over what is good for our agency, without worrying about who I am sleeping with tonight. Now let's get down to the bare bones of why you needed this meeting, sir."

"Very well Wright. Let me tell you, I do not like a junior officer telling me when we are going to start, especially one who is young enough to be my son. Do you understand what I am saying?"

Yes sir, sorry sir, it won't happen again."

"This KGB Director, when did he start working for you?"

"Over a decade ago, sir. You were there when he and Isla graduated off the farm. He met another cadet, while training, an agent recruited by me. Now he and that agent are married."

"Oh yes, I remember, they are both foreigners, Russian, aren't they? Why wasn't my office informed they were working for us? Over ten years and I was never told. Who did he report to, after you left?"

"Tobias."

"He's a Mossad Agent? You have some explaining to do young man. Hold on, what else was kept from me and the agency, over all these years?"

"Sir, I have financed and set up a sub agency for the past three years. This unit is now being used to monitor Middle East hot spots, in a half dozen locations."

"Get me another drink, can't wait for that waitress, I need something now, go get me scotch."

Handing him his drink, he started again after taking a large swallow, with, "While you were getting my beverage, I thought about what should be done with a young sitting General who is close to going off the reservation."

On the way up to the bar again, gave me the time to

think of a way to win the man over to my side.

Placing the General's triple scotch and soda in front of him, thinking this may last a little longer, I said, "General Thibodeau, in the past when I set up the three safe houses in Soviet territories, you not only rubber stamped your approval, you Neuhofer and Simpson approved salaries for three foreign agents, who were under my supervision. Not to mention providing over three hundred thousand dollars to keep everything in place. I will carry the water for you, if that helps the agency out, sir."

"No one has to carry my water, you pompous acting know it all. Let me handle our new President."

By the way, he wants to talk to you on Tuesday morning. Do you know when we left England, he stayed up front in Air Force Two, never coming back to the rear of the plane to say hi or recognize that his CIA Director was on board."

After finishing his drink he started where he left off with, "I know he was interested in what you said, especially about the wall coming down this year or next, you better be right, or you will be tried for attempting a coup de etat on the CIA."

"It isn't only me who thinks that will happen. The Russians in power have an idea their President is going to do something outside the realm of a dictator."

"Well Wright, they are your informants, so you are responsible for broadcasting their concerns."

"Yes sir."

"I have to go to see what the wife is doing, see you in the morning."

"Sir."

Good, it worked, he is now going to sort of stand on his own two feet, that is until the fire gets to hot to stand close to it's heat.

Els walked in just as I put my glass on the bar, asking, "Fancy a walk on the beach?"

"Sure. Nice outfit Dannie, beachy."

"Thank you Sir. Where is your girl friend?"

"It's complicated."

"Was my being here the reason?"

"Yes. Let's walk."

We walked and talked until we reached the North end of the Island, where a small pass separated Big Gasparilla Island from Little Gasparilla Island. She did most of the talking while I wished it was Fran who was with me.

That evening Dannie and I had supper together and a night cap on the veranda overlooking the Gulf of Mexico.

Our conversation eventually reached the area where she asked, "Your friend is she ill? I haven't seen her for some time now."

"Fran decided to leave, she went back home."

"Are you two having problems, I hope it isn't because of me?"

"Els, lets talk about your duties tomorrow while the briefing is going on."

"Sir, I suppose my job is to take notes, listen and discuss what was said later with you."

"Precisely, you are quite good in assuming some things. Are you able to take your notes in short hand, not letting on you are taking notes?"

"Yes sir. Do you think General Thibodeau is going to require a stenographer, or maybe the British Agent will want a recording of the minutes?"

"I hope not. If that is the case, something will have to be done."

The next afternoon Chesterfield and Petro had arrived with their separate entourages. I was worried about the Russian, who seemed to have two minders watching his every move.

Luck would have it, General Thibodeau walked in and said to the Russian contingent "Get those boys out of this room, they can wait outside."

Petro and I smiled at each other without telegraphing our association to the other Russians. One assistant for each side was allowed in, to provide legal and logistical help, no security agents were allowed in. The Russian helper set up an electronic dictation machine, with Petro telling us that his superiors wanted a transcription of everything said.

Lord Chesterfield protested that our conversations were going to be in written form. I looked over at him, slightly shaking my head, miming, it's okay."

Thibodeau started, "Everyone here knows the reason why we are here, we will skip over the long boring thoughts of General Wright and anyone else who seems to think they have the power of some gift. This briefing has nothing to do with seances or witch craft."

While everyone was quietly laughing and staring at the big General, a wooden handle ice pick was taken out of my pocket, and shoved into an electric receptacle next to me. The lights went off, with the Russian electronic machine shutting down.

The Russian tried turning the light switch on and off to see if he could get the electrics back on.

General Thibodeau barked at the man, saying, "It's not coming back on, we're in Florida, this happens all the time. Sit down."

He looked back with a blank stare, making his boss the KGB Director tell him in Russian, "Leave the room, you are embarrassing our country."

That was a good thing, one less important witness

to our amalgamation.

When the minder was gone, I went to the front of the room and said, “We are here to carve up the Middle East, and have the Soviets police their own ethnic populous.”

Lord Chesterfield rudely interrupted, “Now see here General Wright, who appointed you our leader?”

“I did.”

“See here old man, we must put it to a vote.”

Thibodeau spouted,”Lets hear him out.”

“Thank you sir. Lord Chesterfield, we are not going into our past weaknesses of recognizing hot spots of ethnic agendas of seizing available power in small and large communities, whose citizens have been indoctrinated by religious zealots.”

Petro interrupted, with, “The Brit is right Will, we need to have a showing of hands on who our spokes person is going to be.”

“Okay, listen first to why we are here. A minority of Arabs will be indoctrinated into believing some religious leaders pushing their hate. We have a chance to stop this aggressive caliphate or what we in the West would end up calling a twentieth century crusade. If we use that name, we will be seen as anti-Islam. Quite the opposite, we are anti-Islamist extremists who are willing to kill anyone in their way. Any questions on how we are going to monitor these preachers of hate. Let me express my aim, it is not to eliminate these enclaves, it is to rid them of hateful propagandists."

For the rest of the afternoon we hashed out guidelines where our countries would not be seen as anti any religion. The next morning which was Sunday, we had an hour in the early morning for a debriefing on the outside deck.

A last minute off the record mop up was essential, so Moscow, London and Washington could report that this collusion of the three governments never happened.

General Thibodeau being the elder, stood up and said, "Before we adjourn, I want you all to write down on a piece of paper who you want to be your spokes person."

Captain Els collected the votes, and read them out loud, saying, "Petro Apostolic three votes."

Petro rose and said, "Thank you for your confidence in me as your chairman. Russian concerns are for Egypt, England having special relations with Pakistan and is going to play huge in our attempt to keep the peace in the Arab Lands. America has to consider its own numerous ethnic minorities; they have their own racist purveyors of hate. Again, thank you for your confidence in me. Please go in peace, be safe. We need to meet in London this summer. We are are adjourned."

Sunday afternoon Captain Els and I lay on the beach again, this time discussing where we came from, how school had shaped our lives. She was not glad to be born a female in a male dominated high school with its importance on sports and winning.

Male participants were loathed, especially with the ones wearing garish jackets exhibiting their letters. Now I know why she seemed to have a belligerent demeanor.

She asked, "Why did everyone vote for Petro?"

"David and I have agendas, he doesn't."

Els and I flew to Washington the next afternoon, getting to the downtown Hilton at five pm. We were in the lounge at seven when my old friend Clint walked in. After a few hugs and introduction we all sat there for two hours discussing old assignments and how Clint was now over his Hanoi Prisoner of War torturers and their sadistic officers.

The next morning, General Thibodeau took us to the White House to meet and see our new President.

When we walked into the Oval Office the Presidents minders told us where to sit, just before the man himself walked in.

He shook my hand and while grasping it he said, "I have thought over what was said at our last meeting, and if you are right, your next posting will be here in

Washington. You will be instructed by General Thibodeau on what is expected of you. There will be a list of things that you will not be allowed to do."

"The President picked up a document and reading, "Keeping agents in one's back pocket is illegal, foreign or domestic. Are you willing to take an oath of allegiance to these United States, forsaking all others to whom you have associated with in your past or in your future?"

"Yes sir. Do you mind if Captain Els sits in on this briefing?"

The President then said, "Please sit down Captain Els. General Wright, now tell us why you think the Berlin Wall is about to come down."

"Mr. President, repeating the same information you were told months ago and probably know verbatim from reading our briefing on this subject is somewhat tedious to repeat it all over again. Sir, my opinion on this subject is still the same."

The President had a look of disbelief, causing General Thibodeau to stand up and say, "Now look here General Wright, you cannot talk to the Commander in Chief like he was one of your underlings. There is a price to pay for this insolent behavior."

Els and I were quickly excused, General Thibodeau stayed behind to kiss the old man's boot, while we left to get packed and travel back to London.

Two days later I was at my London desk, Els was back in Amman, when a call came in from Thibodeau. My CIA Director was put on hold by Miss Peabody, he couldn't wait to get started chewing on my rear end. Before he started I knew what he was going to say, this wasn't anything to do with having the gift of clairvoyance tendencies, just old country boy logic. After a few minutes I answered the dreaded phone call.

His first statement was, “You are in deep dodo mister, the President was not happy with your rudeness, I am sending you on a six month Officer's Candidate School refresher course at Fort Dix New Jersey, starting next Monday. Pack your bags Lieutenant for a MATS flight out of Mildenhall this Friday.”

“Sir, I take it, these are the President's instructions.”

“Look dam you, it doesn't matter where these orders comes from, does it?”

“No sir, I just wanted to make sure who I am dealing with.”

“It doesn't matter you're only one soldier in a million. We believe you need a little polishing before you go up the proverbial ladder.”

“Can you tell me who is taking over the London Office?”

“Simpson is coming back for six months. Is that

okay by you?"

"Yes sir. I need to take a one year sabbatical, could you please arrange the paper work General."

"No way Jose, you are going to OCS, you need a little polishing before climbing up the proverbial ladder. You understand me my young General?"

"Sir is there, hello, call me back I can't hear you."

I gently hung up the phone, thinking I had better leave London now, where no one could find me.

Before leaving the Embassy for the last time, I asked Miss Peabody to write down a contact address, in some obscure area, where it was possible to get a hold of me. She crawled under her desk and wrote it in ink on the right wall, where the middle drawer stopped.

Just as I left the phone was ringing. Making me start to think about a charge of AWOL will be waiting for me when I get back off an extended absence.

Spending a couple of days in Harrow to think and contemplate my future was quite safe as no one had the phone number at Nicola's Parents. It was essential to leave Friday evening for somewhere foreign. I flew to Amman, arriving at the Jordanian Airport, where I registered under an alias, staying for three nights.

Without attempting to contact my team, on Monday I took a flight to Egypt, staying at the airport hotel. The next morning I took a cab to the Cairo Museum. I went inside to speak to the curator about the places his foreign volunteer archaeologist were billeted.

He sized me up and probably saw I could stand to pay more than most, he came out and gave the cab driver instructions where to take me. It wasn't far, across the main road and down a tree covered lane was a walled in hotel complex, within one hundred yards of the museum.

Visiting the museum for a solid month, I tried get through the whole history of ancient Egypt and Nubia or Lower Egypt. The time spent here, a place totally divorced from the real world was needed so much.

During my time alone, I played out in my mind different rolls of Eastern Europe, or the Soviet controlled territories, in their quest for independence. What if my instincts were born out in a few years, or even months? How could assets be accumulated, some that would be considered unsavory, for instance, the Stasi leadership, like Herr Wolf, no not him, he's a die hard Communist, probably a commie until the day he dies.

My biggest fantasy is to think exoneration may be granted by none other than the President. If that was the case, what would be my price to come back in, scary thought, holding the Commander in Chief accountable, yes that is the word, he is the reason for my exile.

Showing up at the Amman American University Campus the morning our Amman team was to graduate, Captain Els approached me with open arms.

She had so much to say, starting off with, “Everyone has been trying to contact you. Are you hiding from anyone in particular?”

“No. Is the team excited to have another degree in their resume?”

“Yes sir, do we call you sir?”

“What have you heard? Was I decommissioned?”

“Rumor is all. One of the team found out.”

“Was the inquiry generated in the States?”

“Yes sir. Jeff sent a letter to Hank's parent’s home, asking if they knew of your whereabouts.”

“Have you been back to Florida to see Fran?”

“No, I went to Egypt six weeks ago, doing a lot of soul searching.”

“Will, is this over your confrontation with the President?”

“That is it in a nut shell.”

“I think you were a little out of order, speaking to our President like you did. What is to happen with us?”

“You and the team have to stay here until this blows over.”

“That's very optimistic of you sir, I have a feeling you are going to be left out in the cold for a very long time."

"Time is on my side Captain, remember those words."

My team trained for the summer throughout Egypt, using Nile Cruises for cover. Congregating around the Cairo Museum when our positions were seen to be compromised, while eaves dropping on radicalized groups of idle men. The only place to blend in with Europeans and tourist from North America was the Cairo Museum.

At the beginning of October, the team was given two months paid leave, and airline tickets back to their home towns.

When the group left, I traveled the same day to Passau to stay with Elke and walk the mountains, occasionally traveling to Prague to see Leila and hike those hills close to the East German Border.

It was necessary to make sure my safe houses in Czechoslovakia, Leipzig, Kaleningrad and Moscow were still operational.

I was back in London in the first week of November, feeling the cold and thinking of going to Florida.

As it happened I was close to buying a ticket to Tampa and get out of my London Flat, when the 9pm. news of the Berlin wall being breached by Germans on both sides of the border got my attention.

The night of the 9th of November a telegram was delivered, asking me to meet and board a CIA jet to Templehof Airport in West Berlin, from Mildenhall RAF Base, the next morning.

Citizens from both German Countries were working together, tearing down the most hated wall in the whole world.

This was an exciting time to be alive, no one really knew how this new found freedom would play out, is Russia going to stand by. For now, these people should be left alone to celebrate. I can't see us getting involved there will be time to chase shadows in two or three days.

Having second thoughts about meeting the plane was drawing near, may have consequences, put into Fort Leavenworth for sedition was one of them.

Epilogue

General William Wright would soon become CIA Director and given the oath of office, by an arrogant elitist President.

CIA One departed just before 0800 the next morning, for Berlin. Leonid Miska had orders to Check into the British Smuts Barracks, known as Spandau Barracks by American Forces, on Wilhelmstrasse, to make sure the building was secure before meeting the arriving CIA Flight.

During the two hour flight six pages of orders were read, mentioning everything from a shadow agency in place, one that was operating under Wright's tutelage.

Understanding the possibility or more importantly, not confirming the rumor was beneficial from keeping a charge of sedition being leveled against the Presidents new CIA Director. The question was, does he have an alternative nominee? Hmm I wonder.

Half dozen foot lockers were stacked in the rear of the plane, suspiciously banded with Treasury seals. They had to be dollars, but what denomination, 20's 50' or 100's.

If lady luck was Wright's companion in this new world, General Wright is in a position to be King maker and power broker, in all NATO Countries and DC.

Edited by

Keith Thorpe

Photograph taken by a long time friend- Jeff Jones, a fellow Floridian

About The Author

L.A Wiggins grew up on a small South Florida Farm in the mid 1900's. Volunteering just as the Vietnam War was escalating he went through an arduous Boot Camp at Fort Polk, Louisiana. Even though his training had an Airborne theme suited for South East Asia. Lloyd Arthur Wiggins was sent to a Cold War area of West Germany, where he stayed for 33 months in that cold gray dismal weather, quite different from sunny days in South Florida. After 1989 and the fall of the Berlin Wall, Lloyd and his wife, Nikki, traveled extensively through a once prohibited Eastern Europe. They were socked to see countries left in time, shut out from a modern world. Horse drawn carts were widely used along with small spindly wheeled wagons being pulled down high streets to carry food and feed. This made L.A. wonder why the wall took so long to fall, one reason, the populaces in six countries had their weapons confiscated. Several uprisings were quashed in the Czech Republic and Hungary by heavy Soviet Armour,who had sticks and rocks to deal with so called allies. Today, walls in a part of Budapest still shows bullet holes in walls purposely left to remind the world what went on behind a tall Iron Curtain.

www.ingramcontent.com/pod-product-compliance
Lightning Source LLC
Chambersburg PA
CBHW051243250726
48656CB00004B/1107